FOREIGN MUD

FOREIGN MUD

BEING AN ACCOUNT OF THE OPIUM IMBROGLIO
AT CANTON IN THE 1830S
AND THE ANGLO-CHINESE WAR
THAT FOLLOWED

by Maurice Collis

A NEW DIRECTIONS CLASSIC

Foreign Mud is dedicated to Tony and Mary Keswick

Manufactured in the United States of America
New Directions Books are printed on acid-free paper.
First published as a New Directions Classic (NDP938) in 2002
Published simultaneously in Canada by Penguin Books Canada Limited

Library of Congress Cataloging-in-Publication Data

Collis, Maurice, 1889-1973
   Foreign Mud: being an account of the opium imbroglio at Canton in
   the 1830's and the Anglo-Chinese war that followed / by Maurice Collis
   p. cm — (A New Directions Classic)
   Originally published : London : Faber and Faber Ltd., 1946.
   ISBN 0-8112-1506-7 (alk. paper)
China — History — Opium War, 1840-1842. I. Title. II. New Directions
Classics

   DS757.5.C6 2002
   951'.033 — dc21

                                                                2001055772

New Directions Books are published for James Laughlin
by New Directions Publishing Corporation
80 Eighth Avenue, New York, NY 10011

Contents

Contents

Illustrations

Illustrations

Illustrations

Maps and Plans

Chapter I

INTRODUCTORY

Introductory

The vision of Cathay danced before the eyes of the early navigators. To furnish the enchantment they had Marco Polo and a thousand rumours. And since to get to China by the way he went was impossible, because the Silk Road was no longer a safe caravan route, but swept by the wars of Central Asian kings, a sea passage had to be found. The Portuguese were the first to discover it. In 1557, fifty-nine years after their great navigator, Vasco da Gama, had reached India, they obtained leave from the Ming to settle on an island, or more precisely, on a hilly isthmus three miles long which jutted from the south coast of a deltaic island, divided only by narrow creeks from the mainland south of Canton. The town they built there came to be called Macao. Though they were not allowed to go beyond the confines of the isthmus, they enjoyed the monopoly of the sale in Europe of those commodities which the Chinese let them buy.

The next to come into those seas were the Spanish, who soon after took the Philippines, inhabited by savages, and trading from Mexico via Manila used Macao as a terminal port, especially after 1580 when Portugal became part of Spain.

There followed the Dutch. In 1619 they seized from its rajah Jacatra in Java, renaming it Batavia. Well situated there to make contact with China, they sent envoys to

Peking in 1655 asking for a port and for free trade. But suspected of being pirates, they were granted nothing by the Chinese, now ruled by the Ch'ing, a Manchu dynasty that had established itself in 1644. Still hoping, they sent a second and a third embassy with a like result, the Emperor taking pains to make clear to them that China was a closed country, that he regarded them as barbarians from beyond the outer confines, but was glad to receive their tributory presents, for, as Lord of the World and the Dispenser of Light, it was proper that they had come to admire and worship him. The Dutch deplored this view of their efforts to open trade relations, but utterly failed to modify it.

The third European nation to appear in the China Seas was the British. Their eastern headquarters was India, where at Surat and Madras they had holdings on shore. In 1626 Captain Weddell put into Macao on a venture backed by Charles I, but he was taken for a pirate and turned away. During the seventeenth century the British were so occupied in developing the Indian trade that their attempts to obtain a footing further east were not supported with sufficient force. The Dutch drove them from the Islands after a horrible massacre at Amboyna in 1623 and the Siamese from Siam in 1684 when Phaulkon rose to power in that kingdom.

By the turn of the eighteenth century, however, the Portuguese Empire had fallen into decrepitude, having lost the key points of Ceylon and Malacca to the Dutch. The Dutch in their turn got the worst of their brush in home waters with the British, and though firmly set in the great Islands, which they were developing as colonial possessions in the same way as the British were developing India, could not dispute the passage of the British towards China. This conjuncture in European affairs coincided with a modification of Chinese policy towards barbarians. The Emperor K'ang Hsi (1662-1722) had made his dynasty one of the most powerful that had ever ruled China. He had, through curiosity and taste for novel ideas, allowed Jesuits to live in his employ at the capital and had acquired a smattering of the history, sciences, and geography of Europe. At first inclined to be enthusiastic, his final view, after discovering that the Jesuits harboured secret plans for undermining the Confucian system, was that Europeans were dangerous people who, though possessed of certain material secrets of value, were essentially barbarians since by guile they would use their mechanical cleverness to overthrow others and, being without virtue, were not, as all states in the world should be, convinced that Chinese civilization was the only one. But in spite of his disillusion he felt strong enough to make some money out of them and decided in 1685, to open under precautions, his ports to European merchants in general, the dues they would have to pay being his perquisite; but this favour he soon afterwards reduced to permission to trade only at Canton.

Britain was on the rising tide of her fortunes and was able to take better advantage of this opening than were the Dutch, nor had she reason to apprehend serious rivalry from the French or the Americans. By 1715 the East India Company, which for over a hundred years has been entrusted by the government with the monopoly of all British overseas trade with Asia, had firmly established itself at Canton as the principal European agency trading with China.

The terms on which the British and the other Europeans were allowed to conduct their business were governed by the Eight Regulations, which had been drawn up with two objects in view, the first to screw as much money as possible out of the Barbarians and the second to keep them in such subjection that the danger of allowing them to come to China would be reduced to a minimum.

As frequent reference will be made to these Regulations in the course of the narrative, for they amounted to intolerable restrictions as time went on, I shall give here their substance: (1) no vessels of war to enter the Pearl River on which Canton stood; (2) no arms to be brought by Europeans to the factories (warehouses) in the Canton suburb, where the merchants were allowed to carry on business, provided they only stayed during the winter shipping season (September to March) and did not bring their wives and families with them; (3) all the pilots, boatmen and agents working for the foreigners must be licensed; (4) not more than a fixed number of servants might be engaged by them; (5) sedan chairs and boating for pleasure were forbidden them as were excursions into the city or its neighbourhood, though three times a month a visit might be made to the public gardens on Honan Island, in the river opposite the city, provided that the visitors, who were to be conducted, did not go in droves of more than ten, got home before dark and did not get drunk or mix with the public; (6) all business to be carried on through a body of monopolist contractors known as the Hong merchants, who would also receive all complaints or petitions addressed to the local government authorities; (7) no smuggling and no credit allowed; (8) the ships coming to trade must anchor at Whampoa, thirteen miles below the city, where the loading and unloading was to be done.

It was calculated that these regulations would render the Barbarians harmless and expose them to the maximum of exactions without possibility of redress. They were not made subject to Chinese law except should any be guilty of the homicide of a Chinese when the culprit had to be given up. Misbehaviour and disobedience were punished by stopping the trade for a time or threatening to do so.

During the course of the eighteenth century the trade greatly increased in volume in spite of these restrictions. The merchants of the East India Company, ruled by their President and Select Committee on the spot and by the Directors in London, far outdistanced their European rivals until it could be said that the China trade was the exchange of commodities between Britain and China.

The greater the volume of the trade, the wealthier the

British became, and the stronger their position in their growing empire of India, so much the more tiresome, insulting and stultifying seemed the Regulations. During the last decade of the eighteenth century it was felt the time had come to try and convince the central government at Peking that it would be greatly to the advantage of all parties if the relations between Britain and China, both mercantile and political, were brought into line with the realities of the world. The Macartney embassy was sent to Peking in 1795, but was treated in exactly the same way as had been the Dutch embassies of the previous century, being granted nothing and obliged to take part in the ancient Confucian masquerade in which the Son of Heaven as Lord of the World received tribute from Outer Barbarians come from the darkness to worship the light. With such lavishness and marvellous taste was the masque produced that there was no sting in it, but it was not business, there was no profit, no money, no good in it.

There followed in Europe the Napoleonic wars. From them England emerged the most powerful nation in the world. To the victors of Trafalgar and Waterloo it seemed impossible that the Chinese would refuse the friendly offer of a treaty regulating the trade between the two countries, impossible that, were a fresh embassy sent, they would again stage the classic masque and go through the ritual prescribed for the reception of tribute-bearing envoys. Accordingly in 1816 the Amherst Embassy was despatched. But the Chinese enacted the comedy again. We may suppose that they were to some extent the dupes of their own mummery and believed the pageant of the Son of Heaven to represent the truth, but they were also kept rigid in their determination to refuse all concessions by their conviction that the British were a dangerous subversive force and if allowed freely into China would overthrow the Dynasty, as they had brought down Emperor and Prince in India. Lord Amherst returned with hands as empty as all his predecessors, but more irritated than they; and the merchants at Canton, to ameliorate whose condition he had been sent, continued to ply their trade under the same antiquated regulations to which they had submitted for a century.

But it was now within the power of England to force China to make a modern commercial treaty. Before using force a *casus belli* has to be found. The bland insolence of the Court of Heaven could hardly be said to provide it. The theme of this book is to show how it was provided. An indication of its nature can be given in this way: while up to the time of the Macartney Embassy British trade with China had been the exchange of various English goods for tea and silk, an adverse balance against Britain being liquidated by silver payments, from 1800 onwards a new article had increasingly been offered for sale so as to obviate these cash transfers. This commodity was opium. The East India Company, though the owners of the opium in the first instance, sold it to China through an outside organization. As its import was forbidden, it had to be smuggled in. The Company received the wholesale value of the opium and the funds so credited balanced, and more than balanced, the value of their exports, thereby setting the China trade on a sound financial basis.

But an illegal drug traffic would not have had to be called into existence had the Chinese freely opened their ports and the interior to Europeans, for then the spread of new ideas would have resulted in a greatly increased demand for western goods. Since the Chinese were afraid to do this, and did not do it, the other system had to be devised. Nevertheless, explainable though its origin was, the drug traffic, especially when it had swelled till its value equalled that of the legitimate imports, was itself a blatant disreputability, of which the Company was ashamed, wryly declaring it a *pis aller* about which the less said the better. It was this very drug traffic, inextricably bound up as it was with finance and British business firms, which provided the *casus belli*.

To understand how this came about we shall examine from every angle what happened at Canton between 1832 and 1842. Just as in a court of law the merits of a complicated civil action cannot be determined without hearing a great deal of evidence, so an historical imbroglio of the kind before us cannot be sifted unless it is set out in the fullest detail. But the reader will not find this sifting to be tedious, so curious, droll and revealing is the story. When all has been said, there will be found little malice, little cause for moralizing, but a great deal of humanity.

CHAPTER II

THE MISE-EN-SCÈNE

(i)

Macao

Since the events to be recorded take place at Canton and its neighbourhood, it will be useful to begin by acquainting ourselves thoroughly with that region. The map opposite page 33 gives the main features. Canton is seen on the Pearl River some forty miles from its mouth, known as the Bogue or the Bocca Tigris. This is situated at the head of a great bay, on the western horn of which, forty miles south, is the Portuguese town of Macao. The eastern extremity is Lantao Island, behind which is the island of Hongkong. Across the mouth of the bay are the Ladrone Islands, and in its middle Lintin Island.

A lively impression of what travellers in the eighteen-thirties used to see as they sailed up to Canton may be obtained by dipping into a book called *The Fan-Qui in China in 1836-7* written by a certain Doctor Downing who visited the city at that time.

It was about July or August, in the middle of the south-west monsoon, that merchantmen from Europe and India used to enter the China seas. The wind being aft allowed studding-sails to be set, and like black-bodied birds with white wings extended they would drive steadily to the northward at a rate of a hundred miles a day. On such a following wind the Ladrone Islands were often sighted ten days after leaving the Straits of Malacca, if the course were from India, or Banka if from Europe.

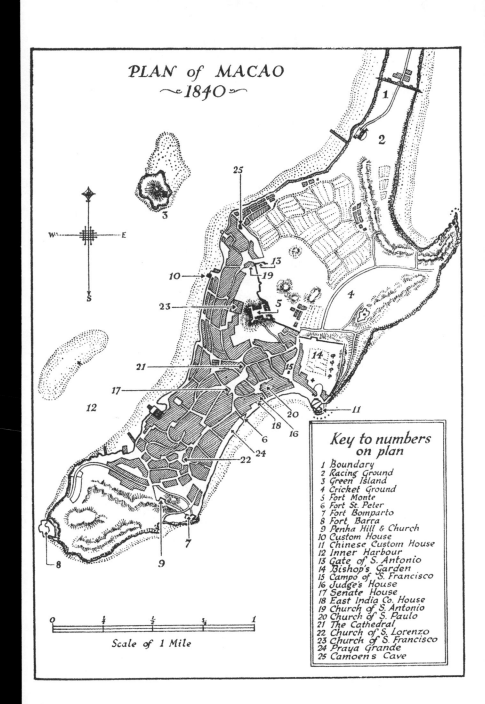

PLAN of MACAO
~1840~

Key to numbers
on plan

1 Boundary
2 Racing Ground
3 Green Island
4 Cricket Ground
5 Fort Monte
6 Fort St. Peter
7 Fort Bomparto
8 Fort Barra
9 Penha Hill & Church
10 Custom House
11 Chinese Custom House
12 Inner Harbour
13 Gate of S. Antonio
14 Bishop's Garden
15 Campo of S. Francisco
16 Judge's House
17 Senate House
18 East India Co. House
19 Church of S. Antonio
20 Church of S. Paulo
21 The Cathedral
22 Church of S. Lorenzo
23 Church of S. Francisco
24 Praya Grande
25 Camoens Cave

W — E
S

0   ¼   ½   ¾   1
Scale of 1 Mile

At the Grand Lemma, the principal of the Ladrones, a Chinese pilot used to be taken on, a simple fellow, more fisherman than pilot, but capable of steering the ship through the island channels to Macao roads. Dr. Downing, who was young and in a hurry to land after the long voyage, left his ship as she beat up through the channels and went ahead to Macao in the pilot's boat with the mail. Everything was fresh and delightful to him. The boat, a sort of large sampan, high aft, the cabin amidships, with its latteen sail and eyes painted on the bow, seemed a quaint and happy craft. The pilot's mate in charge was an amiable old man, the sailors talked and joked together. After some hours they sighted Macao jutting out on its peninsula. The first glimpse of the city was entrancing. Downing saw a little bay, a waterfront of old houses. Though in the tropics and on the other side of the globe, he might have been entering an Iberian port, for the white buildings shining in the sun were in the Spanish baroque of the sixteenth century. They formed a crescent along the edge of the clear sea, a promenade called the Praya Grande. Behind the ground rose steeply, so steeply that in places the streets were stepped. Towers of churches and monasteries were everywhere. The hilltops were crowned with forts whose cannon were now used only for saluting.

The Portuguese had been at Macao for nearly three hundred years; they had lived under the Ming for a hundred and by 1830, had been for a hundred and eighty-six under the Ch'ing. Up till 1685, when K'ang Hsi had opened Canton to all western ships, they had had a monopoly of the China trade. The breaking of the monopoly completed their ruin, already far advanced by the general decline of Portuguese power. The Macao of the eighteen-thirties was a tarnished old place. There was a Governor, a Senate-house and twelve churches, but the atmosphere was less that of a port than of a museum. The tonnage owned by its merchants was only five thousand and the customs were worth hardly £20,000 a year. Yet as the summer residence of the British and other merchants of Canton, whom the Chinese obliged to leave the factories there about March when the laden ships had sailed for home, it had a gay social season.

The waterfront was provided with jetties and steps, and Downing naturally supposed that he would be landed at one of them. But the sampan anchored some distance from the shore. On asking the pilot's mate the reason for this, the man told him the water was too shallow. Presently the real reason came out. The Chinese Government maintained in Macao its own officials, for at no time had the Portuguese had undivided control of the city. The pilot's mate was in the bad books of the local mandarin; he dared not bring his sampan right in.

In a moment, however, an egg-boat came up. This was a most singular conveyance, being eight feet long, six feet broad, flat-bottomed and wall-sided, with the gunwale only six inches above water. For cabin it had a mat bent over like an archway. Two Chinese girls were in charge of this tub. They invited Downing to come ashore in it.

Nothing loath, the young man complied and was given a stool under the circular roofing, which apparently had suggested the local name of egg-boat. The girls sat fore and aft, and began to row. They were dressed in blue trousers and smocks; their hair was in two plaits tied with red cotton. Being the first women Downing had seen for a long time, he found them both delightfully attractive. They seemed so good-natured, too, as they smiled and showed their splendid teeth. The one at the back was only a foot from him. He noticed now that she had artificial flowers in her hair. While striving to converse in the fantastic patois known as pidgin-English, he took hold of her arm in his efforts to make his meaning clear. This seemed to perturb the young woman, for she drew back and looked nervously at the waterfront. 'Na, na!' said she. 'Mandarin see, he squeegee me.' On Downing expressing astonishment at this remark, she gave him to understand that by port regulations egg-boat girls were not allowed while on duty to dally with passengers, and more particularly with foreign devils, and that if one of the port police had seen her just now he might misconstrue, perhaps wilfully misconstrue, her passenger's gesture and she would have to tip him or else he would report her. Downing waxed indignant over this oppression. So sympathetic was he, that she hastened to reassure him, and smiling demurely murmured: 'Nightee time come, no man see.'

On landing, Downing started out to explore. He had no introductions. In point of fact, the British merchants had just left for Canton, though their wives had not gone with them, as the Chinese did not allow that.

There were, however, some permanent British residents, like George Chinnery, a member of the Royal Hibernian Academy. In 1830 Chinnery was fifty-six and had been in the Orient over thirty years. There is a self-portrait of him in the National Portrait Gallery, painted at Macao, showing him in black frockcoat and white trousers, seated before an easel. He has white curly hair and spectacles half down his nose, an ugly little man with a typical Irish face. He was the most distinguished British artist who has ever lived in China. He died at Macao in 1852. His drawings are very sensitive and accomplished, and his best oil paintings have a quality which entitles him to rank as a minor master. Downing, had he called, might have spent an amusing evening, for Chinnery had the reputation of being a spirited raconteur.

As it was, the young surgeon strolled along the Praya Grande. Being afternoon the Portuguese were indoors enjoying their siesta. A pleasant sea breeze was blowing, but the sun was very hot. In the centre of the crescent stood the large building long used as its summer headquarters by the East India Company. Next to it was the pillared gateway of the Governor's residence, outside which Downing saw some Portuguese soldiers on guard, black troops, mulattos or negros it seemed. The crescent was altogether about a mile long. There were no shops, all the buildings being either public offices or private houses. At the northern end stood the old Spanish factory, its pillared frontage the most handsome in the whole promenade. Behind it was the Bishop's garden. Downing did not go round the point beyond the Church of San Francisco, but turned back and took one of the streets which led uphill behind the sea-front. On the way he admired the Church of San Lorenzo; its famous steps had for centuries been a loitering place for the fidalgos. It was situated behind the house of the Company's President. Climbing to the top of the ridge he was rewarded by a wide prospect. The peninsula which is three miles long is here only half a mile broad. On the far side glimmered the inner harbour, an expanse of sea leading to a passage known as the Broadway, which wound through creeks to Canton, a short cut closed to European shipping. At the southern extremity of the peninsula, about half a mile from where he stood, was Penha Church on a high hill. Looking northwards he could make out, beyond the Church of San Francisco at the top of the esplanade, the race-course and cricket ground, used only, it need hardly be said, by the British. Close to these was Camöens' grotto where the epic poet during his banishment to Macao in the sixteenth century is supposed to have written the *Lusiads*. Downing had not time to go as far, though most visitors included it in their rambles. Ellis, who accompanied Lord Amherst to Peking in 1816, records in his *Journal* that he saw a bust of Camöens in the grotto, adding characteristically, for he was a disgruntled fellow, that it was 'ill-executed and placed within a grating resembling a meat-safe'. For all that, it was a most revered relic of a great age, and was as romantic a thing as would be a bust of Milton in the crater at Aden, had our bard composed his masterpiece there in exile.

Beyond this grot of sacred memory the Macao peninsula narrowed down in less than a mile to a breadth of a hundred yards, a stretch known as the Stalk of the Lotus. Here it was that the Chinese had built a wall called the Barrier, barring ingress towards the mainland, for during the three hundred years of their tenure under lease of Macao the Portuguese merchants were never allowed to enter China.

The identical scene which Downing was able to enjoy from his view-point on the ridge has been preserved for us in numerous contemporary pictures. Besides Chinnery's many drawings in ink and pencil, we have the delicate and charming lithographs of Borget, a French artist who was at Macao in 1838. The work of Allom is no less distinguished, and there are many others, such as Captain Elliot, R.N., R. Beechey, R.N., and J. Wathen, whose drawings and water-colours are well composed and topographically most informing. Reproductions of them may be conveniently studied in the catalogue of the Chater Collection published by James Orange in 1929. After looking through that book one is left with the impression that Macao was a captivating little port. Of the several cities built by the Portuguese in the Orient Goa was the most imposing; its churches, monasteries and public edifices were larger, more numerous and of greater artistic importance than elsewhere in their empire. But the site of Macao was infinitely more pleasing than Goa's. Moreover, as the Jesuits proved in the case of the buildings they erected for the Emperor Ch'ien Lung at the Summer Palace of Yuan Ming Yuan, the baroque blends admirably with Chinese architecture, the combination resulting in a true rococo.

Downing now learned he would have to stay the night. The regulations obliged the pilot's mate to report the arrival of the British ship and obtain from the Chinese customs office on the Praya Grande written permission for her to proceed up river. This business could not be completed till next morning, so Downing booked a room at the English hotel. This was run by a man called Marquick. The servants were Chinese youths, dressed smartly enough in blue tunics, white knee-breeches and loose silk stockings. 'You catchee dinner? Can?' said one of them to the doctor, raising his eyebrows. 'Can,' replied Downing, nodding vigorously: he was already getting hold of the lingo. The table d'hôte was good. Afterwards, instead of joining a group at the billiard table, he strolled out again onto the Praya Grande. The sun had just set and the upper class Portuguese[1] were taking their evening promenade. They were in full evening dress without hats, and passed backwards and forwards, saluting and bowing with all the punctilio of their race. Little circles were formed. There was animated conversation, wide gestures. Downing watched for a while and then, in the failing twilight, walked on till he found himself again at the north end of the crescent and, turning the corner this time, continued past the Church of San Francisco, on its mount to the left. This took him out of the European quarter to where the Chinese lived, of whom there were some 30,000 in Macao. It was now getting dark but he could see numbers of both sexes seated facing the sea with their legs dangling over the masonry embankment, enjoying the cool evening breeze and admiring the last reflections of the sunset. On hearing him pass, they looked round and perceiving a European seemed to receive a shock, he says, and quickly got to their feet and hurried home. Word of his approach spread along the road and soon not a Chinese was to be seen, except one old man who continued to dangle his legs. Supposing him not to share the anti-foreign prejudices of his companions, Downing went up and addressed him from behind. He took, however, no notice whatever, being apparently absorbed in meditation. Could he be a philosopher, wondered Downing, and to attract his attention touched him gently. The old man started, looked over his shoulder, shuddered, scrambled up and hobbled away. His inattention was due not to philosophy but to deafness.

[1] There were in 1830 about 3,000 Portuguese of pure and mixed blood resident at Macao.

As will appear frequently, the Chinese as a body disliked Europeans, but individual Chinese who got to know them or who were used to them in general became friendly and attached. This dislike sometimes took the form of avoidance and sometimes of hostility. The government encouraged the people in their attitude because it had various reasons for fearing intimacy between them and Europeans. Downing was rather dashed by this his first experience of Chinese dislike; young, eager, friendly, it was not very agreeable to be treated as a foreign devil, as you strolled through the twilight in a beautiful seascape. He retraced his steps, turned into the waterfront and made his way back past the empty Company's House to his hotel, where he spent a dull evening, since there were no public entertainments and he knew nobody. Had it been the summer season with its round of balls, fêtes, theatricals and dinners, in which the Portuguese joined, he would no doubt have called on the British merchants and been entertained. He might even have been lucky enough to meet someone like Miss Low, the young and very lovely American girl who had been staying with her uncle in Macao shortly before. She kept a diary which was published in Boston in 1900. Of a dinner in 1829 at the East India Company's House she writes:

'This evening we are to dine with the Company at half past six, where we shall be as stiff as stakes and, I suppose, shall not enjoy ourselves at all.'

But it was more amusing than she expected:

'Everything on the table was splendid—a whole service of massive plate. There were about sixty at table . . . The time passed very pleasantly.'

At the close of dinner they played snap-dragon. In another entry she writes of looking out of the window of her house, which was on the ridge commanding the splendid view:

28

'Saw one of the Company's ships with the sun shining on her well-filled sails. How I wished for Mr. Chinnery's talent for painting that I might sketch for you the beautiful scene before me, the large and handsome Church, milk-white, with a splendid flight of stone steps. . . . Just beyond, the port, stretching into the bay. Beyond this again you can see the roads, and the little boats skimming over the surface.'

And she adds:

'But I want someone to enjoy it with me.'

So great was the fascination which Macao exercised over some of those who during their active career as Canton merchants lived there in summer, that when the time came for them to retire to England, they could not bear to leave their houses upon the ridge and stayed on for the rest of their lives. But it is well known that many places in the East have this power of overcoming in British hearts nostalgia for home. All over the South Seas and Oceania, Burma, Siam and China you find Englishmen growing old and who yet cannot tear themselves away from an unhurried life of soft wind, rich sunsets, sweet scents and black-haired beauties, and would rather be buried in a palm-grove within sound of the surf and mourned by their progeny of half-bred sons, than face English cold, English haste and English women. Yet such men cannot altogether escape nostalgia. The day the boat comes in with mails and newspapers is a great day; and there are moments when they would give their bliss for a bus-ride or to be able to order an English dinner or perhaps to look again on a field of buttercups. But such moments pass, the pain of them is half sweet; like memories of a lost love, they but enrich the present.

Foreign Mud

Next morning, after the ship's pass had been issued at the Chinese customs office and Downing himself had paid the landing-fee of thirteen and fourpence, he took an egg-boat and boarded the sampan. This carried him back to his ship, yet barely clear of the Ladrone channels. With the delivery of the pass, and negotiation of the shoal water, the pilot's work was done and he prepared to leave. The sampan was brought under the stern, where it wallowed in a choppy sea, its mast now knocking against the taffrail above, now swinging largely away. The pilot had his small boy with him and at a moment when the mast pitched in, he lifted the boy who clutched it and slid down. The pilot himself followed at the next lunge. This was done with great skill, which he enjoyed displaying before the foreign demons who for all their sea lore could not have emulated him. Smiling and waving he stood by the mast-foot as the sampan cast off and sail was hoisted.

Downing's ship—her name is not mentioned—set course for Lintin Island in the centre of the great Canton bay twenty miles N.E. of Macao, from which it is clearly visible, being in appearance a mountain some two thousand feet high, a fact which explains its name, which translated means 'Solitary Nail'. Though a small island only three miles long, much importance attached to it as the entrepôt of the opium trade. That trade supplies the dramatic motive of this narrative, but at this early stage, while we are sightseeing with

Dr. Downing, it will suffice to describe the general look of things at Lintin, for we shall be returning to the subject again and again.

The ship anchored in the open roadstead under the mountain, where were lying some smart vessels of 300 tons burden, barque-rigged, perfect models of marine architecture. Downing remarked their clean lines, their twenty gun-ports and guessed at once they were opium clippers. Close inshore were three curious hulks. They had no masts, the whole of their decks being walled in and roofed, so that they looked like floating warehouses, the after end evidently a dwelling house, for you could see a chimney there, some windows and a verandah with flower pots. These were the so-called receiving ships. As soon as a clipper arrived, her opium chests were transferred to them. Their commanders were British, their crews Lascars, their boatmen and carpenters Chinese. The little garden of flower pots may be explained by the presence of Chinese, who cannot abide to be without flowers. The wives and families of the commanders often lived on board.

Downing then observed some fifty-oared Chinese boats, long two-masted craft, and enquired their purpose. He was informed they were called centipedes and scrambling dragons, and were owned by Chinese smugglers who loaded them with opium bought for cash on the receiving ships or through brokers at Canton, and evading the custom's patrols ran it ashore at small creek villages, whence their agents distributed it over the countryside.

'The opium trade is then illegal?' enquired Downing, who had but the vaguest idea of the situation.

'Of course,' said his informant, 'why else should our clippers resort to this island instead of going to Canton? Why have floating warehouses here if we could land the opium at the Canton factories? If it were lawful, no need for the cannon on those hulks. And look at the swivel guns, the

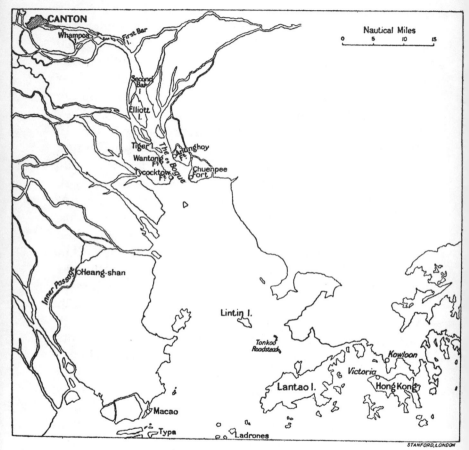

CANTON ESTUARY

MACAO SEEN FROM TYPA
Artist uncertain

CHINESE BOAT GIRL
from an oil painting by George Chinnery

muskets, the pikes on the smug-boats. It is a well-organized, a well-armed contraband traffic.'

'The Chinese authorities, then, are unable to suppress it?'

The man smiled. 'The authorities are in it.'

Downing was puzzled. 'Why then all the secrecy and precautions?'

'Because the officials are in it unofficially.'

'But are the higher authorities involved?'

'Certainly the provincial government of Canton is.'

To illustrate this, his informant told an amusing story of the way local officials pretended to demonstrate their zeal. When the clippers had discharged their cargo of opium and were ready to return to India with what lading they could get, the preventive service of the Chinese customs, which never attempted to sink the hulks or otherwise render Lintin unpleasant as a receiving station, would stage an imaginary pursuit. As soon as the British tars began singing at the capstans and it was evident the clippers were about to weigh, thirty or forty large men-of-war junks would begin to bear down on them. The clipper captain, who appreciated the joke very much, used to clap on all sail as if much alarmed, being careful, however, not to sail too fast, so as to give the lumbering junks the chance of a fair chase. Sometimes a captain would heave-to, so as to let a junk get within cannon shot, just to see if it would fire a broadside. On such occasions the Chinaman at once shivered his sail and banked his oars, waiting until the clipper resumed its course. The chase would be continued relentlessly, sometimes as far as the Ladrone Islands. Then allowing the clippers to get well away, almost out of sight, the junks would open a furious cannonade. Broadside after broadside would be discharged, the island hills reverberating with the blast and all the fisherfolk witness of the victory. In this way, their duty performed, their face restored, and the smuggler driven off, the officials returned in triumph to Canton. An express letter would be sent immediately to Peking stating that after a desperate conflict the foreign devils had been forced to run for it, such loss being inflicted as to discourage their return. We need not credit every detail of this story, but it is typical of the happy spirit that prevailed and may well have had a basis in fact.

Though the distribution of the opium was mostly done by the Chinese smugglers who took delivery at the Lintin hulks, this was not always the case. Sometimes the British firm which had imported a consignment would itself deliver it at a port further up the coast. In such cases Chinese buyers in Canton used to order so many chests and pay cash in advance, it being stipulated that the firm should undertake to hand them over to agents at an agreed place. Hunter, the American, in his book, *The Fan Kwae at Canton*, gives an entertaining description how this worked out in practice. In 1837, the year after Downing visited Lintin, Hunter, then a young man in the American firm of Russel & Company, was sent on a schooner called the *Rose* to learn how such a delivery was effected. The *Rose* was of 150 tons register and carried 300 chests of opium, valued at 150,000 dollars. Half of this had already been the subject of a deal at Canton and was to be handed over to agents of the buyers at Namoa Island in the Bay of Swatow, some three hundred miles north of Macao. The other half was to test the market in that locality. The schooner, having taken on the opium at Lintin, made a rapid journey and on the third day anchored inside the Island of Namoa close to two brigs owned by the leading British firms, Dent and Company and Jardine, Matheson and Company, which were there on a similar errand. In-shore were riding two men-of-war junks, one of them flying a commodore's flag.

The *Rose* had hardly swung with the tide before a scow was seen to leave one of the junks. As it approached an official wearing a mandarin's button in his hat was observed on board. He was seated comfortably in an arm-chair under a large embroidered silk umbrella, and was smoking a long pipe. Servants stood behind him with fans and he was supported by a number of official attendants in grass cloth robes and conical rattan hats, bound with the usual red silk cord.

'Who is this personage?' enquired Hunter, slightly apprehensive at seeing him come from a government junk.

'He is the official in charge of the port of Namoa,' said Captain Forster, the commander of the *Rose*, without any sign whatever of alarm.

'But is it all right about his coming?'

'Quite,' said the Captain. 'In fact, it is indispensable. Certain formalities have to be gone through before the agents take delivery. That is the purpose of his visit.'

After making this somewhat cryptic remark, he posted himself at the gangway and when the scow came alongside assisted His Excellency aboard. The Chinaman's manner was easy and dignified. He was conducted to the cabin, requested to seat himself, offered a glass of wine and a choice of cigars. After a polite interval devoted to compliments, he asked why the *Rose* had anchored at Namoa, since no foreign ship might enter any port but Canton.

CAPTAIN FORSTER (through his Shroff or Treasurer who was acting as interpreter): As Your Excellency may well believe, I would not have dared to enter Namoa, had not contrary winds and currents driven me from my course, which was from Singapore to Canton, and so compelled me to seek this haven to replenish my water and provisions.

HIS EXCELLENCY (having listened with complacent attention): Any supplies required may be obtained on application, but I must insist that as soon as they are delivered you depart at once for Canton. No loitering is permitted by Imperial Decree.

Having declared himself in this manner he stooped down and drew from his boot a long red document, which he handed to his secretary, requiring him in a grave voice to read it out.

The secretary (reading in a high official voice): True copy of Imperial edict dated Tao-Kuang, 17th year, 6th moon, 4th sun. As the port of Canton is the only one at which the Outer Barbarians are permitted to trade, on no account can they be allowed to wander and visit other places in the Middle Kingdom. His Majesty, however, being ever desirous that his compassion be made manifest even to the least deserving, cannot deny to such as are in distress from lack of food through adverse seas and currents the necessary means of continuing their voyage. When supplied they must not linger but put to sea again immediately. Respect this.

The secretary returned the Edict to His Excellency, who restored it to his boot and then rose to his feet. This was the well-understood signal for all his followers except the secretary to withdraw to the scow and leave him to discuss the real business. It was silently obeyed and he resumed his seat. After his glass had been refilled he came bluntly to the point, the Shroff as before acting as interpreter.

HIS EXCELLENCY: How many chests of foreign mud have you on board?

CAPTAIN FORSTER: About two hundred.

HIS EXCELLENCY: Are they all for Namoa?

CAPTAIN FORSTER: We want to try the market here.

HIS EXCELLENCY: You are wise. Further up the coast the officers are uncommonly strict. I am informed that at Amoy smugglers have recently been decapitated.

CAPTAIN FORSTER: We have no intention of going to Amoy.

HIS EXCELLENCY: You are wise, I repeat. We can assume then that you are landing your chests here.

CAPTAIN FORSTER: With Your Excellency's permission.

HIS EXCELLENCY: My permission, if I may put it so, depends on your offer.

CAPTAIN FORSTER: (Lapsing into pidgin) All same custom.

HIS EXCELLENCY: (Satisfied) All same custom.

36

Captain Forster had the money ready and handed it over to the secretary. The business being thus amicably concluded, His Excellency lit a cheroot, the glasses were recharged, the conversation became general, with everyone in good spirits. At the proper moment His Excellency rose to go. 'I announce my departure,' he said with some formality. The Americans hastened to conduct him to the side. He entered his boat, sat down in the arm-chair and with the umbrella above him was rowed to his junk. His departure did not pass unnoticed by those who were waiting on shore to buy. They now came aboard freely and trade began. Later two junks anchored close by after showing a pre-arranged signal at their mastheads. The 150 chests already paid for at Canton were quickly transferred to their holds.

(iii)

The Bogue

Though Downing did not know of this little comedy, since it took place the year after he was there, he heard all kinds of stories about the drug trade, as would any traveller who had gone that way, for it was in full swing, more than 20,000 chests of opium, worth two or three millions sterling according to the market, being smuggled annually at this time.

From the peak of Lintin to the Bogue the distance was some twenty miles up the great bay. Here the Pearl River discharged itself through an opening which at its broadest was three miles and at its narrowest less than a mile. It was almost a defile, for on both sides steep hills fell to the water. Nature had thus substantially assisted the Chinese in fortifying the gateway to Canton. They called the mouth the Lion's Gate and had built five forts to command it, the first at Chuenpee at the right entrance and opposite the second, Tycocktow, at the left entrance; the third at Anunghoy, the Woman's Shoe, at the upper extremity of the defile, four miles in, and the fourth opposite to it on an island called Wantong, where the passage was under a mile broad. The fifth fort was on Tiger Island, so named by the Portuguese because they thought it looked like a tiger's head, though English travellers tended to declare that they could see in it no resemblance whatever to a tiger. The Tiger Fort—it was two miles on from Wantong—looked down the defile.

Thus described, the Bogue sounds a very strong place. A ship attempting to force it would have to tack backwards and forwards for an hour or more and would necessarily come under point-blank range of each battery in turn. Yet on four occasions British ships had forced their way through; in 1637 Weddel on the *Dragon*,[1] in 1743 Anson[2] on the *Centurion*; more recently, in 1816, the frigate *Alceste* attached to the Amherst mission; and, only three years before Downing was there, the frigates *Imogene* and *Andromache* at the behest of Lord Napier, of which more hereafter. The explanation is quite simple: the cannon of the forts were not on carriages but fixed in the masonry of the loopholes. Their balls could only hit a ship if it happened to be directly in front, while the ship's gunners could traverse their pieces and pour in again and again broadsides from any angle. The garrisons of the forts never could stand this and always fled. That in two hundred years the Chinese had not put right this fatal defect was characteristic, less of their conservatism than of official ineptitude. After each forcing of the Bogue

[1] See my *The Great Within*, Part Three, Chapter One.
[2] See same volume, Part Three, Chapter Two.

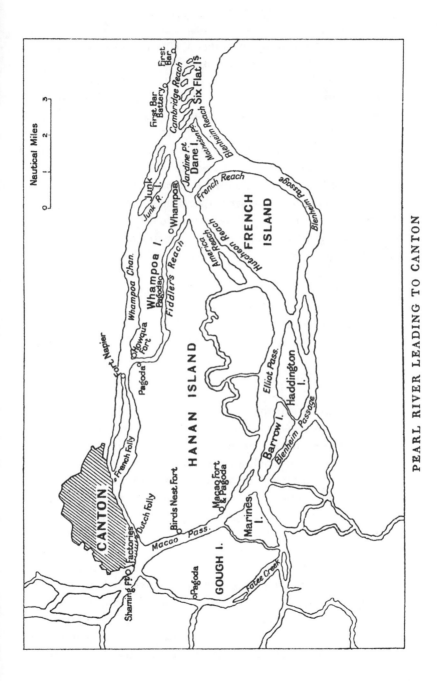

PEARL RIVER LEADING TO CANTON

the Emperor invariably cashiered the persons responsible and directed that all necessary measures to render the Bogue impregnable should be taken. But to comply with such orders would have involved a serious study of European gunnery and wide reforms in the local armed forces. Very possibly this was always beyond the competence of the authorities at Canton and in any case would have cost more money than they were inclined to spend. In the event, nothing was done. Like many other things in China the Bogue forts had only a paper importance. On paper the gateway to Canton was inexpugnable; in reality there was nothing to prevent British men-of-war from entering the river and holding up the city. This fact with all that it implied has much bearing on what is to follow and it is well to have it clearly in mind from the first survey of the ground.

After the Bogue the river widens and the hills recede. An extensive rice plain is disclosed, divided into islands by many streams which are arms of the main river, the country here being in the nature of a delta. This was the first broad view of the Chinese landscape for travellers arriving by sea. Pictures, painted on silk, on porcelain or on furniture, which they had seen in Europe, had prepared them for a countryside laid out as a parterre with gravel walks and pavilions, flowering trees and hump-backed bridges. The park of the Summer Palace was such an artificial scene, but the Canton rice plain, as you viewed it from the deck of a merchantman during the monsoon, was a green expanse edged with pale blue hills, dotted with villages and isolated country houses, a pagoda on every eminence and hardly a tree to be seen. It was a land of humming life, where a patient industrious people worked from dawn till dusk, tending their fields, fishing the streams, looking after their livestock and trudging to market. Of that life, the immemorial round of rustic China, with all its virtues and all its talent, the European traveller was necessarily quite ignorant. What he came into contact with was the life of the river, a more boisterous, a more disreputable life, from the spectacle of which he drew his conclusions and formed his picture of the Chinese nation.

(iv)

The River People

From the Bogue to Whampoa was a distance of thirty miles or so according to the course steered. There were two bars en route at about the tenth and the twenty-third mile. Vessels of more than 1400 tons sometimes anchored below the former bar, but the great majority of merchantmen trading to China were of less than that tonnage. The bars were crossed at the flood. If the wind failed, six-oared bar-boats were ready to give a tow. After the upper bar the course of the river was due east. You came very soon to the Six Flat Islands and then to Dane Island, the eastern end of which was called Matheson Point, and the western Jardine Point, after the two partners of the firm about which we shall hear so much before we are done. Adjoining Dane Island to the westward was the island of Whampoa, the name being a corruption of the Chinese word Wang-po, Yellow Anchorage.

Whampoa, lying thirteen miles short of Canton, was the place where all European ships anchored. They were not allowed to approach any nearer to the provincial capital nor would the water have allowed this except in the case of the smallest. At Whampoa they discharged their cargoes into barges and waited in the road for three or four months, until the teas came down and were loaded aboard. During the season from October to March there might be seen any day in the reaches between Dane Island and Whampoa fifty or sixty of the most splendid ships in the world. The sailing ship, which was to be ousted gradually by the steamer from about 1840 onwards, was then at the peak of its development, a complicated bit of craftsmanship, over which contemporary writers continually became eloquent. 'As the Reach winds round Danes Island in a gentle curve,' says Downing, 'you have a view of a whole semicircle of shipping, drawn up and moored as if in the order of battle . . . a large forest of masts and rigging . . . Cargo-boats and junks, some of them highly adorned, are seen winding their way with great skill between the Indiamen, while the whole surface of the water appears covered with an infinity of small craft, paddling about in every direction.' Downing's ship came to its moorings dressed with flags, a band playing on the poop. The sailors were in a state of wild excitement, looking forward to their shore leave, for stronger drink could be got at Whampoa and Canton than at any port they knew. 'Slowly she proceeds, and at last, when near the place which had been chosen for her, the topsails are lowered and clewed up, and the order "Let go the anchor" is pronounced. Close by was an Indiaman of the largest type, a double-decker, her tall slender masts towering above the others, and with her yards squared and delicate rigging extended with the minutest nicety; the well-bleached awning above the deck, stretched with the greatest care; the gilded figure-head and ornamented stern, and the sides fresh painted and shining with varnish. As she lies thus moored in the centre of the stream, she only requires a few guns peeping out of her open ports to transform her into a man-of-war, and one of the finest in the British Navy. Borne lightly on the water, her tall spars are reflected towards you and her double side, checkered with black and white, is portrayed in the water immediately beneath, resembling the squares in a chessboard made of ivory and ebony.' Downing as a rule is an indifferent writer, but the vision of great British ships floating majestically in the Pearl River gives him wings for a moment, and his thoughts involuntarily turn to war, though during the hundred and fifty years of trade between England and China there had never been more than the cannonades in the Bogue, which were not naval engagements but efforts on the part of the Chinese port authorities to enforce the regulations that no ship of war should enter the Pearl River. The English, however, were very conscious of the power of their ships. Many of the seamen at Whampoa remembered Trafalgar; some of them had actually fought in that action. Here in China they went softly, for they had come trading and wanted no trouble. But at the back of their minds they felt ready and able for whatever might come and supremely confident in the event.

Even before the anchor was down, the wash-boats were alongside. These were decked and twenty feet long, the roofing of split bamboo, its walls of curtains. The crew was three or four girls, who washed and mended for the sailors and petty officers, active cheerful creatures, good natured and robust, who year after year were employed by the same ships, and were so honest that should you leave behind some clothes you found them ironed and folded ready for you the next season. As the ship swung, they would bawl out to the chief mate: 'Ah, you missee chiefee mate, how you dooa? I saavez you long time, when you catchee Whampoa last time. How missee captinee? I saavez him werry wen. You saavez my? I makee mendee, all same you shirtee last time.' The sailors were delighted to see them; they were easy-going and ready to be anyone's sweetheart. The atmosphere here is of the South Seas and the little ports of Indo-China, where some of the labour is done by stout independent wenches of this kind, but is not at all of more staid inland China, where rules and regulations, custom and tradition, lay far heavier upon female shoulders.

43

The compradore was the first functionary on board. The paternal government liked to order every act of the Barbarians and insisted that each firm should have a compradore, one of whose duties it was to meet the firm's ships on their arrival at Whampoa and see to the supply of fresh meat and vegetables. To have allowed the pursers to negotiate as they did in other ports, directly with contractors on shore would have conflicted with the policy forbidding foreign devils to have contact with the Chinese public. But though the compradores were forced on the firms, they were much liked, because they were so obliging, good natured, took such trouble, were so human. At the time we are writing of, the senior compradore at Whampoa was an old gentleman called Acow, the name a corruption, as were all the names of the various go-betweens, for the English in the regions where they wander have their own insular fashion of pronouncing names and places. As Acow came on deck, grey-headed, his beard grizzled, with the stoop of venerability and a whimsical expression, the officers would hasten to shake him warmly by the hand. All who had been there before knew him well and he himself never forgot a face. An animated conversation began in pidgin, so laughable a language that it was almost impossible to be serious in it: the most weighty matters it transformed into drollery, one of the reasons why the great Anglo-Chinese imbroglio we shall be describing was never taken quite seriously on the spot.

The second person on board at Whampoa was a representative of the customs, for a long list of port charges had to be paid, involving a great deal of discussion and measurement. Attached to his staff was a factotum whom the sailors used to call Jack Hoppo, and whose duty it was to hang about the deck and see that nothing was smuggled on shore. He was ready for a consideration, however, to look the other way or even to advise how best to arrange a deal. Always on the best of terms with everybody, we may listen to him talking to

44

the boatswain of Downing's ship, to whom for some reason or other he was under an obligation.

'In England so, you catchee wife, can?' says he, smiling widely.

'Yes, I've a wife, what of it?' enquired the boatswain.

'You catchee chilo, can?'

'One child, Jack; well?'

'Bull chilo, cow chilo?'

'A little girl. Why do you ask?'

'Ah yah! Can do!' exclaims Jack Hoppo, apparently much delighted. 'You catchee cow chilo! I catchee flowers, all same put round head cow chilo.'

Next day the boatswain received neatly packed in a wooden box some artificial flowers for his daughter's hair.

As the merchantmen had to lie anchored at Whampoa for three or four months waiting for the firms at Canton to buy the teas and send them down, the officers and seamen had plenty of shore leave. They were not permitted by the Chinese to land on Whampoa Island, but Danes Island, and French Island, which adjoined it, were thrown open to them for walks, and excursions were made to Canton. Each sailor was allowed two visits to that city. They used to go up in parties of twenty under the charge of an officer and get very drunk indeed in Hog Lane, a thoroughfare adjacent to the British factory. The drink-shops in that street sold a concoction guaranteed to give the greatest satisfaction in the quickest time. Its ingredients have been preserved for us in the *Chinese Repository*, a quarterly publication edited by a Protestant mission to China: they were alcohol, tobacco juice, sugar and arsenic. Downing has described the scene in Hog Lane as he saw it with his own eyes. The seamen would be sauntering up the dirty alley when they were hailed in a hearty manner: 'Fine day, Jack! How you do, old boy?' No British tar could resist such a salutation, even had he the wish, which these had not. Soon they were all seated inside the drink-shops and pouring the potent liquor down

their throats. Those who became insensible had their
pockets picked and were then thrown into the lane. Others
not completely stupefied set on the shop-keepers with their
fists when the attempt was made to rob them. The whole
street sometimes became embroiled in a free fight, which
the Chinese did not always lose, for the inhabitants of Hog
Lane were extremely tough. Though violent riots were
rare, the street at certain hours was very disorderly. You
would see sailors on the way back to the boat, quarrelsome,
insulting everyone they met and kicking over the heaps of
bird-seed piled on the ground for sale; or reeling and surrounded by a jeering riff-raff, at whom they made rushes,
till they toppled over. There they would lie, when presently
their officer would emerge from the factory where friends
had been entertaining him, round up his party as best he
could, bundle them into the boat and take them back to
Whampoa. Some of the older hands remained sufficiently
lucid to buy liquor to carry back with them. This they had
to secrete because the captains, though obliged by long
custom to allow their men the occasional drinking-bout
ashore, did not permit liquor on board. But the Chinese were
ingenious in helping their customers. You could buy the
stuff in a bladder and hide it in your trousers; or could get an
unobtrusive teapot filled with it; or, best of all, the ballast
casks. Arriving back with these supplies the crew would keep
up the carouse all next day. The reader will not be surprised
to hear that the death-rate at Whampoa was very high.
There was an extensive cemetery on Danes Island, the
ground being the property of Chinese residents who charged
a good price for each grave. But Jack's money did not all go to
the publicans and undertakers. The mandarins, as contemporary writers always called the executive officers of the
police and preventive service, had their percentage. Hog
Lane could not have continued for generations to be a sink
of iniquity, had not the guardians of the law been in league
with its purveyors. This connivance did not prevent the

authorities from adopting, when it suited them, a high moral tone, when in edicts they would animadvert upon the behaviour of the Barbarians and the beastly manner in which they comported themselves, coming as they did from beyond the pale of civilization. Our sailormen were admittedly a carefree high-spirited lot in the eighteen-thirties. But if they were illiterate, hard to discipline, wild and reckless, they were also human, loyal, dauntless and long-suffering. Rowlandson, who died in 1827, has many drawings of them. His *Landing at Greenwich*, for instance, gives you Jack to the very life.

Our cicerone, Dr. Downing, has a lively description of the thirteen-mile row from Whampoa to Canton. Provided you caught the tide, it took two and a half hours in a ship's boat. As the map shows, various courses might be steered, but usually one went either north of Whampoa by the Junk Channel or south of it by Fiddler's Reach. Half-way was marked by a pagoda nine storeys in height, which stood on the left bank shortly after leaving behind the west point of Whampoa. The sailors, as they rowed, says Downing, always disputed the exact spot of the half-way. Was it when you saw daylight through the windows of the pagoda or when a certain temple gave you a bearing upon it? The reason for this dispute is readily understood: it was the custom to serve grog at the half-way halt, and the men were angling for their refresher. When the officer agreed they were truly half-way, 'Jack had his quid out and in again, with the spirits between, in a moment,' as Downing puts it.

As they rowed along, sometimes girls sculling small sampans loaded with oranges and bananas would approach from a bank and offer their wares. 'These women are remarkably strong, and manage their sampan so well that I have occasionally seen one of them', says Downing, 'with a single scull at the stern come up with a four-oared cutter, and keep up the chase as long as she thought there was a chance of selling her stores.' So naïve and fresh were these celestial greengrocers that some of the younger Fan-quis—the British found it fun to refer to themselves as foreign devils —would pretend as a joke they wanted fruit, but, when the girl was nearly alongside, would pull away, tempting her to follow, yet keeping just out of reach. A girl taken in by this trick would have given a brilliant display of her oarsmanship before, undeceived, she dropped astern. The sailor boys then ceased pulling and beckoned her to come up again. This she would do, calling out: 'You wantshee fruit, all same plantaine, all same orange?' Then just as it seemed a hand was extended from the stern to grip her gunwale, the rowers gave way again and she was left bobbing in their wash. At about this stage she generally lost her temper and a torrent of abuse flowed from her mouth, partly Chinese and partly English. The sailor boys found it so funny to hear pidgin obscenities, that they all burst into open-hearted laughter, laughter in which she could not help joining, however vexed she was before. Feeling now it was too bad to have treated the poor girl so, they tried to make it up with her, holding out money to pay for oranges. But it was her turn to make a fool of them. Beckon and call as they might, she kept out of their reach and to all their importunities answered: 'No, can.'

To get the full bouquet of this farcical scene you must picture the broad river puckered with little waves, the green sweep of the rice, on the horizon blue hills; you must conjure the many sorts of passing craft, the Mandarin house-boats, dainty and lacquered, the streamers and lanterns of passenger boats, the high tilted junks with demon-painted sterns; and you must plunge these images into a light more intense than we know in these countries, into a warmer wind and an air, purer and more scented than we can sniff except in dreams.

As one drew nearer to Canton the river became more crowded. While some of those frequenting it were passengers, fishermen, smugglers or police, there was also a

THE PRAYA GRANDE, MACAO
From a painting by Thomas Allom

ENTRANCE TO HOUSE USED BY THE SENIOR MEMBER OF THE EAST INDIA CO. AT MACAO
WITH STEPS LEADING UP TO THE CHURCH OF SAN LORENZO
from a drawing by George Chinnery

permanent water population, people who lived in boats
always and conducted the trade of the creeks and estuaries.
Their habitations were large commodious junks, often to
be seen moored in midstream, as if waiting for the tide,
and were crowded with men, women and children. These
were a rough and insolent class, who did no business with
foreigners and so had no reason to modify the national
prejudice against them. When, say, a British cutter was
passing, they would pop their heads out of every door and
window, staring unpleasantly and soon beginning to gibe,
pointing, making obscene jokes and roaring with laughter,
as the English sailors, red-faced, hairy and sweating, pulled
by. If within range, they threw what came handy, not dead
rats or anything conceivably edible, but refuse, fruit-skins,
broken bricks or bilge water. Mothers held up their children,
crying 'Look, look, Foreign Devils!' and naked urchins of
four or five stood on tiptoe on a bale or box, and raising one
hand clenched as if lifting a head by the hair, drew below it
the other, open and with a horizontal sawing motion, as if
cutting a throat, and chorused the while 'Demons! Devils!'
As a rule the British tars paid little attention to these demonstrations, for they were thinking of Hog Lane and the
welcome awaiting them there. But on occasions when the
river people went beyond all bounds or when the seamen
were returning drunk in charge of a midshipman in his
teens, there was a fight, the junk was boarded and the
seamen used their fists or laid about them with ropes' ends.
Such a retaliation always seemed to surprise the Chinese, as
if it had never occurred to them that people so beastly and
degraded as foreign devils would dare to raise their hands
against Celestials. Yet it chastened them and they accommodated themselves, observing for a time a greater decorum,
thereby exhibiting traits of the national character, which
will frequently be observed later on in more important
transactions.

Quite close to Canton, where the suburbs straggled along

the north bank, a river population of a different sort would
be met with. You saw moored off shore house-boats of the
most elegant variety. Gilded, painted and minutely carved,
with flower pots in rows on the roof, these were the Flower
Boats, by which euphemism the Chinese denominated floating brothels. On balconies in tiers with curious banisters,
women sat waiting robed in silk and jewelled or toddled to
exhibit the smallness of their crushed feet. 'As the foreigners
pass along close to the Flower Boats', writes Downing, 'the
girls come out from their apartments and use all their little
arts of attraction. They chatter and whisper to one another,
and sometimes laugh out and nod their heads. It is not easy
to understand the utility of these manoeuvres, as these
houses are frequented by the Chinese alone, no Fan-qui
being allowed to enter.' He puts down their solicitation
either to force of habit or to a desire to hint that 'nightee
time come' a visit could be effected without the knowledge
of the police. In point of fact, Europeans did not frequent
these places as a rule; it was considered dangerous to do so.
In Downing's book there are unpleasant stories of men
who had gone there. 'A party of young men returning
from town one night ran their boat alongside one of them.
One, who was a little in liquor, jumped on board and was
quickly assailed by eight or ten men, who seized upon him
and were going to throw him into the water, and it was
only by the greatest exertions of his mess-mates that he was
rescued from their hands. One poor fellow, at another time,
went on board by himself and insisted on penetrating into
the interior. It was ascertained that he had gone in, but he
was never heard of afterwards.' Whether the Flower Boats
were run by quite such ferocious roughs may be doubted.
But it seems to have been a fact that Europeans did not
resort there. They had other more discreet and comfortable
rendezvous. 'A tradesman', says Downing, 'once invited me
to call upon him at Canton, and, as an inducement which he
thought it impossible for me to withstand, said he would

show me some ladies "all same foot, so so, all same; werry little, can do," at the same time holding his finger and thumb about three inches apart from each other and looking delighted and significant.' Besides, at Whampoa there were plenty of girls, and some of a better class who through long acquaintance with the captains and officers used to come on board for a chat and a cup of tea.

By the time you were level with the city the number of boats was so great that you had the impression of a town on the water. Travellers were reminded of Venice on a gala day. The various vessels were anchored from the middle of the stream to the shore in rows which made lanes and from which side lanes branched off. The river was here half a mile broad, becoming a mile broad beyond the west point of Honan Island which jutted halfway across the frontage. As the tidal current was rapid, to get to the stairs was no easy task. You had to take your boat down one of the lanes and soon were entangled among a host of small craft. When the oars became useless, resort was had to paddles. A boathook was handy for pulling yourself along. The din was tremendous; on all sides the hammering of carpenters, the cries of salesmen, the thud of gongs, the snapping of crackers and, not least, the yells of abuse as old women leant over banisters and accused you wrathfully of scraping their paint. Through the maze you tried to keep in sight the landing steps below the water-gate of the British factory's garden. After a long tussle you reached it and disembarked.

The Factories

Up to this we have been keeping our eyes as far as possible on the river. But it is not to be supposed that the traveller did this. He will have been straining to catch sight of the Factories. They used to come into view in this manner: first you saw the great walled city of Canton, a square, each side of which was over a mile long, and in which more than a million people were reputed to live. The walls were thirty feet high, with towering gates, and outside them were extensive suburbs. On the south side, which was that facing the river, the space between the walls and the water was a third of a mile. This area was the port of Canton and a most busy quarter, full of warehouses, shops and stores of all kinds, with water-steps at frequent intervals. As your eye travelled along this frontage you perceived flags flying at the western end of it. Three quarters of a mile brought you opposite the flags, which in the eighteen-thirties were those of the British, the Dutch, the French and the Americans. They were flying from tall flagstaffs in front of a row of buildings of a semi-European character. On account of the press of junks and sampans, it was hardly possible to distinguish much more for the moment though one gathered that the buildings stood back about fifty yards and that between them and the river was an open space of some sort. Not until you landed at the stairs in front of the British flagstaff could you get a detailed impression of the general features. You were in a garden or shrubbery, bounded east

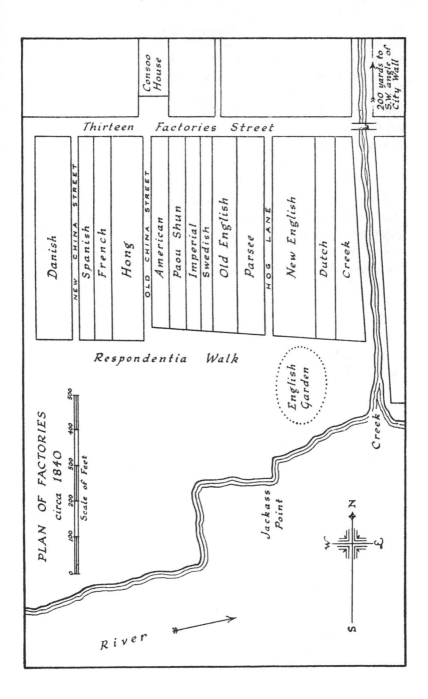

and west by walls. North of you was the pillared façade of a two-storeyed building, which you knew already was the British Factory. A little further exploration disclosed that to your left, over the west wall of the garden, was a square, a hundred yards across, at the other end of which was the American flagstaff and beyond it the French, while to your right, over the east wall, was the Dutch flagstaff. You had arrived at one of the most curious and famous places in all Asia.

The plan opposite page 52 shows the lay-out, but it requires some little explanation which, if the reader desires to enjoy the flavour of the episodes to be recounted, he will do well to master. In the first place, what precisely were the Factories? They had nothing, of course, to do with manufacture, but had the old-fashioned sense of the word and were offices, showrooms and treasuries where the business of the trade between China and Europe (and India) was transacted and where from August to March the European merchants lived. From the front they looked like a row of single houses, but actually they were a congeries of buildings arranged in depth and opening on inner courts. When it is said that their depth was a hundred and forty yards, and that the frontage of the British Factory was a hundred and twenty feet, the number and size of its rooms behind can be estimated. It was a regular warren of a place, the store-rooms, offices and treasuries on the ground floor; public apartments, dining and sitting rooms, on the first floor; and on the second floor, for many of the inner structures had three floors, were the bedrooms. Among its buildings was a church. It was, in fact, as large and self-contained as a monastic foundation, to which it had the further resemblance that no women were allowed by the Chinese to live there.

A second point to notice is that though, as the plan shows, the Factories bore the names of most of the maritime nations in Europe, they were not, except in the case of the British, Dutch, American and French, occupied by the merchants of those countries at the time of which we are writing. They had been leased in the past by Danish, Swedish, Austrian and Spanish companies, but these had gone out of business by the late eighteen-thirties. Nevertheless, the old names were kept on. The East India Company, which up to 1834 had the sole right in Britain of trading to China, leased till that date for a rental of £20,000 per annum the factory into whose garden we have already penetrated. It was twice the size of any other factory and its internal appointments were far superior.

The factory marked Old English was old English in the sense that it had once been rented by the Company. Not all the British merchants lived in the British factory. Before the Company's monopoly was terminated in 1834, it used to grant trade licenses to a few London houses affiliated to it, and also allowed a number of British houses, with offices in Calcutta, to engage in what was called the country trade, that is the exchange of commodities between India and China and the countries en route. These merchants leased accommodation among the various buildings along the front. After 1834, when the Company and the houses affiliated to it ceased to hold the monopoly, there occurred an influx of other merchants and these, too, had to find accommodation. The total number of British merchants, partners and individuals, was sixty-six in 1834 and rose to a hundred and fifty-six in 1837 after the trade was free. The leading firm, Jardine and Matheson, leased the Creek Factory, the one situated on the extreme eastern end of the line, and so called because it was bounded on its east by a creek. The Chinese had their own names for these blocks. They called the British, Assured Tranquillity; the Creek, Peaceful Justice; and the American, Wide Fountains: nor in employing so picturesque a nomenclature were they acting with particularity, for most Chinese place names are highly fanciful. Yet, to choose Assured Tranquillity for the British was more fanciful than usual, for as this book will show the troubles, destined to plague China for seventy years, had their rise there.

Looking more closely at the topography, we should note certain features. Hog Lane has already been mentioned. The plan shows its location immediately west of the New English Factory. There were two other streets running through the frontage, Old China Street and New China Street. At the back of the factories ran Thirteen Factory Street. North of it lay the suburbs dividing the Factories from the city wall, which was pierced at this place by the Petition Gate, so called because there petitions, on the special occasions when it was necessary to address the authorities, had to be presented. On the river side of the Factories we have made reference to a square. This was in front of the buildings between Hog Lane and Old China Street. It was named Respondentia Walk or Jackass Point, and was supposed to be a place where merchants could take the air. In fact, it was generally so full of Chinese of the lower orders, who crowded into it from Hog Lane and Old China Street, that it was no place for relaxation. Pedlars, hawkers, peep-show men and loungers, cobblers, tailors, and sellers of tea or nuts, not to speak of men who just stared or begged loudly, packed this little promenade, and though from time to time, when it became unbearable, the police would be sent for to clear them out, they filtered back again and continued as before to shout, beg, accost and stare. The merchants for their part were not allowed to enter the walled city or to make excursions into the country round. For privacy they had their rooms in the Factories and there was the walled-off British garden. But as soon as they went outside, they were among the rabble of the square, of Hog Lane and of the other narrow alleys adjoining. The Chinese here were well used to them and normally offered no incivility. For a century and a half it had been as safe to live in Canton as in London. Yet the merchants had many causes for complaint, one of which was confinement in a quarter with a frontage of only a thousand feet and a maximum length of a fourth of a mile.

The Official System of Trading
to China

In the introductory chapter an outline was given of the
events which led to the founding of the Factories, of the
attitude of the Chinese Government to trade with the West,
of how the English out-distanced their European rivals, and
in general of the anomalous state of affairs at Canton where
Britain, victorious in Europe and mistress of an Empire in
the Middle East, continued to be treated by the Chinese as
if she were a chieftancy beyond the borders of civilization.
That outline will now be filled in with sufficient detail to
make the drama which follows intelligible.

When Canton was first opened to overseas trade at the end
of the seventeenth century, the Emperor sent down a
representative to milk it on his behalf. The duty of this
officer was to impose on the trading Barbarians as many
dues as he could get them to pay, and remit his takings to
Court. To call these dues a custom's tariff is to employ a
modern term which obscures the reality. The port payments
were not revenue in our sense, but imperial perquisites.
This explains why no tariff was ever published: it was a
private matter; moreover the amounts payable varied according as more or less could be squeezed from the merchants. There was no department of foreign commerce; no
board or ministry had any control; and so there was no
provincial officer to whom the merchants could appeal
against exactions, for none had jurisdiction.

The officer sent to manage the trade was a Court grandee, a Manchu who was generally a member of the Imperial Clan, and so a relative of the Emperor. His official designation was Hai Kwan Pu, which the British corrupted into Hoppo, a comical word, which reflected the amused contempt with which they viewed the whole Chinese administration and was a-piece with the farcical atmosphere distilled by pidgin English. The Hoppo, of course, was not salaried. He was expected to pay himself from the takings. Indeed, he had to purchase the appointment, which was considered one of the most lucrative in the Empire.

As described, the system was a foreign squeeze. But it had a further refinement, a monopoly within a monopoly, which yielded both the Emperor and the Hoppo additional funds. The Eight Regulations laid down that foreign merchants were not allowed to buy in the open market, but only from a corporation known as the Co-Hong, a body of contractors appointed by the Hoppo. The whole trade passed through the hands of these persons, who by charging far more than the current rates made very large incomes. But for a man to get the post of Hong merchant he had to pay an enormous sum to Court, a sum which he repaid himself out of the trade. The Hong merchants may therefore be described as Emperor's agents, the Emperor himself trading through them. In this way the Court got a share of the profits of the trade itself as well as the taxes. In short, the whole was a cleverly arranged Imperial monopoly.

For the privilege of conducting the Emperor's trade the Hong merchants had, in addition to buying their posts, to make many further payments and presents. On behalf of his master the Hoppo frequently squeezed them under various pretexts. Hunter in his book already mentioned describes the sort of conversation you might find yourself holding any day with Howqua, the leading Hong merchant, who had been clever enough, in spite of a long course of exactions, to amass a fortune reputed at the time to equal five million sterling.

'Well, Howqua,' you would begin, 'hav got news today?'

'Hav got too muchee bad news,' he would reply with his old wan smile. 'Hwang Ho hav spilum too muchee.'

This reference to flooding by the Yellow River warned you of what was coming. You knew by experience that fires, floods, storms, famines in any part of China, even if a thousand miles away, gave the Hoppo an opportunity to call on the Hong merchants to subscribe, nominally, for relief. Accordingly you said, a note of condolence coming into your voice:

'Man-ta-le hav come see you?' pidgin for the enquiry whether the Hoppo had actually sent one of his subordinate mandarins to ask for a subscription. But it was worse than that. Poor Howqua had received a notice calling upon him to pay a stated sum and expressed this fact as follows:

'He no come see my, he sendee come one piece chop. He come to-mollo. He wanchee my two-lac dollar.'

Astounded by this demand for £50,000, for that was what it amounted to, you asked with commiseration:

'You pay he how muchee?'

'My pay he fitty, sikky thousand so,' replies Howqua.

'But s'pose he no contentee?' you suggest.

'S'pose he number one no contentee, my pay he one lac.'

If in spite of squeezing to the tune of £25,000 a time, Howqua possessed five million pounds stowed away, one may suppose that the Hoppo did pretty well during his three years' tenure of office. In 1804 the then Hoppo's takings were estimated at £200,000 a year, and that in spite of what he found it necessary to pay the local officials, like the Viceroy and the Governor, to keep them quiet.

When Dr. Downing was in Canton in 1836-37 a new Hoppo took office and one of his first acts was to inform the British merchants that he proposed to call on them. Such an act of condescension on the part of holders of his appointment was very rare, and it was supposed at the time that he had a practical reason, the one suggested being that, as he had never seen Red Bristles before and was liable to be asked questions by the Emperor in an approaching audience, he thought it prudent to inform himself by an inspection. Whatever may have been his precise object in unbending to such an extraordinary degree, he decided to make it a formal occasion, and putting on his Court robes set out in his sedan. He had the decoration of the peacock's feather and the knob on his hat was a ruby, which denoted that he had attained the second rank in the Mandarinate.

As it had been decided to return his politeness by offering him breakfast, the state apartments in the English Factory were aired, the silver plate was got out, the best wines brought up, while the leading merchants assembled on the steps to welcome him as soon as his sedan was reported in the suburbs. His procession passed down the narrow thoroughfare of Hog Lane, in Chinese Green Pea Street, the footmen who preceded it clearing this seven foot passage with their sticks and commanding its famous gin-shop proprietors to kneel, Old Jemmy Apoo, Ben Bobstay, Tom Bowline, Jolly Jack, Young Tom and Old Sam's Brother, for so the British sailors nicknamed the principal purveyors of the noted cocktail called in pidgin 'first chop rum number one curio', a violent intoxicant and aphrodisiac combined. The singing birds twittered in their cages, the junk-shop keepers bowed; Hog Lane was not accustomed to sight of the quality. The procession was of some length, for the great man was followed by the Hong merchants, each in his sedan. It entered Respondentia Walk and swinging left through the gate in the factory garden wall drew up under the pillared façade above the main door.

His Excellency alighted. He was a prepossessing old gentleman of sixty years of age with a straggling grey moustache and a tuft of a beard. His clothes were of the finest silk, blue and red tones predominating, and on his breast was richly embroidered a bird. When the bowing was done, he was conducted indoors and up the stairs to the state dining room, where hung, among other pictures, a Lawrence portrait of George IV and a portrait of Lord Amherst, the nobleman who twenty years before had been so very glad to get the imperial breakfast sent him on the morning of his ignominious dismissal by the Emperor Chia Ching. Not that the Hoppo deigned, as they led him past, to remark on these works of art; to him they were beastly things, everything that a painting should not be. He was ushered to a seat, a handsome armed chair, at the head of the table which was loaded with dishes, beef, fowl, plum-puddings, jellies, in short everything, as Downing says, 'to form a first rate breakfast after the English fashion.' The British merchants, however, did not presume to sit down with him. They stood in a row behind a rail or banister which ran across the room a little to his left. In this way he was able to see and study them at leisure without being oppressed by their barbarian presence or obliged to speak with them more than he desired. The Hong merchants had been left downstairs, but he was attended by his secretary, his interpreter, and a staff of servants.

On taking his seat he viewed the viands and motioned to a servant to hand him the beef. When the dish was brought he observed it attentively, not altogether as one inspects an article of food but rather examines what is unknown and curious. When he had completed his examination, he smiled thinly as with distaste and waved it away telling them to bring him up something else. Dish after dish was then offered to his view. It was supposed by the merchants, who stood watching his progress, that eventually he would light on a thing he liked. But the inspection went on: he dismissed in sequence the fowl, the cutlets, the ham and kidneys, nor was more favourable to the plum-pudding. Would he then rise without tasting anything? No; he was a gentleman; he knew what was expected of him. 'Bring me a cup of tea,' he sighed at last.

Some of the Red Bristles behind the barrier could not bear

this and left the room. The others whispered among themselves and their remarks were not complimentary to His Excellency. He, however, sipped his tea contentedly and presently announced his departure in formal terms. They conducted him with ceremony to his sedan at the hall-door and bowed respectfully as he was carried away.

The significance of this scene will soon be clear enough. The Hoppo's behaviour was in no way singular; had he acted otherwise he would have shown singularity. What he did was in perfect accord with the attitude of the Court of Peking, not only towards western merchants, but everything western. For a century and a half the Honourable Company's servants had been treated precisely in this manner by all Chinese grandees. A system had been elaborated under which they were allowed to trade but were held at arm's length. The Emperor's point of view has already been stated. He desired to encourage the westerners enough to take their money, but not so much that they became difficult to manage and strong to make demands. The Hoppo, and his colleagues in the administration, the Viceroy and the Governor, had to sail between these two points, and make the dues, the restrictions, the regulations as stiff as was consistent with maintaining the trade at a figure which yielded what was held to be a handsome squeeze, but not so stiff as to enrage the Barbarians. Complaints, alleged wrongs, applications for improved facilities should never be considered on their merits. To milk the trade till there was left just enough profit to make it worth the merchants' while to continue it, and to refuse all concessions short of causing a rupture, that was the ideal and it was consistently followed. Such a policy was not business: it was a racket: and the British had found that the way to combat it was to meet refusal to consider wrongs with a degree of unpleasantness sufficient to cause the Court to fear for its perquisites, and the local officers to fear, not only for theirs, but also punishment for failing to soothe the Barbarians. To a certain extent the Company had followed this course, but from the first its policy had been to conciliate and to bear. It was persuaded that any other course inevitably led to conflict, and that conflict meant expense, and expense cut dividends. For a century and a half its merchants at Canton accommodated themselves and declared the steady increase of the trade to be proof that it paid to do so. It probably did pay a monopolist company to act with the greatest mildness, for Britain as a nation was not behind it; moreover, throughout the eighteenth and early nineteenth century the Company was in the process of consolidating its position in India. When that consolidation was complete and when it had acquired territories in Burma and Malaya on the road to China, the necessity for so utter a circumspection was less apparent. But not till the opening of the China trade to all British merchants in 1834 did a change of tone become apparent. These free merchants had England behind them, particularly manufacturing England, an England made conscious of her power by victory in Europe. The stiffening of attitude did not happen in a day. Some years elapsed before opinion at home was awakened. The partners, Jardine and Matheson, were the men who did more to rouse opinion both in Canton and London than anyone else. Yet in using this language we must be careful not to forget about the skeleton in the cupboard. Opium was the staple commodity the free merchants had to sell and the Company provided them with it. We shall return to this frequently, for to understand and assess its weight is extremely difficult.

The Co-Hong besides being the agency through which the Emperor sold tea and silk to foreigners, had many administrative duties arising from its primary function. For the system to work properly it was essential that the Company's servants should not be able to correspond with or interview the authorities. That would have made things far too easy for them; it would have facilitated complaints, made refusal more difficult if the complaints were reasonable, and would, moreover, have been the thin end of the wedge, leading the British to think they had the same rights as Chinese subjects, and have encouraged them to hope they might petition at Court. In short, it would have allowed them entry, when the principle was to keep them out. A buffer was essential; the Hong was the buffer. All requests and complaints, all business no matter of what nature, had to be addressed to the Hong. From the Chinese point of view there were great advantages in this: it gave excuse for delays; and it provided scapegoats. The Hong merchants were made primarily responsible for everything. If any of the regulations were disobeyed by the Barbarians, if their drunken sailors broke out and killed somebody, if their warships approached, if they brought their women up, the Hoppo, and the other heads of the administration, rounded on the Hong and it was another case of 'fitty sikky tousand'. Indeed, the worse the Barbarians behaved, the better it was, provided they did not go too far. One feels that some of the regulations were drawn up for the express purpose of being disobeyed, and that the good behaviour of the Honourable Company was sometimes a disappointment, an expense, as it were, a dashing of reasonable expectations of squeeze, so much so that its abject compliance did not pay, obviously did not pay the Hoppo, but also did not pay the Company, for then the regulations were tightened to make compliance impossible. It will be noticed that though the Barbarians lived entirely within the power of the Chinese authorities, they were not personally punished for breach of regulations. It was considered an easier, more prudent and more subtle procedure to punish the Hong.

But we must now particularize. The Hong merchants numbered eight or a few more according to circumstances. In our period the most solid were Howqua, Mowqua, Tingqua and Puankhequa. Needless to say, these were not their real names. The final syllable corresponded to our Mister and the first was a shot at their surnames: Howqua's

THE GROTTO OF CAMOENS AT MACAO
from a painting by Thomas Allom

W. C. HUNTER
from a painting by George Chinnery

was Wu. Chinnery has left us portraits of Howqua and Mowqua, both painted in 1830. The first was a wizened little fellow, with a half whimsical, half sad expression, who looks almost like a man of letters, though of course none of the Hong merchants belonged to the scholar class. For all that, Howqua has a distinguished, rather aristocratic appearance, and reminds one faintly of the present Lord Halifax. Mowqua, on the contrary, was stout, slow-looking, also rather sad (they all had grounds for sadness) and had honest eyes. His expression suggests that he had been badly bullied all his life, as, indeed, was the case. Eventually he was so squeezed that he went bankrupt.

At the beginning of each season the Hoppo used to post a notice in front of the Factories admonishing the Hong merchants to be of good behaviour. The document is so droll that it demands to be quoted. 'It is very difficult for the Barbarians to understand the proprieties of the Celestial Empire,' it begins sympathetically. 'Hence Hong merchants have been appointed to control commercial transactions. It is the duty of these merchants continually to instruct the Barbarians; to repress their natural pride and profligacy, and to insist on their turning their hearts to propriety, that all parties enjoy glad repose and gain, with each person in his place and minding his own business. Since the Hong merchants are men of property and good family, it becomes them to have a tender regard for their face, nor to cheat but trade justly, and so win devil confidence.'

The Demons themselves were admonished in a separate notice, which was posted up alongside the other. 'About this time the devil-ships are arriving and it is feared that lawless vagabonds will again tread in their old habits. It is highly important that all have regard for their face and repent bitterly of their previous faults. Let them not dare to employ young boys as servants to lead them to brothels nor to bring prostitutes into the Factories.' Chinese edicts all tended to be written in this manner. Authority had two duties, to admonish and soothe, in accordance with the Confucian fiction that the Government was paternal and tender. The Chinese themselves loved the fiction, for it gave a polish and elegance to life, a surface propriety which appealed to them strongly. That it happened to be a fiction was part of its charm: the myth had carried them happily through two millenniums.

If the Hong merchants had had only to lecture the licentious Barbarians, they would have had no cause for that sad look in their eyes. Reproving them for their bad behaviour could only have been congenial, but unfortunately they had to go surety for their good behaviour. Their duties were multifarious, they were regular factotums; they could not hope to escape constant blame. When a ship anchored at Whampoa, a particular Hong merchant was deputed to conduct all its business until it sailed. Men appointed by him took the cargo ashore; he procured the tea and saw it aboard; he dealt with all complaints, made all arrangements. In such a business, involving contact with many sorts of people and the solution of numberless problems, it was impossible for him to avoid giving a handle to the Hoppo who was watching and hoping to see him slip. For a small unpleasantness he was heavily fined; for a great, put in chains and made to pay enormously for enlargement. And this in addition to handsome contributions to the Hoppo's income, of presents to the Emperor and to the local officials. Dr. Morrison, the Company's interpreter and the only Englishman in Canton who knew Chinese, gives a table in his *Commercial Guide* (1834) of the donations annually expected from the Co-Hong. The birthday and other presents to the Emperor cost £56,000; the Hoppo's presents £14,000; tips to officials came to £14,000; the Yellow River (whether it flooded or not) £10,000; and the compulsory purchase of a medicinal root called ginseng £46,000, an item like the Yellow River, which covered some anonymous recipient, presumably the Hoppo. But the total of £140,000 must be

66

regarded as a minimum fixed annual charge. The real total was much greater, for there were many extras.

It is not surprising to hear that Hong merchants were frequently in debt and sometimes went bankrupt; no business could stand such overheads and be solvent for long, unless reinforced by an enormous reserve. Howqua managed to remain in funds because he had sufficient capital to run a big export trade of his own. But others could not do this. Some of the Hong merchants, unable to find the cash for advances to the tea men, who had to buy the crop far inland, borrowed from British firms, only to find that at the end of the season they could not meet their liabilities. But the bankruptcy of a Hong merchant did not altogether suit the Hoppo. He had to find another person to take his place. True, he would get a handsome sum for the appointment, but it was not easy to secure a suitable man, a man with the knack of getting on well with the Barbarians and with the executive capacity to manage a complicated and special line of business. To obviate bankruptcies it was decided to create a common reserve pool, and to create it out of the subscriptions paid by the Barbarians themselves. This appealed strongly to Chinese sense of humour. It amused them, just as it had amused Peking when Lord Macartney in 1796 was accommodated there in a palatial residence built by a Hoppo out of the spoils of the Canton trade.

This reserve became known as the Consoo Fund, after the Consoo Hall, the Hong Council Chamber which was situated at the north end of Old China Street. It came into existence in 1780 and was an *ad valorem* charge of 3 per cent, increased in emergency to 4, 5, or even 6 per cent, on all goods which passed in or out of the customs. In 1829 the annual charges are given as amounting to £330,000. One cannot estimate the total sum in the fund at one period, for by this time it had come to be looked on as a reserve into which the authorities could dip in any emergency or, indeed, whenever they liked. Eventually it helped to meet the cost of the opium war and its indemnities, so that the British, instead of compensation, only got back part of their own money. That the East India Company should have submitted to such a charge is to be explained by their fear of disturbing the trade and because, in this case, their monopoly enabled them to pass on the 3 per cent to consumers of tea in England.

It is hardly possible to imagine anything more disheartening for business men than to have been obliged to engage in such a commerce. But, paradoxically, the corruption of the local officials afforded a way of breaking out of the tight box in which the system confined the merchants. The Ch'ing Dynasty, a military domination, had begun to go down hill and when that happens to an autocracy of the sort official corruption increases beyond measure. The demoralization of the bureaucracy was perhaps greatest at Canton because more money was to be made there than elsewhere. When officials throw off all semblance of uprightness, every rascal in the place crowds in to share the loot, for he knows that bribes will protect him from punishment. China had preserved its identity for so many centuries because it had a sound core of opinion, a sufficient body of men who really believed in the Confucian virtues and were ready to sacrifice even their lives to uphold them. But in Canton the protests of such people were drowned and only lip service was given to the old canons of conduct. So debauched was the local government, so ruffianly were the persons who swarmed in under its shadow, that they undermined the very system on which they battened.

A bad order of things is as dependent on loyal servants as a good. But the Canton bureaucracy was not loyal to the Emperor. They were ready to go wherever profit was to be made, and no difficulty was found in securing their unofficial co-operation when the merchants of the country trade developed a counter-system to the Hong, a system directly contrary to all the rules and regulations we have just seen, but which gave the local authorities from the top of the scale to the bottom great opportunities of enriching themselves. The nature of this alternative method of trading to China is explained in the next section.

(vii)

The Unofficial System of Trading to China

A clue to the nature of this unofficial trade has already been provided. In an early section of this chapter we supplied as much information about it as a traveller to Canton might be expected to pick up as he sailed from Macao to the Bogue. The reader knows that its headquarters was Lintin Island, the Solitary Nail, in the centre of the great bay of Canton. He knows that it was a trade in opium or largely in opium and that it was a smuggling trade, the sort of open smuggling which develops when officials combine to defraud the revenue by allowing for a consideration what it is their duty to suppress.

The best way to get the bearings of this trade is to look at the import figures both for it and the legal trade. Taking the complete trade table for 1831, one notices that the imports were in two categories, western products and eastern products. Western products were merchandise imported from Europe and America, to be exchanged principally for tea and silk; they consisted of woollens, cotton goods and furs.

The value of those imported by the East India Company that year was two and a half million dollars, by private British firms under licence from the Company half a million dollars, and by the Americans nearly two million dollars. Imports by other European nations were very small. This five million worth of goods was the legal trade and went through the customs at Whampoa, paying duty as assessed by the Hoppo.

The eastern products came chiefly from India and were imported, not by the Company or the Americans, but by the British country firms, which included Parsee firms of Bombay. They imported nearly four million dollars' worth of cotton, eleven million dollars' worth of opium, the total, after adding a few spices, coming to over seventeen million dollars. These goods were not, for the most part, taken to Whampoa. They were not handled by the Hong, nor did they pay the imperial dues. The firms landed them at Lintin through the connivance of the Chinese officials, who were bribed to let them in. As opium was a prohibited article, these officials were guilty of more than defrauding the customs: they were abetting an illegal trade.

The figures quoted show that this smuggling trade was more than three times as valuable as the Company's and the American trade combined. Lintin became a greater emporium for handling foreign wares than Canton. The Emperor lost his revenue on the non-prohibited articles, which went wholly to his officials. These levied private tolls also on the prohibited article, opium, equal it is said to what would have been the duty if it had been unprohibited.

Looking now at the export table for the same year we find that the Company exported nearly eight million dollars' worth of tea and that that was their sole export; the licensed firms five millions' worth of various goods; and the Americans nearly six millions' worth. Subtract these figures from the import figures, and in the case of the Americans you get an adverse balance of four millions. This was discharged by paying cash in Spanish dollars, imported for the purpose. The adverse balance in the case of the Company was greater, being five and a half million dollars. But the Company is shown as exporting silver worth over a million dollars. One may well ask how they managed to do that?

For answer we must look at the eastern produce figures again. The country firms imported seventeen million dollars' worth and exported five million dollars' worth of goods. That gave them a favourable trade balance of twelve million dollars. A great part of this was in silver, for opium was bought for cash in advance. The country firms gave the Company the use of as much of this silver as it required to redress its adverse balance and pay for its tea, or more if desired, taking in return bills on London, thereby avoiding the cost and risk of sending overseas a great quantity of bullion, an arrangement highly advantageous to the Company for analagous reasons.

After all payments had been made there still remained a considerable silver residue for export. In 1831 the Company exported over a million and the firms three million dollars. But there was a further connection between the Company and the firms. The Company controlled the cultivation of opium in India, having in fact almost a world monopoly of the drug. The eleven million dollars sold by the country firms in China was procured at Company auctions held annually at Calcutta. Thus the Company was the source of the opium traffic. And it reaped a double advantage from it. The sale of opium to the country firms provided an important percentage of the Indian revenues, and their sale of it for silver to the Chinese provided the funds to finance the Company's tea trade.

Under cover of this indirect method the Company could say, 'Our ships do not carry opium, we are concerned only with the tea trade. We go to Canton and pay all dues and duties, and have every right to complain of our arbitrary treatment by the Chinese authorities.'

71

A few quotations from the records of the Company, as given in Morse's book *The East India Company trading to China*, will illustrate the various points summarized above, and show how it was careful to dissociate itself from the drug traffic on the spot. Thus the Select Committee, that is the Company's board of management at Canton, wrote under date of 3rd September, 1827: 'The very extensive Contraband Trade now carried on at the anchorage of Linting, not only in the Importation of Opium, but in the transit of goods of every description to and from Canton, by means of such vessels as are entering the river, renders it necessary in our opinion to issue a strict prohibition against any communication between our ships and the above vessels, which might eventually form a subject of discussion to the Officers of Government and a pretence for levying exactions upon the Hong Merchants.'

In 1831 something of what was taking place at Lintin was reported to the Emperor. He sent an edict to the Viceroy and Governor, declaring he had heard that brokers in Canton were buying opium from British firms, delivery being made at Lintin to 'fast crabs', the smuggling boats, and by them distributed inland and up the coast. Immediate action, he said, must be taken to stop this. It does not appear that he understood how large the traffic was and that it included other goods. The Viceroy, though involved in the smuggling equally with his subordinates, some of the smug-boats being actually owned by him, was obliged to make a show of compliance. Moreover, the edict enabled him to threaten and so screw more bribes out of the dealers. On 1st September the Company recorded: 'Private accounts from Canton inform us that an active persecution has been commenced by the Governor's orders against the Opium brokers, several of whom have been put in prison, and report says that one of the leading men has been twice subjected to torture in order to compel him . . . to name his associates.' The report was probably true enough, for the Chinese authorities did not hesitate on other occasions to imprison and even execute smugglers, if they thought it necessary to impress the Emperor with their devotion to duty. Following their measures against the brokers, the Hong merchants were commanded in a viceregal edict 'to expostulate with earnestness and persuade the Barbarians that they must not . . . appoint vessels to be Opium depots at Lintin . . . hoping there to sell by stealth. . . . This is a strict interdict respectfully received from Imperial authority, and the Hong merchants must honestly exert their utmost efforts to persuade to a total cutting off of the clandestine introduction of the foreign mud. Let there not be the least trifling or carelessness, for if opium be again allowed to enter the interior it will involve them in serious criminality. Oppose not.'

The Hoppo joined in and also pointed out to the Hong merchants their duty: 'Of late years foreign ships have continually anchored at Lintin. Repeatedly have orders been issued to the Hong to communicate the commands of Government to the respective nations' Chiefs, requiring them to compel the vessels to quit the port . . . but all these foreign vessels continue to anchor as usual, with insolent haughtiness disobeying.'

The Hong merchants had, of course, no way of compelling any ships, far less armed merchant clippers, to leave Lintin. All they could do was to write to the Select Committee of the Company and forward a copy of the orders they had received. On receipt of such a letter the Committee invariably returned the same answer: 'We have no responsibility whatever for what may be happening at Lintin. The vessels there are not owned by the Company, their owners are not members of the Company, but are country firms whose business is quite separate and over whom we have no authority.' If any reply was received to their disclaimer, they put it in the wastepaper basket.

In addition to these letters to the Co-Hong, the Chinese authorities thought it as well to have it on record that they had ordered the admiral to take the necessary action. This worthy either made the sort of demonstration described earlier in this chapter when his junks pretended to pursue the clippers or else he did nothing at all but reported that he had driven them away. Needless to say, he too was in the business.

After a certain interval the Viceroy would prepare a detailed report for the Emperor, describing at length the measures taken, stating with truth, for the season was over, that the clippers had departed, and expressing the conviction that they would never dare to re-appear. Meanwhile the smuggling had been going on without interruption or, if the importers had deemed some reduction was necessary, it was now renewed with greater vigour than ever and in the cheerful atmosphere of prices increased by the temporary shortage.

In a despatch to the Governor-General in Bengal on 25th October of the same year, 1831, the Select Committee sums up thus: 'The illegal trade at Lintin as it is now conducted is a proof at once of the imbecility and corruption of the Local Authorities.' Yet we may suppose that they would not have had them less imbecile or corrupt, since the more they exhibited both these characteristics the better for the tea trade and the Indian revenues.

(viii)

The Drug Trade in Operation

The drug traffic had been fostered by the East India Company with careful deliberation over a long course of years.

Opium had for centuries been cultivated in Bengal. When that province passed into British hands in the eighteenth century, the cultivation of the drug was steadily increased and a monopoly created by forcing growers to sell the whole crop to the Company. As the Company's dominion was extended over India, it became evident that to supply opium to Indian subjects was a short-sighted policy on account of its pernicious effects. A decision was taken at the time of Warren Hastings to decrease home consumption and develop an export trade. It was well known that the Chinese would buy; the Portuguese had been selling them for generations opium they procured at Malwa on the Indian coast north of Bombay. The Company therefore resolved to build up an export to China. This was done very methodically, possession being obtained later on of the Malwa crop, a move which completed the ruin of the Portuguese at Macao and created a Company monopoly for all India. Though opium was also exported from Turkey to China, chiefly by the Americans, this brand was very inferior and had only a small market, so that the Company had obtained in fact a world monopoly. At first some of their ships carried it, but they soon abandoned this practice, because, the drug being contraband, they feared altercation with injury to the tea trade. They never believed that the local authorities at Canton had any moral objection to opium, but since the Court of Peking had forbidden its importation, experience told them that the imperial edicts against it would be used by the Hoppo and the Viceroy as an excuse to squeeze the legitimate trade. A way therefore had to be found of selling it in China which would give the authorities no handle against the Company. Neither the Dutch nor the Portuguese had the ships, the capital, the enterprise nor indeed the courage to undertake such a trade in the big way which the Company had in mind. Nor was it desirable that a valuable trade should be abandoned to foreigners. But there existed a British agency competent to undertake it. The country firms whose business had always been to handle trade inside Asia, were able and willing to assume the whole risk. The additional attraction that this would provide silver to finance the tea trade has already been explained. Having worked out this policy in close agreement with Parliament, they nursed the country firms at the risk of these merchants becoming one day more powerful than themselves. The firms were most successful in selling the drug and were able to take up larger and larger quantities. The Company's revenue from their sales of it at the Calcutta auctions rose steadily. In 1793 it stood at a quarter of a million pounds; in 1809 at over half a million; and in 1832 at just under one million, a figure which, representing as it did about a sixth of the whole Indian revenue, was clearly of great importance to the administration. The increasing sales of opium can also be represented by the chests of a hundred and fifty pounds weight each, actually disposed of in China. Thus, at the end of the eighteenth century the figure was in the region of two thousand chests; in 1820, 4,770 chests; in 1825, 9,621 chests; in 1830, 18,760 chests; and in 1836, 26,018 chests. The profit made by the firms varied greatly, the operations of speculators, the amount of stock in hand and the attitude of severity or the reverse adopted by the Chinese authorities causing the price at Canton to fluctuate between 1,000 and 500 dollars per chest, so that it was very difficult to forecast the precise figure at the time the auctions were held. Indeed, it was a highly speculative trade, where great fortunes were possible, but where those firms which sold only on commission did sounder business in the long run. Jardine and Matheson generally sold on commission unless they could buy at rock bottom, and they reckoned on an average profit of £20 per chest. As the firm handled up to 6,000 chests in the later eighteen-thirties, its income at that time was £100,000 per annum. It was by a long way the greatest of the opium firms and some quotations from its archives showing how in practice the trade was carried on will illustrate very well the manner of the traffic.

Since they did not bid for the opium at the Calcutta auctions, their practice was to place their selling organization at the disposal of those who had bought lots there. This organization became very elaborate. Its components were: (i) a fleet of fast armed ships to carry the opium from Calcutta to Lintin; these were the famous opium clippers; (ii) hulks anchored at Lintin, of the kind already described, to which the opium was transferred from the clippers: these were known as receiving ships; (iii) an office in one of the factories at Canton, to which Chinese smugglers of opium might come and contract, for silver paid in advance, to take delivery of the opium stored on a receiving ship at Lintin, whence it was distributed by the smugglers' men in the armed galley-like boats called 'fast crabs' and 'scrambling dragons' to a host of receivers living in the creek villages in the vicinity of Canton. This was the organization employed to place the opium in the hands of consumers in the Canton province. When supplies increased this market became saturated and prices fell. It became necessary to seek other markets and for this purpose Jardine and Matheson acquired a second fleet of ships, runners which loaded opium at Lintin and sailed up the coast, disposing of it at various little ports. This was known as the Coast Trade. Here the firm's ships took the place of the Chinese in the crabs and dragons. It was not sale to smugglers but direct smuggling; it required much local knowledge and experience, and entailed the braving of many dangers both on sea and land. We have already had a glimpse of the Coast Trade in section ii of this chapter, where Hunter describes the scene at Namoa near Swatow, three hundred miles N.E. of Canton when the *Rose* on behalf of the American firm of Russell and Company put in to sell her cargo. Further down will be cited examples from the Jardine-Matheson archives. The Coast Trade may then be seen as an attempt to meet the

Chinese demand for opium over much larger areas and to introduce the drug to markets which had been out of reach before. Here it was not always the case that the consignment was paid for in advance in the Canton office and was delivered to specified receivers at a coast port. Sometimes a cargo was hawked round the ports and sold for cash on the spot as occasion offered.

The firm of Jardine and Matheson came into existence in 1828, when these two men, who were leading country merchants, joined forces. At that date William Jardine, a Scotsman by birth, was forty-four years of age. He had first visited India in the capacity of surgeon on board an East Indiaman in 1802. In 1816 he gave up medicine, having made sufficient money by private trading to establish himself in London as a merchant. In 1819 he sailed East again, this time as a partner in a country firm, and visited Canton, where he made the acquaintance of Matheson. In 1820 he was established in Bombay in partnership with the Parsee merchant Framjee Cowasjee, but moved in 1822 to Canton, where he lived in quarters rented from Matheson. His business was an agency for Cowasjee and other firms, who dealt in Malwa opium. He was so successful in selling this contraband that in 1824 he was given a partnership in the firm of Magniac, at that date the leading opium firm. About this time Hollingworth Magniac recorded the following opinion of him: 'You will find Jardine a most conscientious, honourable and kind-hearted fellow, extremely liberal and an excellent man of business in this market, where his knowledge and experience in the opium trade and in most articles of export is highly valuable. He requires to be known to be properly appreciated.' Jardine was widely held to be a man of great strength of character, and, while a good friend, to be an implacable foe. The Chinese called him the Iron-headed Old Rat, a name dating from an occasion when he remained unruffled by a heavy blow on the head while presenting a petition at the city gate. Hollingworth Magniac retired to England soon after Jardine's appointment, Daniel Magniac taking his place. Two years later Daniel transgressed the code of the firm by marrying his Asiatic mistress, probably a half-caste Portuguese of Macao, by whom he had had two children, and was retired by his brother on a beggarly pension, for these opium firms were, it seems, very particular in some matters. This left Jardine in sole executive charge till he took in Matheson in 1828. Hollingworth Magniac remained a sleeping partner till 1832, when the firm was then formally registered as Jardine and Matheson.

James Matheson, the son of a Scottish baronet, was twelve years younger than Jardine, and so thirty-two years old when he entered the partnership. But he had had considerable experience. After passing through Edinburgh University he entered the Calcutta firm of Mackintosh at twenty. In 1819, when twenty-three, he began his career at Canton. At twenty-five he was partner in a Spanish firm and Danish consul, a term meaning that he acted for such Danish ships as came in and had the right to fly the Danish flag, a convenience when he wished to disobey the orders of the East India Company or to dissociate himself from them if they were in trouble with the authorities. It was he who discovered the possibilities of the Coast Trade, the direct smuggling of opium along the Chinese seaboard. In 1823 he set out in his Spanish firm's brig the *San Sebastian*, and flying the Spanish flag. The Spaniards held certain concessions at Amoy, which had fallen into disuse, but which he found very convenient, and which enabled him three months later to dispose of £33,000 worth of opium. His success could not be kept secret and in the following year other firms entered that market, particularly Dent and Company, after Magniac and Company the most considerable at Canton. Matheson had his ups and downs, but he acquired wide experience. This, and the Danish flag and a capital of £20,000, were the assets he brought with him when he joined Jardine in January 1828. They were the ablest men in the opium trade and, united in one firm, built up a selling organization far more efficient than any other.

Their fleet of clippers was to take the place of the old carriers, the so-called country wallahs, teak ships of between five and eight hundred tons from Indian yards, very old-fashioned for they were replicas of seventeenth-century caravels, carracks and galleons, with a round-house over a cuddy looking on gilt quarter galleries and a short waist for guns, their ports carved with wreaths. Some of them had been at sea for a hundred and fifty years, and were rather survivals than replicas. But though built to endure they were slow and unhandy. They could not beat up against the monsoon. With it behind them they had been known to get from India to Lintin in a month, but generally their voyage occupied two or three. With the expansion of the market and the necessity of catching it as early as possible, a faster type of vessel was essential, a ship which could make two or even three round voyages a year and which could be driven into the monsoon. The first of the new fleet was the *Red Rover*. She was a copy of a famous American privateer and was launched in Calcutta in 1829. Her displacement was 254 tons, she carried three rakish masts, and was flush decked with little or no shere. Long and low, she was a greyhound of the sea, and once ran from Calcutta to Lintin in 18 days, and regularly did three round trips a year. 'The voyages of this vessel are quite astonishing and unparalleled, and until now considered perfectly impracticable from repeated failure of the finest men-of-war to make passage up the China sea against the monsoon,' wrote a correspondent in the *Bengal Courier*, as reported in the *Asiatic Journal* of September 1831. There was one steam tug at that time in Calcutta. It was tried over the distance but was not as fast as the *Red Rover* and cost far more to keep up.

More clippers followed the *Red Rover* and enabled Jardine and Matheson to be first in the opium market every

VIEW OF WHAMPOA FROM JARDINE POINT, DANE ISLAND
from a painting by Thomas Allom

THE FACTORIES AT CANTON
from a painting by Thomas Allom

year and to make their fortune. When the East India Company withdrew from Canton in April 1834 they fell naturally into the position of leaders of the British community.

The Coast Trade was developed with the same thoroughness. To illustrate more particularly how the business was done in the first years we may cite the voyage in 1832 of the *Sylph*, a 251 ton barque, carvel built, two decked and even faster than the *Red Rover*. As has been pointed out, the drug traffic up the Chinese seaboard was more a direct form of smuggling than was the delivery of opium to Chinese smugglers at Lintin. It entailed entering a port or anchoring off a village in a river-mouth and there getting into touch, often without previous arrangement, with local dealers, who had to be induced to come aboard and buy. To effect this an interpreter was essential. The so-called Chinese linguists available at Canton were nearly useless, their English being very poor and their honesty doubtful. It was remarked further back that the only Englishman who knew Chinese was Dr. Morrison, the Company's official interpreter. But there was also a Prussian who knew the language, a medical missionary, the Reverend Doctor Charles Gutzlaff. He lived at Macao in a little house on the ridge and was a noted character. We have a description of him in a letter of Sir Harry Parker, then a lad of sixteen. 'He was a short square figure,' wrote the future old China hand, 'with clothes that for shape might have been cut in his native Pomerania ages ago, a broad-brimmed straw hat, his great face beneath with a sinister eye.' Hunter says he had a rather Chinese appearance. He spoke Cantonese and wrote it fluently and had also mastered other local dialects. His practice was to tour where he could among the villages of the mainland or along the coast, distributing translations of the Bible and tracts, as also ointment and Cockle's pills. He had a persuasive way with the inhabitants and was used to roughing it in all weathers.

It occurred to Jardine that here was the very man to go with the *Sylph*, though it meant persuading a missionary to translate for opium smugglers, and a doctor to help in the distribution of a deleterious drug. But Jardine knew his man and how to address him. His letter to the reverend gentleman is dated October, 1832. It begins by stressing that the *Sylph* will carry £4,000 worth of piece-goods and then comes a burst of apparent candour:

'But as the expenses of the voyage cannot be defrayed from this source, we have no hesitation in stating to you openly that our principal reliance is on opium. Though it is our earnest wish that you should not in any way injure the grand object you have in view by appearing interested in what by many is considered an immoral traffic, yet such traffic is so absolutely necessary to give any vessel a reasonable chance of defraying her expenses, that we trust you will have no objection to interpret on every occasion when your services may be requested.'

We may assume that previous to this letter Gutzlaff had been offered a passage as if Jardine's sole intention had been to oblige him in his missionary labours and that this was the first news of what was expected of him in return. He would be rewarded, of course, for his services, the letter went on:

'The more profitable the expedition, the better we shall be able to place at your disposal a sum that may hereafter be employed in furthering your mission, and for your success in which we feel deeply interested.'

As a further inducement a magazine which Gutzlaff was printing in Chinese was guaranteed for six months.

On receipt of this letter Gutzlaff hesitated for a moment. 'After much consultation with others and a conflict in my own mind, I embarked on the *Sylph*,' he wrote.

On 20th October they weighed from Macao Road and headed into the N.E. monsoon. Their final destination was the far north, the Gulf of Pechili, where the Pei-ho River flows from Tientsin on the approach to Peking, a distance of 1,600 miles from Canton. 'Furious gales, accompanied with rain and a tremendous sea, drove us several days along the coast, threatening destruction to our bark,' wrote Gutzlaff in his published account of the voyage. 'But God who dwelleth on high did not forsake us; and though often engulphed in the deep, His almighty hand upheld our sinking vessel. Only one lascar was swept away; we heard his dying groans, but could lend no assistance.' His narrative continues in this strain, laying emphasis on their perils and hardships, thanking God for their escapes from death, and detailing how he distributed pills and Bibles in large quantities. No mention whatever is made of sales of opium, but at the end when summing up his experiences he refers obliquely to the matter, thus:

'Our commercial relations are at the present moment on such a basis as to warrant a continuation of the trade along the coast. We hope that this may tend ultimately to the introduction of the gospel, for which many doors are opened. Millions of Bibles and tracts will be needed to supply the wants of the people. God, who in His mercy has thrown down the wall of national separation, will carry on the work. We look up to the ever blessed Redeemer, to whom China with all its millions is given; in the faithfulness of His promise we anticipate the glorious day of a general conversion, and are willing to do our utmost in order to promote the great work.'

And he concludes:

'After a voyage of six months and nine days we reached Lintin near Macao on the 29th of April 1833. Praised be God for all His mercies and deliverances during so perilous a voyage.'

Dr. Gutzlaff's conscience may appear still to have been a little tender. Surely he was justified, he seems to urge. His aim was so high, to convert to Protestantism at last the teeming millions of a country, which for millenniums had been plunged in darkness, and bring to it not only light and truth but the uncounted blessings of free commercial intercourse with those chosen nations to which God had revealed Himself. As Mr. Jardine had so truly said, the exchange of commodities more respectable than opium was impossible unless funds were provided by sale of the latter. And there must be commerce if there was to be evangelization; the two were indissolubly bound together. The greater the trade, the more the conversions. No doubt, later, when the natives had been won, it would be possible to dispense with opium, because the value of other western products would then be demonstrable and the Chinese would buy largely what now they rejected. But it was needless to anticipate the ways of Providence. In His good time God would save Asia. It was not for an instrument like a poor missionary to criticize God or look too closely into His methods. God must have decided that the drug traffic was necessary, if the wall of national separation were to be breached. Had He not saved the *Sylph* from tempest and reef, though she was loaded with hundreds of chests of opium? No, he could not doubt; the day of general conversion was dawning; it was incumbent upon him to do his utmost, to do anything, so that that glorious sun might rise.

We should be falling into error were we to suppose that Dr. Gutzlaff was hypocritical in entertaining such views or that in believing such rubbish he differed from the majority. It is true, as Jardine's letter shows, that the drug traffic was criticized by some people, but it had been encouraged by the East India Company, a most solid and respectable body of merchants, and had been sanctioned by Parliament. Its critics did not represent the general opinion of the day. The fact that Gutzlaff hesitated at all before consenting to help shows that he was somewhat in advance of his age. As to the conversion of the Chinese to Christianity, that was held by all Europeans to be highly desirable. When Jardine wrote of Gutzlaff's 'grand object', he really meant what he said. He was strongly in favour of Christianity for China. Moreover, it would help to open the country to trade and make the population more amenable to western influence. Where he differed from some was in not seeing anything incongruous between smuggling and preaching. Or, if he did he was not troubled by it. Yet those good people who were troubled by it were not averse, after the defeat of the Chinese in 1842, from using the power which arms had given them to force Christian missions upon China. In this way their point of view is seen not to have differed very profoundly from Jardine's. He wanted to force everything western upon China, including opium, which he considered indispensable. They wanted to force everything western upon China, except opium, for, being without commercial experience, they were not convinced of its indispensability.

Though Gutzlaff suppressed all mention of his activities as interpreter on the *Sylph*, we have a glimpse of him on board the *John Biggar*, another of Jardine and Matheson's fleet, to which he transferred four months after his return from his first voyage. The *John Biggar*, like the other opium ships, was heavily armed. On the 6th August she put into Chinchow Bay, a little north of Amoy, about 400 miles up the coast from Macao. So far there had been no difficulty with the local administrative officers, who took their percentage and looked the other way. But at Chinchow Bay six mandarin junks anchored close by after sunset in such a way as to suggest that the officials on board intended to prevent dealers from coming to buy. Captain McKay, who was in command of the *John Biggar*, asked Gutzlaff to row over and tell them to go away. In a letter to the firm McKay describes what happened: 'Doctor Gutzlaff, dressed in his best, which on such occasions is his custom, paid them a visit accompanied by two boats made to appear rather imposing. He demanded their instant departure and threatened them with destruction if they ever again anchored in our neighbourhood. They went away immediately, saying they had anchored there in the dark by mistake, and we have seen nothing more of them.'

It was disclosed afterwards that the officials, though really willing enough, had not dared connive at the smuggling because the *John Biggar* was lying out in the roadstead in full view of the town. A mandarin had always to reckon on the danger of rivals or enemies reporting him if he openly flouted the law. Such a report might not mean punishment, but certainly entailed a heavy bribe to escape it.

The *John Biggar*'s cruise was highly successful. Captain McKay returned to Lintin with silver worth £53,000. He was very pleased with Gutzlaff's devotion to duty and reported to Jardine on the 14th September:

'I have received much assistance from Doctor Gutzlaff whose services, as the trade increases, will become invaluable. His zeal is unbounded, but in his ideas he is perhaps a little too sanguine . . . The trade at Chinchow may now be considered to be placed on a firm footing, although the mandarins may occasionally make difficulties.'

So much for the Reverend Doctor Charles Gutzlaff, who in this narrative stands for the religious, as Jardine stands for the commercial, assault upon the Far East. His voyages when he interpreted for the Coast merchants are symbolic: trade and the Bible were allies, and after them came the flag.

Owing to the Doctor's discretion we have not yet had a very detailed impression of a smuggler at work, but as Jardine and Matheson had a third ship out in 1832, the super-cargo or business agent of which kept a diary, we can easily supply the deficiency. The super-cargo was James Innes and the ship the *Jamesina*. That year, besides the British staff of the East India Company, numbering about twenty-five, there were permanently resident at Canton and

Macao thirty-two other Englishmen, of whom nineteen belonged to the country firms and thirteen were unattached. Of these thirteen, seven were private merchants, four shop-keepers, one a watchmaker, and the last, Chinnery, the painter. James Innes was one of the seven private merchants. These men had no licence from the Select Committee of the East India Company, the body which all merchants, whether in the Company or not, were supposed to obey. But the Committee, though from time to time it ordered one or other of the unlicensed merchants to leave, was loath to press its authority and they mostly contrived to linger on some excuse. James Innes had been asked to leave, but he was a very tough customer and rather than provoke a scene, the Committee let him be, for their monopoly was shortly coming to an end, when Innes and any number of private merchants would be able to come and go as they pleased. He was the sort of forthright and intrepid character who appealed to Jardine, and as the *Jamesina* was likely to require just such a super-cargo, Jardine secured his services. On board were ten Europeans, a crew of fifty-four Indian lascars, and four Chinese, belonging to Innes' staff. Of the latter he wrote:

'The Chinese stand as under: old Awee (Humbug) and a partner of his own choosing for brokers; the brother of Ajee to act as courier, and he promises strong and fast; old Olio, his son, a good man from Canton, and a halfcaste Portuguese will be our shroffs . . . We carry as many arms as we can stand to.'

Leaving Lintin on 8th November, they reached Chin-chow Bay on the 29th. The following extracts from Innes' diary give some idea of what coast smuggling was like.

'Just before daylight I sent ashore two Chinese with a list of 28 opium dealers' names to ask them to come off and do business. . . . Last night two regular smugglers came off, and after a hard set to over price, they this day paid 870 dollars a chest and took away 36 chests. Before they were away two more boats came and took away 40 chests at the same rate.' This was £174 per chest, about £50 more than the then rate at Lintin.

On 2nd December Innes records: 'Employed delivering briskly. No time to read my Bible, so to keep my journal.'

On the next day they were still delivering briskly: 'Today several small mandarin junks sailed round us once or twice, when some smuggling boats were alongside . . . They gave us no trouble and the opium boats came and went easily close to them.'

Against date 6th December he describes the scene at night in the cuddy where the dealers crowded aboard, bargained for the opium and paid in dollars, which the shroff Olio weighed. 'During this bargaining,' he says, 'which often lasted deep into midnight, were received all comers, high and low. Some head merchant was generally extended on my couch attended by his personal servant. All had tobacco pipes, some were with abacus at table settling their balances, others buying by signs or Morrison's vocabulary small articles or offering gold for sale. Once or twice in the evening to high and low a glass of Mareskino or Hoffman was served. Before midnight the rabble was generally as close as they could pack, stowed head and feet asleep on the carpet floor. . . . We were on a kind footing with the natives and though the cabin was full of articles of value to them, I never missed a pennyworth.'

The weather now became very wild. Under date 24th December 1832 Innes writes: 'Bay of Chinchew. About midnight came one of those sudden gales of wind for which this coast is celebrated. By daylight it had assumed the aspect of a typhoon, with a heavy wind and irregular sea which put us all to what was proper to be done, when the captain decided to try to ride it out, so 160 fathoms were let go to our anchor, but from this we drove, so our heaviest anchor was added and 120 fathoms given, adding a spare chain to the first. This held her and here we celebrated Christmas Day, not so comfortably but quite as cheerfully as we anticipated. Our rigging was struck to the extent possible without applying an axe and yet we rode hard and a tremendous sea.'

Throughout Boxing Day they wallowed in the wild roadstead, the clouds driving on the face of the sea like a dark mist, the rain a deluge, the cold numbing their limbs, and the wind the fiercest the *Jamesina* had ever met, though the barometer rose a little. Dawn on the 27th revealed the same savage tumult. 'Gale and sea nothing abated,' wrote Innes, 'as dark as a wolf's throat and the ship occasionally riding very uneasily, but fast to her ground tackle. I regret three days of a good place for doing business being lost, but nothing else. The rest is not a lasting source of sorrow. I noticed many flights of wild waterfowl going at a rate of a hundred miles an hour down wind to a warmer climate, and we are now regularly attended by albatrosses, whom I, by prejudice, supposed a bird of the far north or south.'

So passed the 28th and the 29th. 'We have not seen the sun since this moon came in.' On New Year's Eve the gale blew itself out, and by 3rd January they were again delivering briskly. On the 5th Innes notes that Jardine and Matheson should station a receiving hulk in the vicinity of Chinchow Bay and keep up a steady supply of opium, a suggestion afterwards adopted. His business finished at Chinchow, he headed north towards Foochow, which is opposite Formosa. 'But we were not destined long to keep up our sky scrapers,' he says. On 11th January they ran again into foul weather, 'a thick mist and tremendous sea.' They tried to meet it, but could not. 'At twelve o'clock with great regret bore away and were well pleased to get tolerable shelter in a sandy bay about abreast the Lamyets in 12 fathoms water.' On 19th January they went ashore for water and Innes distributed some of Dr. Morrison's books. As Dr. Morrison was a missionary as well as a Chinese scholar, we may suppose these books were tracts, and so have a closer and more startling example of opium and the Bible operating together. On the 26th they reached Foochow, having hung suspended on a reef for two hours. 'From the time we grounded till we were in safe mooring nothing could have been more seamen-like than the conduct of our officers and crew. Captain Hector and the chief, Mr Burnett, calm, clear and without flurry, the men with spirit flying to where their exertions were ordered.'

At Foochow the port officer at first made difficulties. He caught and beat some of the Chinese dealers who tried to trade. But Innes had him told that if he interfered again, they would man boats and trade on shore. The mandarin, being satisfied that he had sufficiently demonstrated his zeal for the government, privately intimated that he was an opium buyer himself and offered an unusually good price. The interpreting had become difficult, for up to this they had depended upon one of the Chinese on the staff, but he could not speak Fukien, which was the local dialect. 'I would give 1,000 dollars for three days of Gutzlaff,' exclaims Innes. However, they managed as best they might and on 5th February turned for home. With the N.E. wind following fresh, they scudded down the coast, reaching Lintin, which is 500 miles from Foochow, in six days in spite of putting in to a little port for a day and a night to sell the last of their opium.

These extracts, which all come from the Jardine-Matheson archives, suffice to give some idea of the Coast Trade in opium during the years 1832-33. It was then in an early stage of its development. Dent and Company and other firms had not yet seriously begun to compete. Jardine and Matheson had it all their own way. They had had more experience with opium and were more far-seeing than the others. Their organization had been built up first and was more thorough; in their purchases of ships specially suited to the trade they had anticipated the rest. Later on, as we shall see, they improved their organization yet further, increased their ships, which became still more sea-worthy and faster, gathered round them a body of captains, as staunch and fearless as those who commanded the privateers of the old days, and maintained their supremacy over all competitors. The Coast Trade, at first only a branch of the opium trade at Lintin, grew to be the more important. It was, moreover, further out of reach of any counter-measures which the Chinese Government might seek to take. That Government, having no deep-sea fleet, could not prevent the opium ships prowling along the coast; and even had local officials been honest, the coast was so long, and cover and inlets so numerous, that the most efficient preventive service could hardly have stopped smuggling. Lintin, on the other hand, was very close to the centre of Chinese authority; the Chinese boatmen who took delivery from the receiving hulks could be intimidated; and pressure could be brought to bear by suspending the legitimate trade of the port of Canton or by constraining in some way the European merchants there who, as residents on the mainland, were in the power of the Chinese administration. But the Coast Trade was free from these curbing restraints. From the Chinese Government's point of view, it was much more alarming, not really because it was a drug traffic but because it was wholly beyond their control and was a demonstration of what British ships of war might do, should England one day decide to use open force.

Some readers will have asked themselves the question— was it legal under the Navigation Act for armed ships, without licence for their guns and without port clearance, to operate along the China coast in the manner described? It was not legal. They were liable to seizure by the warships of any navy, including their own. Thus the Coast Trade contravened not only the laws of China against opium and against smuggling and against entering any port but Canton, but also international law. But then, it was argued, China hardly fell within the purview of international law. She did

91

not recognize its existence; though earnestly requested to do so, she had refused again and again to enter into international relations with the West. Why then should she expect to enjoy its advantages? If she desired those advantages, let her enter the comity of nations, throw open all her ports to overseas trade, reform her civil service, receive diplomatic representatives at her capital, and abrogate those irritating and old-fashioned rules and regulations, which for so long had been used to keep foreign merchants at arm's length.

We know the Court of Peking's answer to that kind of reasoning. It was not safe to let the Barbarians move freely in the celestial lands. They had swallowed the Middle East, they would certainly attempt to swallow the Far East. Their influence upon the population was very disturbing; where they came honest men turned rascals, propriety was forgotten and rebellions were hatched. Emperor after Emperor had weighed and found them wanting. Everything in the Confucian code demanded their exclusion.

That China would not, or could not, accommodate herself to events, though too weak to stem them, had brought about by 1830 a situation, not only unprecedented in Chinese history, but ominous for her, full of peril, extravagant, hardly credible. The most powerful nation in the West, whose strength depended wholly upon overseas trade and whose people were resolved to extend that trade by every means, to push it with valour and undergo hardships to carry it to the ends of the earth, now pressed against the old closed market of China and was resolved to break into it. Neither the Chinese people nor the civil service was in practice behind their Government in its policy of seclusion. Though in law all the ports were shut except Canton, many of them were open in fact and though opium was forbidden it was in immense demand. For a very long time the East India Company had sought to find a staple to send to China. But the Chinese had so little use for any of the commodities offered and made their demand for opium so clear, that it became inevitable that it would be satisfied. Taking the broadest view, one perceives that a rebellion against the Chinese Government was actually in being. A section of the people and the civil service had opened China to the West. They had not done this for economic or political reasons, but because they wanted a certain drug and the money which went with it. But the practical effect was as if they had acted from policy. A fleet of ships was now passing up and down their coast, bringing not only opium, but Bibles and medicine, western notions and novelties of thought. These ships would not have been there, had not the Chinese in sufficient numbers facilitated their presence. But inasmuch as this amounted to a covert rebellion against the Government, these ships and all they represented became a potential menace to the state, for so paradoxical a situation could not persist indefinitely. The British who manned them were charting the harbours and approaches and acquiring a detailed knowledge; they were, in literal fact, spying out the nakedness of the land. Jardine and Matheson knew with greater precision than any other men how weak and defenceless was that land. Informed by the first-hand reports of their captains they were in a position to give well-founded advice. And so, when the time came, they spoke with authority. Their character and experience had already made them the leaders of the British community in Canton: now they were to become the men who, from behind the scenes, inspired the policy of the British Government. But before the crisis became acute, as it did in 1839 in a manner no one expected, many things were to happen. The stage had to be cleared by the departure of the East India Company in 1834. The curious drama of Lord Napier had to be played through. The temper of the British Government had to be given time to rise. These events were the preliminaries which enabled Jardine afterwards to convince the Cabinet that a line of policy, which he and Matheson had long advocated, was the right way to resolve the problem of China.

The Dragon Memorializes Heaven

Before concluding this chapter it will be proper to take a peep at the Dragon. Like all his predecessors for three millenniums he was called, not by his name, but by the title of his reign, which was Tao Kuang, Glorious Rectitude. In 1830 he had been ten years on the Dragon Seat. No one has ever pretended that in character or attainments he equalled or, indeed, approached the two great sovereigns of the Ta Ch'ing Dynasty, K'ang Hsi, Lasting Prosperity, and Ch'ien Lung, Enduring Glory. Yet he was a respectable figure, somewhat parsimonious, say some, or businesslike, say others, with a strong sense of duty and a desire to act rightly. As his three successors were debauchees or simpletons, each of whom was murdered by the usurping concubine, the Motherly and Auspicious, it may be said that he was the last Manchu sovereign of worth.

But already were apparent ominous signs of those internal stresses, which, combined with pressure from without, were to wreck the Dynasty. In the history of China certain evils recur. One of these took the form of the interference by Court eunuchs with the administration. This was so notoriously fatal, for it had undermined many dynasties, that the Manchus from the first took great care to prevent it, and there was no sign of it in 1830. But the administration, if it had not been tampered with by irresponsible elements at Court, had become for a variety of reasons very corrupt, as the preceding pages have amply demonstrated. Perhaps the ultimate cause of this corruption was the fact that the Manchus were not native sovereigns. They could not count, even after two hundred years of rule, on the unquestioning support of the whole population. But the civil service was solidly behind them, because the promotion and prospects of each individual official depended on the maintenance of the *status quo*.

This loyalty to a foreign House had two results: it made the Emperor disinclined to alienate their chief body of supporters by exercising too strict a supervision; and it widened the distance between the general population and the bureaucracy, so that public opinion, always against corruption, was less able to make itself felt. The civil service was more independent than it would have been under a strong native sovereign. Being the agent of the foreign domination, it was against reforms originating among the people. It was less sensitive to popular feeling than, as a Confucian organization, it should have been. All these factors tended to make it irresponsible. Its feeling of duty to the public was much diluted. A Governor was less the father of his province than a man who regarded his powers as a lever to get money.

Nevertheless, the China of the nineteenth century still kept green the memory of past officials who had been incorruptible. Their names were household words; stories about them had been treasured for centuries. Thus, the Ancestral Hall of the Yang family was still called the Hall of the Four Knows because of what had happened there seventeen centuries earlier. In A.D. 1221 when a friend remonstrated with Yang Chen for leaving nothing to his sons, he replied: 'If posterity speaks of me as an incorruptible official, will that be nothing?' And when a man offered him a bribe and said: 'It is after dark and no one will know,' Yang Chen was recorded as saying: 'Not know? Why, Heaven will know, Earth will know, you will know, I will know.' There was a later Yang, Yang Ch'eng, who lived a thousand years before the time of Tao Kuang. Ordered to collect taxes during a famine, he refused, and threw himself into prison where he slept on a plank. Many other old stories of official rectitude were current. For instance, such was the example of probity set by Lu Kung in the first century A.D., when magistrate of K'ai Feng-fu, that even children were unusually humane to each other, a Confucian way of pointing the belief that if a ruler was of good character his influence permeated society to the very bottom. This belief was even carried further, for it had been held from the beginning of history that the quality of rulers was reflected in the crops. Thus the case of Chang K'an of the first century A.D. continued to be quoted: when he was Governor of Yu-Yang, every blade of corn bore two ears. One could multiply instances. Opinion ascribed, and had always ascribed, a transcendental power to goodness in high places, and, conversely, attributed such calamities as flood, famines and rebellions to lack of virtue in the Emperor and his subordinates. The notorious corruption of the civil service in the nineteenth century caused therefore misgiving, not only because of its everyday results in practice, but because it was likely to be attended by natural calamities, the sure warning of Heaven that the Confucian standards were not being maintained. Heaven always delivered its warnings in that way, and if no notice was taken withdrew eventually its Mandate from its Son, the Emperor, whose dynasty, supported no longer, fell into ruin.

In the eighteen-thirties Heaven had begun to visit the Chinese population with signs of its displeasure; there were portents abroad of the kind which had invariably been held to mean that all was not right with the Government. Thus, following upon autumn floods, there was a serious famine in May 1832 in four of the central provinces. Furthermore, the hill people living on the border of the Canton province broke into open rebellion on 5th February of that year under a leader calling himself the Golden Dragon King, who, using all the magical arts to which rebels in China always resorted, defeated the regiment of imperial troops sent against him, partly because two hundred of the soldiers were opium addicts. The Governor of Canton, in reporting to Court, tried to excuse his defeat by laying emphasis on the demoniacal powers of the Golden Dragon King, for which he received a sharp reprimand, the Emperor himself noting with the Vermilion Brush: ' "Demoniacal arts" are words which should never appear in a Memorial to Us.' Nor was this the only rebellion. The same year a serious outbreak occurred in Formosa. The public there, infuriated by official extortion, suddenly surrounded the barracks and massacred twenty officers and seventeen hundred men, thereafter abrogating all authority on the island. A large military expedition had to be sent to restore order.

Even in Peking itself there was trouble. A manure-gatherer, who had saved some money, collected a rabble of distressed soldiers and desperate paupers. Calling himself the Old King, as if he were a Taoist Immortal returned to earth, he appointed as his lieutenant a man styled Lion of the Recumbent Buddha, a cripple who could not open his right hand, which defect proved, it was said, his knowledge of magical arts. Together they planned to seize Peking and inaugurate a native dynasty once again, with the manure-gatherer in the Dragon Seat. They were arrested the very day fixed for the outbreak, a date in February 1832.

Apprehension, however, continued to be felt in the capital, for no rain fell. Spring gave way to summer and still not more than a few showers. It seemed to the Emperor that this prolonged drought, coinciding as it did with two insurrections, an attempted *coup d'état* and a famine, denoted the extreme displeasure of Heaven and he decided to address a Memorial thereto. As is well known, the Emperors of China sacrificed to Heaven once a year on the night of the winter solstice. This sacrifice took place on the Altar of Heaven, a great open marble dais in a park near the main gate in the outer enceinte. A solemn and lengthy ritual was observed.

After the cremation of the sacrificial buffalo came phases of the ceremony called the Offering of Incense, the Advent of the Spirits and the Offerings of Jade and Silk, which were followed by the Oblation of Wine and the Recital of the Prayer. Finally the Emperor kneeling before the altar entered into communion with Heaven after drinking the Wine, and eating the Meat, of Felicity. When Tao Kuang memorialized Heaven, which he did at dawn on 24th July 1832, he did not do so at the Altar of Heaven but at an altar dedicated to Heaven inside the Purple Forbidden City and probably situated in the Hall of the Blending of Heaven and Earth, which is behind the Palace of Heavenly Purity. His dress was the antique costume always worn by the Sons of Heaven when acting as the High Priests of the Children of Han. On his head was a hat which had some resemblance to a mortar-board, twenty-four pendentives swinging from the brim. He wore a pleated yellow gown and a purple surcoat, wide sleeved and embroidered with the Twelve Ornaments, to wit, the sun, the moon, the stars, the key-fret, the grass, the pheasant, the axe-head, the mountains, the dragon, the cups, the rice-grains and the fire. From his girdle, of leather studded with sacred gems, there hung metal pendants, and across his breast was a golden stole. His high boots had thick white soles. After alighting from his sedan, he slowly moved towards the blue altar in procession, his gait stiff and hieratic, an antique gait as rigorously ordered as the steps of a formal dance. Gongs and drums were sounding a classic march.

The precise details of the ceremony used on this occasion are not on record, though they will have followed in part the liturgy used at the winter sacrifice. The words of the Memorial to Heaven, however, which at a stated moment, kneeling before the altar, the Emperor read out in a high-pitched ritual voice, are preserved: 'Wu Hu, oh, alas! Imperial Heaven, were not the world afflicted by extraordinary ills, I should not dare to present extraordinary supplications. But this year the drought passes all precedent. Summer is past and no rain has fallen. Mankind is bowed beneath calamity, even the beasts and insects cease to live.

'I, the Son of Heaven, am Lord of this World. Heaven looks to me that I preserve tranquillity. My bounden duty is to soothe the people. Yet, though I cannot sleep, nor eat with appetite; though I am grief-stricken and shake with anxiety; my grief, my fasts, my sleepless nights have but obtained a trifling shower.'

His Majesty then proceeds to consider wherein he has erred, for it must be his errors which have brought down Heaven's censure: 'Looking up, I reflect that Heaven is benevolence. The atrocity alone of my sins is the cause, too little sincerity, too little devotion. Had I been more devoted and sincere, I had moved Heaven to confer a blessing. Let me now therefore examine myself. Have I wanted in respect at the winter sacrifice? Has pride or prodigality a place in my heart, springing like weeds by my neglect? Have I been negligent in public business, lacking in the diligence and effort which was due? Have my rewards and punishments been equitable? In building mausoleums and laying out gardens have I distressed the people by extravagance?'

He then turns to the conduct of the civil service, which if not, as we should say, the cause of the drought, was certainly one of the principal evils of the day: 'Have unfit persons been appointed to official posts, and petty and vexatious acts oppressed the people? Have my officials punished only with justice? Have the poor not found means of appeal? Have magistrates refused their ear to petitioners? Have there been massacres in frontier fighting by officers seeking imperial rewards? Has famine relief been properly distributed or have the people been left to die in the ditches? Have the operations against the insurgents been taken as an excuse for trampling on the villagers?'

Having in this way laid bare where the evil which had offended Heaven might well reside, he comes to his con-

cluding apostrophe: 'Prostrate, I implore Imperial Heaven to
pardon my ignorance. Summer is past, autumn is close at
hand. Truly to wait longer is not possible. I have made the
Three Kneelings, I have made the Nine Knockings. Hasten
and confer clement deliverance; with speed send down the
blessing of rain. Wu Hu, Oh, alas! Imperial Heaven, give
ear to my petition! Wu Hu, oh, alas! Imperial Heaven, be
graciously inclined! I am inexpressively grieved, alarmed
and shaken. Reverently this memorial is presented.'

This remarkable Confucian document was published in
the *Peking Gazette*, the Court's newspaper, on July 29,
1832, and a translation of it was made by Dr. Morrison for
the *Chinese Repository*, the quarterly newspaper edited by
Protestant missionaries at Canton. The *Repository's* first
issue was in May, 1832 and it continued to be published
regularly during the period covered by this book. It is a first-
hand authority and contains many other original documents.
The editors recorded a narrative of current events, reviewed
all European publications about China and the Far East in
general, and offered translations of the Chinese classics. Its
rivals were the *Canton Press* and the *Canton Gazette*, the
organs of Jardine and Matheson and of Dent and Company.
But it was the more weighty and scholarly magazine, for it
had Dr. Morrison and Dr. Gutzlaff behind it, the only two
men who knew Chinese. Its tone and bias were, of course,
strongly Protestant and missionary, but, as has been pointed
out above, this was also the approach of the merchants, who
were as convinced as the missionaries that the conversion of
China was both feasible and to be desired. The editorial
comments on Tao Kuang's Memorial to Heaven are, therefore, more significant than might appear. We may give a few
citations, some of which, in fact, show remarkable pres-
cience. 'This is a most singular production,' they begin. 'It
is one too of great value; it is worth more than scores of
quartos and folios of the vain speculations which have been
published concerning China. Even allowing that much of

the colouring has been given to it for effect merely (which we are slow to admit), still it exhibits an exalted personage in a most interesting and affecting point of view. It is withal a very serious document. As it conducts us to the ante-chamber of the Celestial Court and there shows us the "minister of heaven" scorched with grief, poring over his atrocious sins and with trembling anxiety recounting the errors of his public and private life, our sympathy is excited and we instinctively re-echo his lamentations, Woo hoo! Oh, Alas!'

There follows this pregnant comment: 'The document shows very distinctly, if we mistake not, the symptoms of an oppressed and declining empire. We predict nothing. We should rejoice to see "the great Pure Dynasty" long stand strong, flourishing in all the glory, peace, tranquillity and prosperity, which it now proudly and falsely arrogates. . . . But our own minds, in accordance, we believe, with the minds of millions, forbode an approaching change.'

The nature of that change, the editorial suggests, would be a revolution and the fall of the dynasty, followed by anarchy. As we know, the dynasty was carried away eventually by a revolution, though this did not happen for another eighty years. But changes of deep import were close, which sorely tried it, and without whose operations it would not have fallen at long last. There was to be an inrush of the West, with all it stood for. But this was largely hidden from the editors of the *Chinese Repository*. Neither they nor the merchants believed as early as 1832 that in eight years England would turn its armed forces against China. Though the possibility of this was not entirely absent from the minds of a few, the office of the West was conceived rather to be the bringing in of Christianity and of international trade.

In concluding their comments the editors reveal the narrowness of their sectarian outlook. Lest anyone should suppose from their sympathetic references at the beginning that they identified Imperial Heaven with God, they are at pains to make clear that they think nothing of the sort and esteem Tao Kuang no better than a pagan. 'The conduct of the Emperor in praying, fasting and self examination ought to reprove the sluggish Christian. But we shall do exceedingly wrong if we attempt to excuse such abominable idolatry, and to throw the mantle of charity over that which God abhors.' To us, of course, it is indisputable that the Confucian belief in Heaven was deism. The eighteenth century had been ready to concede this; even the Jesuits had made the identification the basis of their proposed syncretism. But the outlook of nineteenth-century Protestantism was much narrower, and as it was shared by the merchant community in Canton and by Parliament it tended to colour the whole attitude of Britain to China.

According to the *Peking Gazette*, the Emperor's Memorial to Heaven received a favourable answer. At 8 p.m. that very evening there was a thunderstorm followed by a substantial downpour. During the ensuing week six inches of rain fell altogether. For this manifestation of heavenly compassion the Emperor issued an edict expressing deep devotion and intense gratitude.

In summary we may draw one or two conclusions which will be found relevant to what is to follow. Though the corrupt bureaucracy merely used the Confucian terminology as a patter which they uttered while they continued to fleece the people, the population in general, and particularly a minority of scholars and gentlemen of the highest character, were as devoted to the tenets of the Master as had ever been the best of each generation for the two millenniums which had elapsed since his death. This public opinion obliged the Emperor, particularly at times of public calamity, to declare openly in accordance with precedent his responsibility to Heaven and his determination to see carried out by his subordinates the national sage's moral precepts, which had a more direct bearing on the conduct of public affairs than is generally to be found in state religions.

Had the Emperor neglected to respond to this public opinion, he would have shocked millions of his subjects and endangered his throne. We may therefore take Tao Kuang's Memorial, not as an expression of personal contrition or necessarily of any conviction that the administration in fact was failing in its duty, but rather as a ritual act enjoined on him as Son of Heaven. But if he was doing no more than performing, as in duty bound, what was both a religious service and an act of state, the public opinion which obliged him so to do was quite genuine. That there existed in China a force of this kind will be found to throw light on the drama to be related. It should be noted, however, that the British did not believe such a public opinion existed. The Confucian phraseology, in which all government announcements were couched, was conceived of merely as an official style, so at variance with the acts of officialdom as to have no real meaning whatsoever. That ultimately the words were not empty but rested upon the deeply felt convictions of a sufficient number of men to give them weight at a crisis never occurred to anybody, and when this was demonstrated to be so, there was first incredulity, then surprise and finally consternation.

In conclusion, we should note that the Emperor makes no reference to the opium trade, either at Lintin or along the coast, or to the connivance of the local officials which made it possible. This omission can only mean that public opinion had not yet been roused to protest. There were three directions from which protest might come. It could be alleged that opium was a deleterious drug; that its import had grown so much that the exports did not pay for it, resulting in a drain of silver large enough to disturb the prevailing monetary system; and that the coast clippers which delivered it along the sea-board had set at nought the age-old rule that foreign ships must not frequent the ports, a rule founded on the settled policy that western nations be kept at a distance. But in 1832 the mouthpiece of public opinion, such as the

Censors, had not yet begun to memorialize on this subject. The Emperor had two reasons for not referring to it. Commercial affairs at Canton were his monopoly, and he had no wish to bring them into the limelight. The second reason was yet more solid—he had no idea of the magnitude of the smuggling.

Chapter III

THE MISADVENTURES
OF A BARBARIAN
EYE

(i)

A Review of Prospects in 1833

As we have had occasion in passing to mention, the monopoly of the China trade which the East India Company had been enjoying for about a century and a half came to an end in 1834. This was effected by an Act of Parliament dated 28 August, 1833, which provided that after 21 April, 1834, the trade with China should be open to all British subjects. We need not here go into all the reasons which prompted Parliament to pass this measure. Suffice it to say that it was no sudden resolution. The Free Trade school of economists had been gradually increasing their influence, as had the manufacturing interest. The shareholders of the East India Company did not represent much more than the governing classes. The whole conception of monopoly trading was going out of date. The great new middle class was largely opposed to it. Perhaps the most practical reason against continuing to restrict the China trade to the East India Company was that, while the restrictions operated to keep out London houses financially capable of engaging therein, it could not keep out foreigners, particularly the Americans, who traded at Canton to the limit of their capacity and made profits which, had the monopoly not existed, these houses might equally have made. Moreover, by licensing certain firms, which were not shareholders, to export tea to England, and by using the country trade to serve both its Indian and Chinese financial requirements, the East India Company had already so diluted its statutory monopoly that the change over to free trade had gone a certain distance before 1834. And the Company was not asked to face grave losses. It still had the monopoly of opium in India. The free merchants would have to apply to it for the drug and as many new merchants would come in, the demand would be much larger. Indeed, the Company was likely to make more money by selling opium, without risk or overheads, in its own city of Calcutta than it had by selling tea in London after the enormous expenses of the establishment at Canton and the fleet of Indiamen had been met.

But if the transition from monopoly to free trade was no upheaval in the commercial sense, it raised a number of important questions in the political. In its issue of December, 1833, the *Chinese Repository* published an article signed 'British Merchant'. As the opinions it contains coincide very closely with those which later on we shall find Jardine expressing, it is possible that he himself was the writer. Indeed, we may say that either he wrote it or one of those merchants who shared his opinions. Reading it, we see what was being discussed at the time. The British residents had a clear idea of the policy required, if the trade were to be advanced on the departure of the East India Company.

After pointing out that in the century and a half of its trading to China the Company in spite of repeated efforts had failed completely to obtain the smallest amendment to the drastic Eight Regulations, except occasionally in the matter of boating for pleasure, the writer asks why that is so and concludes the reason to be that, to avoid disturbing the even course of trade, a policy of conciliation, almost amounting to subservience, was invariably adopted, when a stiff or threatening front would have served far better. This timidity went so far that on one occasion its Committee handed over an innocent Briton to death in order to avoid interruption of trade, an act which covered them with everlasting infamy. The reference here is to the case of the gunner of

107

the *Lady Hughes* who in 1784 being ordered to fire a saluting gun, inadvertently killed a Chinese boatman, who was alongside. The Chinese threatened to stop the trade, if he were not delivered up to them for trial. Rather than risk a stoppage, the Company handed him over and after a secret trial he was strangled. Though this had happened fifty years previously, it still rankled. The Chinese declared that blood for blood was the law, but it was considered an undying disgrace that the Company should have bowed to such an iniquitous law. 'Has not the Chinese commerce of Great Britain been purchased with the blood of the gunner of the *Lady Hughes?*' asks the writer of the article with bitter anger, and he goes on: 'Has not his immolation up to this day remained unavenged? There is the smell of blood still.'

There is no doubt that we hear the authentic voice of England in this outburst. That the British authorities at Canton should have been intimidated, that to save their pockets they should, with such coldness of heart, have delivered to a lonely and cruel death a poor innocent helpless fellow-countryman, who had only been obeying orders, too, when he fired the gun, was an act which, it was felt, indelibly stained the reputation of the whole English race. Such was the view in 1833, and it would be the same today. So disgraceful a thing must never never happen again, cries the writer, and it never will happen again if we free merchants insist on a strong bold policy.

He then proceeds to discuss such a policy. When the Company leaves, its governing body, the Select Committee, goes with it and the free merchants are left without direction. A Chamber of Commerce could no doubt take the place of the Committee and continue to work with the Co-Hong as before, but such a body would hardly be able to take a stronger line than the Committee. Instead, the Crown should appoint a representative, a person of standing who could speak in the assurance that the British nation was behind him and ready to sanction vigorous measures if an occasion demanded.

The writer then indicates the great difficulties with which such a representative would have to deal. In the first place, he says, it is extremely doubtful whether the Viceroy and the Governor would condescend to recognize his superior status. The rule remained that the Barbarians must conduct all their affairs with the Hong merchants. The King's representative risked being ordered, if he attempted to approach the Viceroy direct, to put in his petition through the proper channel. But supposing, for the sake of argument, that the Chinese authorities decided to recognize him and to amend the rules sufficiently to allow him to consult with them, what would happen if they then raised the matter of the Coast Trade and asked him to stop it on the ground that it was a smuggling trade, and that the smuggled article was a forbidden drug? Could he, as a representative of the Crown, refuse to forbid the merchants engaged in it to desist from illegal acts? He would be obliged to refuse, for the revenues of India were dependent upon the opium trade, yet how could he frame his refusal? It was hard to imagine what phrases he could use which would leave him with a reputation for bona-fides. 'Such are some of the difficulties,' observes the writer, 'and they are of no small magnitude, which a governmental authority would have to encounter, could he effect an impossibility, or what at present may be considered as such, and insinuate himself into a communication with the head authorities of Canton.'

Yet, he goes on, a solution must be found or a crisis of the first magnitude will eventually arise. There is a dynamic momentum on the British side which cannot be dammed. Not only have you the 'patient, thrifty, dextrous assiduity of private and untrammelled enterprise' which seeps through every crack, but there exists a fundamental propelling force, a force more powerful than the normal exchange of commodities for profit. This force which stands poised like an avalanche is 'our capital, our manufacturing interest, our power-looms, which cry out "obtain us but a sale for our

goods, and we will supply any quantity".' Here is the fundamental difference between British and American commerce.
The American merchants are not pushed from behind,
because America is not a manufacturing nation, while their
British confrères are propelled onwards by an economic pressure, which they did not inaugurate and cannot bind.

What, then, is the solution? he asks. The answer is
sketched in the following sentences: 'If a crown authority be
placed in China, he must be an efficient one, and vested
with powers of no ordinary nature, as being placed in a
position that may force him into a state of war in spite of his
best endeavours to the contrary. Nor, indeed, should our
valuable commerce and revenue, both in India and Great
Britain, be permitted to remain subject to a caprice, which a
few gunboats laid alongside this city would overrule by the
discharge of a few mortars. The Governor and Hoppo would
soon find that their freaks of fancy were no longer the
pastime they used to be, and that it was not prudent to
provoke those who were willing to be their friends . . . The
results of a war with the Chinese cannot be doubted.'

There you have it. The British must ply their trade and if
the Chinese refused to trade, it meant war, and war meant a
certain Chinese defeat because they had no navy. But the
British did not want war. War might precipitate an internal
revolutionary crisis inimical to trade. But the threat of
war should be used: 'It is well known that the Tartar
dynasty floats upon a smooth but dangerous sea, and that its
existence depends upon the habit of tranquil obedience to its
authority. Sensible of this, the high authorities view with
abhorrence anything that savours of perturbation.' Therefore cause them to fear perturbation, both within and
without, unless they yield to reasonable requests. The
instrument of that threat is ready to hand. 'The only thing
which has raised our character above its abasement and
created an influence with the Chinese is the conduct of our
men-of-war. They indeed have established a character

which makes the Chinese tremble at the knowledge of their approach.' That is the lever to upset the Eight Regulations and prise a way for British goods into the very heart of China. It will not, he says, be sufficient for the navy merely to show itself occasionally. It must establish an advanced base in the China seas. This should not be in the region of Canton, which is too far from the capital, but much further north at a place from which, should necessity require, ten thousand men could be launched at Peking. To such language the Chinese, or rather their Manchu overlords, would give instant and respectful attention: 'They are sensitive of their incapacity and weakness, their empire is in so crumbling a state that they dread danger beforehand . . . We must practise on their fears. The mere presence of our cruisers on their coast would sufficiently alarm them, however friendly might be our conduct, nor is it desirable that it should be otherwise.'

And he sums up: 'By bold demonstrations through our cruisers, followed up by negotiation through a Commission, we might arrive at arrangements with the Chinese Government mutually beneficial, without any violation of justice or any act of hostility . . . We have permitted the Chinese to doze in error when one rude shock would have aroused them to the sense of it . . . The basis of the new Commissioner's demands should be open trade with China . . . The scrupulous deportment of past embassies should be wholly laid aside . . . A diplomatic Petruchio would be far preferable.' Pitt spoke of calling a new world into existence to redress the balance of the old; to call China into commercial existence would be an act of no less elevated statesmanship.

This is Jardine speaking, the British mercantile community speaking, as it had always spoken out, and, indeed, as it still speaks. That community claims that by its 'patient, thrifty, dextrous assiduity' it has been the creator of England's greatness and will continue to be its conservator. In support of this claim a mass of evidence is adducible. It is

111

from that angle that the historical importance of a firm like Jardine and Matheson must be assessed.

One point in the article raises a question. How was it that the writer spoke of the propelling power of British manufactures, when, in fact, such products of English industry had been found unsaleable in China in sufficient quantities to balance the purchases of tea and silk, and when opium valued at approximately the same figure as the total of all manufactures had had to be brought in? In short, if the China trade depended on opium, and a smuggling system had been perfected by means of which the import of the drug had increased from 6,000 to more than 20,000 chests in twelve years, why was it relevant to talk of opening China to the products of the power-loom? Was not the situation already commercially satisfactory? The Eight Regulations had in practice been largely abrogated; in practice the ports of China were open to foreign trade. Why was it urgent that the British should press for, and threaten to acquire by force, what was already theirs? The answer can be put like this: far sighted persons did not believe that it would be possible indefinitely to continue smuggling opium into China. Though the Company had fostered the drug trade and depended upon it, the Court of Directors, sensitive to more respectable opinion in England, had never dealt in it directly. The dislike of having to do with a disreputable commodity would grow. That the China trade should hinge upon such sales, that it should be mixed up with bribery, corruption and smuggling, that it should have to run the gauntlet of the local police and be carried on by means of armed vessels beyond the pale of international law and contrary to the terms of the Navigation Act, was not sound business, was not the sort of solid traffic which had enabled the British to found an empire and a world-wide trade based on the mutual benefit and goodwill of all concerned, but was a gamble, a racket, certain one day to lead to ruinous complications. Anglo-Chinese commercial relations could never be regarded as satisfactory, until an open and legal exchange of goods was established. As the Chinese Government was unlikely to legalise the importation of opium, it followed that not until the whole vast empire was opened to free trade would a sound commercial traffic be possible. And with the opening of China to western ideas would come a demand for all sorts of British goods. Therefore, on a long view, it was in the interest even of those firms dealing at present exclusively in opium to support a forward policy. This was the general view in 1833, though there were people to declare that if force were used to compel the Chinese to open their country, it would not be necessary to abandon the opium trade, for the dynasty would be too debilitated after the defeat of its armed forces to object to it any longer. A forward policy was therefore correct in any event, for it would put the legal trade on a proper basis and would make easier, more extensive and more lucrative the illegal. Such was to turn out a true anticipation.

(ii)

The Head Authorities of Canton

The civil administration of Canton was under the control of two members of the bureaucracy, the T'sung Fu or Viceroy and the Hsün or Governor. The Viceroy had charge of the province of Kuangtung, of which Canton was the chief city, and of the neighbouring province of Kuangsi. In 1834 this official's surname was Lu. He had recently succeeded Li, who had been dismissed for his failure against the Golden Dragon King.

The Governor was the Viceroy's colleague rather than his subordinate. In official papers he was referred to as 'an Attendant Officer of the Board of War, a member of the Court of Universal Examiners, an Imperial Censor, the Patrolling Soother of Canton and the Controller of Taxes.' In all matters relating to Canton these two officials acted jointly. Both were Chinese.

The military administration was under the Chiang Chün, usually rendered as Tartar General. In rank he was the equal of the Viceroy and it was always a nice point which of them should take precedence on any given occasion. He was invariably a Manchu and generally a nobleman of the Imperial clan. The troops under his command were Manchus drawn from one of the Eight Banners, the standing army of the Manchu overlords, in which all Manchus of military age and approved fitness were obliged to serve. This standing army had kept the Chinese in subjection for the previous 190 years. In equipment it was hardly better furnished than in 1644 when it burst into China; and long years of peace, the habit of opium smoking, a sheltered easy life, and the discontinuance of the hunting and equestrian sports which were so marked a feature of training in earlier days, had turned it into an effete military aristocracy. Five or six thousand of these men were stationed at Canton. In addition there existed a provincial force known as the Army of the Green Standard, a rabble composed partly of Manchus and partly of irregulars enlisted from the Chinese lower orders. The forts defending Canton were small and, as we know, in want of repair, some being in such a state of dilapidation as 'to present nothing more formidable than the frightful paintings of tigers' heads on the wooden lids which block up their portholes', as a contemporary newspaper put it. Of the whole garrison of Canton, only two hundred men, it was said, made any sort of an impression on parade.

We are enabled to take a close view of the Viceroy and the Tartar General because they happened to pay a visit to the British factory on 2nd May 1834, a few weeks after the end of East India Company's reign. As it was May, the season was over and the merchant community had moved down to Macao for the summer recess. The British factory, which after the departure of the Company was to be rented by individual merchants and also used as a hotel, its public rooms being reserved for entertainments, was empty on this 2nd of May, save for two or three assistants left to wind up accounts and sell its various properties to the private firms, principally four million dollars' worth of imports and seven millions of export teas. The Viceroy's visit was therefore unofficial, a morning excursion to explore the place at his leisure. The *Chinese Repository* published a first-hand account of what transpired.

The Viceroy had announced his intention to the Hong merchants and these worthies entered the factory at an early hour and took charge of the arrangements. As is usual in the East, the rumoured hour of the arrival was long before it actually took place. His Excellency was expected at 9 a.m. and before that hour the gate into the garden was thrown open. In lieu of the red carpet of western state, a red hanging was draped over the gate itself and two policemen were posted there on guard. Inside the factory, chairs were put out in the main drawing room sufficient to seat the official party and arranged in conformity with Chinese etiquette. In the dining room the table was laid in the English fashion, for the intention was to offer His Excellency refreshments.

All being in readiness, what the *Repository* terms 'a few vaporing runners from the hoppo's office' made their appearance. These fellows, with the officiousness of underlings the world over, proceeded to interfere and, giving out that they had received orders to that effect, closed the doors leading into the other apartments to prevent, as they said, the foreign devils in the building from staring at His

Excellency. The foreign devils, however, would have none of this impertinence and told the runners to go downstairs and stay there.

A very long wait supervened. It was past one o'clock when a gong was heard and the cry of heralds, a sound not unlike the howling of dogs. This meant that an official of importance was approaching. It was not the Viceroy, however, but the Adjutant of the Tartar General. He was presently seen turning in at the gate, his sedan borne by four footmen and accompanied by a retinue of servants, soldiers and petty officers, all Manchus, tall stalwarts from the north. The Tartar General himself—his name was Ha-Fengah—was in the middle of the procession which followed, carried in a sedan by eight bearers. He was preceded by lictors with bamboo staves, by men with chains in their hands and others with whips. Above his sedan a high state parasol was held up. It was remarked that the swords carried by his immediate bodyguard were of wood.

On reaching the factory porch General Ha alighted and it was possible to see the sort of man he was. He appeared about sixty, and was not Chinese in features, having a narrow thin face, an aquiline nose and a tall spare form. His clothes differed little from those of a civil functionary, being a dark flowered silk robe, worn over another of lighter blue, embroidered on the back and breast with tigers. His hat-button was coral, indicative of the first rank of the Mandarinate and he had been decorated with the Peacock Feather. Immediately going upstairs to the drawing room, he sat down to wait for the Viceroy, filling in the time by briskly conversing with Howqua, the senior Hong merchant, whom he summoned to his presence.

There now appeared a lieutenant-general, and Howqua retired. The next arrival was the Hoppo, Chung, sleek and with a silky beard. As a prince or duke of the Imperial clan he, of course, was also a Manchu. He was followed by another lieutenant-general. These four high mandarins now moved to the pillared verandah over the porch and sat, two by two, facing each other. They chatted among themselves, taking no notice of anybody else nor expressing any wish to speak to the foreign devils in whose house they were.

Another long wait now occurred; not till nearly three o'clock was the Viceroy's approach announced. His procession was similar to the Tartar General's. As his sedan entered the garden, soldiers lining the path knelt. At the porch he got into an open chair and was carried up the stairs, at the head of which the Hoppo received him by bending one knee and lifting his hands in the gesture of supplication. Rising from the chair, the Viceroy, who was tall and stout, also bent a knee, but a trifle less far, and extended his hands to raise the Hoppo. This done, the Hoppo conducted him, leaning on a favourite's arm, to the verandah, where the three military officers welcomed him in turn, bending the knee and raising the hands. It had now to be determined who should move first to the chairs, but this was settled by them all moving together. The actual sitting down, however, was less easy. Four chairs faced each other, looking east and west, and there was a fifth chair at the top, looking south. Who was to take the chair of honour? The Viceroy and the Tartar General were both mandarins of the first rank, and both had the decoration of the Peacock Feather. Each pressed the other to take the principal chair. Finally, the fiction was agreed on that the Viceroy should on this occasion be regarded as host. He took the chair at the top, placing the Tartar General on his left, always the seat of honour in China.

The Englishman, who reported the scene afterwards to the editor of the *Repository*, and who presumably was peeping through one of the doors, was now amused to perceive that, once the formalities were over and they were seated, the Chinese visitors immediately became unreserved, familiar and talkative. They knew each other, of course, extremely well. After a few moments one of the Hong merchants came forward with bowls of birds' nest soup as a restorative. This drunk, hot damp towels were handed in and their Excellencies' faces were wiped, a refreshing custom which still persists in China. Then came tea and pipes, the Viceroy making great use of his snuff box the while.

In the ordinary way the Governor would most likely have been one of the party, but he had been transferred a short time before and his relief did not arrive until 9 May, a week later. He had been far from popular with the British. His surname was Chu, and it was he who three years previously had made a descent upon the British factory, the staff being away, and ordered his men to demolish there and then a small extension of the garden, which the British had made without first obtaining his sanction through the Co-Hong. It had been a most unpleasant affair and in the course of it he had made things worse by eyeing the Lawrence portrait of George IV in a supercilious manner and then deliberately sitting down with his back to it. On the present occasion the Hoppo suggested that the party should get up and have a look at the view over the garden to the river. When they were standing at the edge of the verandah, he was observed to point, while he said to the Viceroy with a good deal of satisfaction: 'That is where Chu knocked the wall down.' Everyone smiled: it had been a Chinese victory.

After this they adjourned to the dining room for something more substantial than birds' nest soup. The table was laid with knives and forks, about which their Excellencies made the same sort of jokes as we are accustomed to make about chopsticks. However, they were more adventurous or less clumsy than the generality of Englishmen, for they set to with these unfamiliar implements and did full justice to the collation, though one of them was seen to take up a slice of cake on his fork and nibble it, while another committed the solecism of mistaking his saucer for a plate. There was some laughter and badinage and the Viceroy remarked that it was just like the Barbarians to eat with kitchen utensils.

The meal was not protracted, perhaps because the birds' nest had taken the edge off their appetites. They soon rose and went into the main reception room where hung the portraits of George IV and Lord Amherst. Considering what Governor Chu had done, and not forgetting that Lord Amherst was hardly admired in China, it was a question whether their Excellencies might not by some gesture or deplorable jocularity wound the susceptibilities of the watching residents. But the thing passed off without incident. They had a look at the Lawrence and the other, at the august pose of His Majesty and Lord Amherst's wooden stare, and, not more interested in these curiosities than we used to be in Chinese pictures before oriental painting became fashionable, turned away, descended the stairs and left in the reverse order in which they had come. From first to last they had ignored the Barbarians, not even sending a message of thanks on departure for their entertainment at table. But during the century and a half of the trade no Viceroy or Tartar General had ever asked to see a British merchant and had invariably refused to see him if requested to do so. It was true that these grandees expected to make a fortune by squeezing the legal trade and were highly interested also in the smuggling. But just because a gentleman happened to benefit financially by a business connection was no reason why he should unbend socially.

These were the people with whom the Barbarian Eye, whose misadventures are the subject of the rest of this chapter, sought to deal.

The Appointment of Lord Napier

When it was decided to terminate the Company's monopoly of the China trade, arrangements had to be made to fill the gap left by the departure from Canton of the Select Committee. The free merchants could not be left without some authority to regulate their actions. A Chamber of Commerce would not suffice alone. In the particular circumstances of the Canton situation, where a miscellaneous body of British merchants was living within the territory of the Emperor of China, who had never accepted the principle of diplomatic representation at his Court, it was clearly essential that they should have at their head a person with authority from the Crown both to oversee and protect them. The Whig administration of Lord Grey, in which Lord Palmerston was Foreign Secretary, was well aware that things were going on at Lintin and on the China coast which could result in consequences hard to foresee, and which, involving as they might matters of high policy, would be too difficult for a non-official head to cope with.

The Viceroy had also given some thought to the matter and had expressed the opinion as early as 1831 that a chief merchant would have to be appointed with authority, like the Select Committee's, over the other merchants. The Co-Hong had conveyed this hint to the Select Committee, which reported it to London. The Viceroy was not suggesting that the chief merchant should be an official or that he should enjoy any privileges which the Select Committee did not possess. The present system would, of course, be continued. In fact, no change in it could have been made without the Emperor's express sanction. And the Emperor had not the smallest intention of modifying the Eight Regulations or abolishing the Co-Hong.

The British Cabinet, though aware that a Crown appointment would be a new departure, does not seem to have realised its full implications from the Chinese point of view, in spite of the mass of evidence which had become available as a result of the Macartney and Amherst embassies and of the report of a Parliamentary Committee recently published. Having decided on its policy, it looked round for a suitable man, and picked Lord William Napier of Meristoun, a Scottish Peer. In 1834 Napier was forty-eight years of age. His career had been in the navy. At the age of nineteen he was a midshipman on the *Defence*, at the battle of Trafalgar. In 1809 he became a lieutenant. In 1815, after the close of the Napoleonic Wars, he retired and married, being elected at that time a Fellow of the Royal Society of Edinburgh. Settling down on the family estates in Selkirkshire, he became somewhat of a model landlord, built roads at his own expense and specialized in sheep farming. He even published a book, his only book, on mountain sheep. In 1823 he succeeded to the title and the following year returned to the navy, serving off the South American coast in command of the frigate *Diamond*. His services in that capacity, if not greatly distinguished, were sound and he became known as a plain, downright and competent officer. As the Cabinet had a feeling that a man with naval experience might turn out very useful if affairs in China ever reached a pass when some of His Majesty's ships would have to go there, he seemed the best man they could find for the post, being the only available peer (and a peer was thought necessary) who had seen service afloat.

Turning now to the letters printed in *Correspondence and Papers relating to China*, a White Paper laid before Parliament in 1840, we may see precisely what Lord Napier was expected to do when he got to Canton.

His appointment was to be called a Chief Superintendency of Trade, and he was to be assisted by a Second and Third Superintendent, the persons to be nominated having been members of the defunct Select Committee of the East India Company. His Commission under the Sign Manual dated 31st December 1833 contained the following points, which denote clearly enough the Chinese policy of His Majesty's Government: he was to take up his residence at Canton; he was to protect the interests of the British merchants, and advise and mediate between them and the officers of the Chinese Government; in his relations with the Chinese Government he was to abstain from all unnecessary use of menacing language, be moderate, cautious, nor ask for the help of the navy except when 'the most evident necessity shall require that any such menacing language should be holden, or that any such appeal should be made'; he should respect the laws and usages of China.

It will be noticed at once that the first of these instructions clashes with the last. He was to obey the Chinese regulations, yet he must reside at Canton. As he was not a merchant but an officer of the Crown holding what today resembles a consular appointment, he had no right under Chinese law to reside at Canton. Under that law persons like him should report their arrival to the Viceroy and await instructions from Peking. The Emperor never allowed such officials to enter China except to come as tribute bearers to the Celestial Court. For him to sanction Lord Napier's residence at Canton in his capacity as an agent of his sovereign would have been a new departure and tantamount to a reversal of the long established policy of refusing to receive resident consular or ambassadorial representatives. It was impossible that he would give such permission, even if the utmost efforts were made to obtain it. But Lord Napier was given no instructions even to seek that permission. He was simply to go to Canton and take up his duties there forthwith. From the very start, therefore, his orders were to break one of the most fundamental of Chinese regulations. He was expected to effect a revolution in Chinese policy by the simple method of ignoring its existence. This revolution was inherent also in the instruction that he mediate between the merchants and the local officers. Under the existing rules no correspondence or contact of any kind with the local officers was permitted: all such business had to be conducted through the Co-Hong, a body of mercantile contractors. Yet at the same time he was directed to be cautious, complacent, to abstain from giving offence, to maintain friendly relations. In short, he was expected to be as mild and discreet as had been the Honourable Company, and yet immediately to do all the things which it had desired to do, but refrained from doing, for fear of exciting hostility. That the Cabinet should have issued such instructions and that he should have expressed a willingness to carry them out, shows that neither had taken the trouble to obtain expert advice nor to read the state papers relating to China. As the Cabinet had no intention at that time of bringing to bear the force which would have been necessary to effect such a revolution in its relations with the Court at Peking, it was sending the unfortunate Napier on a wild goose chase. The merchant who wrote the letter summarized further back was at pains to point out that no change could be effected in China without threatening to use the navy, but to make such a threat was the very thing which Napier was forbidden to do.

Let us now examine Lord Palmerston, the Foreign Secretary's, letter of supplementary instructions addressed to Lord Napier on 25 January, 1834. In this he was ordered to announce his arrival at Canton by letter to the Viceroy. The objection to this we have already seen: it was against the rules for a man holding Napier's appointment to enter China without permission. There followed a number of directions which in view of the fundamental weakness of his position were wholly impracticable: he was to 'omit no favourable opportunity of encouraging any disposition which you may discover in the Chinese authorities to enter into commercial relations with the British Government', as if it were likely that after his irritating irruption he should find any such disposition; he was to 'adopt no proceedings but such as may have a general tendency to convince the Chinese authorities of the sincere desire of the King to cultivate the most friendly relations with the Emperor of China', though how he could convince them, when the whole conception of his office had no warrant in Chinese agreement, is not explained.

The Right Honourable gentleman then touches on another point, a most delicate point, a point which in the merchant's letter already quoted was felt to be very difficult. This was the Coast Trade, the smuggling of opium into the ports on the China seaboard. In regard to this, writes Lord Palmerston, 'it is not desirable that you should encourage such adventures; but you must never lose sight of the fact that you have no authority to interfere with or prevent them.'

This is the only reference to the drug trade in all the written instructions received by Lord Napier. He was to shut his eyes to it, that is what his orders amounted to. He was to shut his eyes to what was strictly forbidden by the Emperor and yet attempt to get into friendly relations with him. In short, he was to follow the policy of the Company and pretend that a commerce, the mainstay of the Indian revenue and the tea trade, had nothing whatever to do with him or the Crown.

Finally—and this suggests that Lord Palmerston knew that one day a crisis might arise—he was to survey the China coastline and select places from where ships of His Majesty's Navy might operate in safety in the event of hostilities.

In pursuance of these instructions, perhaps the most ill-considered ever drafted for the guidance of an officer of the Crown sent on an important mission overseas, Lord Napier, accompanied by his wife and two daughters, embárked on board the frigate, H.M.S. *Andromache*, when the daffodils were in bloom and on 15 July 1834 came to anchor in Macao Road.

(iv)

The Palaver at the Gate

The same afternoon he landed on the Praya Grande, that crescent of old houses faced to a glittering sea and set in a landscape of blue mountains. On the ridge above, a salute thundered from the Portuguese forts, built originally to keep off pirates and whose bronze cannon, sumptuously moulded with leaves and figurines, were now exclusively used for the rite of welcome. The British community was waiting at the stairs, though Jardine and Matheson were not there. The exact date of Lord Napier's arrival could not, of course, be foretold and both the partners happened to be in Canton. They had, however, as the leaders of the free merchants, made all the necessary arrangements. One of their staff, a Mr. A. Robertson, had instructions to place at his Lordship's disposal a well-appointed house belonging to the firm. Soon after stepping ashore Napier was apprised of this and asked to decide whether he would put up there or would prefer to stay at the Company's palatial quarters on the front, where two members of the defunct Select Committee were still in residence. He elected to use the firm's house, observing that it was as well from the very start to mark the beginning of the new era by dissociating himself from the old commercial order. His sedan-bearers were accordingly directed to carry him up the hill, which was done, he and Lady Napier and their two daughters being conducted by Mr. Robertson and other gentlemen to a house surrounded by a flower garden, which seemed after four months' confinement on shipboard a very bower in paradise. That evening Mr. Robertson wrote a letter to Jardine, shortly describing the arrival and adding that his Lordship was 'a tall raw Scotchman with light hair' and that the daughters were 'rather good looking than otherwise.' That Napier's appearance should have been so raw and sandy, so red, for we may assume the voyage had turned him that colour, was unfortunate for a man commissioned to conduct negotiations of the utmost delicacy with the Chinese, for whom such a hue was the very essence of barbarism.

Lord Palmerston had given instructions that on arrival in China Napier should take as his advisers and assistants two members of the Select Committee, who, under the Sign Manual, were given in advance the title of Second and Third Superintendents. Accordingly, the following morning he communicated the contents of his Commission to John Davis and Sir George Robinson, Baronet, the two men who at the moment were at the Company's residence on the Praya Grande. The same day he completed his staff by appointing a Mr. Astell his Secretary, Dr. Morrison his interpreter, and a Captain Elliot, R.N., nephew of the first Earl Minto, his Master Attendant with authority over all ships and crews within the Bogue. It will be evident from the appointment of Mr. Davis and Sir George Robinson, that Parliament was sincerely desirous of continuing the policy of appeasement followed for so long by the Honourable Company, even though Napier's instructions were not likely when put into practice to lead to anything but discord. Had a vigorous policy backed by naval force been Palmerston's intention he would have associated with the Chief Superintendent men with views like Jardine and Matheson's. But, in fact, Jardine later did become his confidential adviser.

Having got his colleagues and assistants together in this way, Napier acquainted them with his orders, the first of which was to proceed to Canton and inform the Viceroy, Lu, of his presence and what it meant. The difficulties involved in this course were no doubt pointed out to him and fully discussed, but he resolved to take it and fixed 23 July for his departure from Macao.

The mandarin in charge of the Chinese patrol boats in the vicinity reported to Canton, as soon as he became aware of it, the arrival on 15 July of a Barbarian Eye on board a British man-of-war, meaning by that curious term to denote that Napier was not a merchant but an official. On 21 July the Viceroy issued an Edict to the Hong merchants, quoting this report and citing the rule under which an officer of a foreign government was not allowed to enter China until, after petitioning for a permit, he might be authorized to do so by the Emperor. 'When this order is received by the said Hong merchants', the Edict continues, 'let them immediately go in person to Macao and ascertain clearly from the Barbarian Eye for what he has come to Canton province. . . . And let them authoritatively enjoin upon him the laws of the Celestial Empire, to wit that, with the exception of the merchants and the taipans, their heads, no other Barbarian can be permitted to enter Canton, save after a report has been made and an Imperial Mandate received . . . The said Barbarian Eye, if he wishes to come to Canton, must inform the said Hong merchants, so that they may petition me, the Viceroy, and I will by express messenger send a memorial, and all must respectfully wait until His Majesty deigns to send a Mandate. Then orders will be issued requiring obedience. Oppose not! A special order.'

On receipt of this Edict a delegation of Hong merchants

hastened down to Macao by the passage through the inner creeks, but they arrived after Napier had started for Canton by the outer passage, which goes by the Bogue. As he had arranged, he embarked on board the *Andromache* on 23 July and came to anchor at midnight before Chuenpee, the fort guarding the eastern mouth of the Bogue. 'Next morning', he wrote in a report to Lord Palmerston, 'a Chinese war-junk weighed, and came to anchor near His Majesty's ship, firing a salute of three guns, which was returned by an equal number. At noon the Superintendents left His Majesty's ship under a salute of thirteen guns and proceeded on board the cutter on their way to Canton, where they arrived at two o'clock on the morning of the 25th.' It had taken them, sailing and pulling, fourteen hours to cover the distance, which, according to the course steered, was between forty and fifty miles. Leaving their heavy luggage in the customs, the three of them were conducted by Jardine, who met them, to the English Factory, where they passed the rest of the night in the bedrooms of one of its many buildings.

After a late breakfast Napier started work, interviewing such merchants as were in Canton and getting his letter to the Viceroy translated into Chinese by Dr. Morrison. It was headed *Letter*, not *Petition* as had been the rule in the past when the Select Committee addressed the Viceroy through the Co-Hong. While he was so engaged, Howqua, with Mowqua the second Hong merchant, arrived with a copy of the Viceroy's Edict of the 21st, which should have been delivered to Napier at Macao. When they announced their intention of enjoining it upon him, his Lordship called on them to desist, explaining that he had been instructed to inaugurate a new procedure, under which he and his colleagues would deal direct with the local authorities. 'The Hong merchants', he wrote in the above quoted despatch, 'were courteously dismissed with an intimation that I would communicate immediately with the Viceroy in a manner befitting His Majesty's Commission and the honour of the British nation.' Howqua and Mowqua were bowed out. They were much alarmed, for they knew from old and bitter experience that when the Barbarians misbehaved themselves, they, the unfortunate members of the Co-Hong, were always fined and ran the risk also of chains and the bamboo. However, no one could be got to listen to their pleading and protestations, and they departed trembling to report to their master.

The next day, 27 July, was very trying. Whether or not what occurred was befitting the honour of the British nation the reader shall judge. The morning opened badly by Napier being informed that his baggage-chests had been broken open by the customs officers, though the keys had been supplied to them. This petty annoyance was followed swiftly by two others—the boatmen generally employed by the firms were withdrawn by order, and certain other employees were intimidated into deserting. Old China hands knew what such pinpricks meant: the authorities were annoyed and hinted their annoyance in their roundabout way.

The letter was now ready and Mr. Astell, the secretary, was ordered to take it to the Petition Gate, there to hand it to a mandarin for delivery to the Viceroy. The custom of presenting a petition to the Viceroy at this gate was a very old one. It was recognised that there might be occasions when a petition could not, or should not, be sent through the Co-Hong. But such communications were petitions, not letters, and in recent edicts it had been emphasized that only in the most exceptional circumstances should resort be had to the gate. Jardine, with whom Napier dined on the previous night, was well versed in these matters. Had he not received at the gate his nickname of the Iron-headed Old Rat? He will have told Napier of the difficulties ahead. But Napier had no option. His orders enjoined this course. Perhaps, Jardine was not sorry that he should be introduced at once to the impossible methods of Chinese officialdom, for, the sooner he realized that force only could serve, the better it would be. Mr. Astell, duly primed and told to use the utmost tact, set out with a deputation of merchants. On their arrival at the Petition Gate, the soldier on guard sent a report of the circumstances to his superior. A quarter of an hour elapsed before a mandarin appeared. Mr. Astell offered him the letter for transmission to the Viceroy, but he excused himself on the ground that a superior officer was on the way.

With admirable patience the British waited an hour, when another mandarin arrived, followed in rapid succession by several others, to each of whom the letter was offered and by each declined, on the same plea that higher officers would shortly attend.

There followed a wait of another hour, during which the crowd, having become very thick, amused themselves by shouting opprobrious epithets and making opprobrious signs. It was very unpleasant and humiliating to have to stand there and bear all this silently, but Mr. Astell and his companions, being resolved not to become involved in a free fight, than which nothing, they suspected, would have pleased the Chinese more, by a superhuman effort maintained their calm and continued to wait for someone who would take the letter.

As soon as the authorities inside, who, of course, were fully informed, considered that their importunate visitors had reached the degree of wretchedness when they would be ready to abate their claims to address the Viceroy direct, some of the Hong merchants were brought on the scene. They came forward smiling, wistful, charming, their hands hidden in their long sleeves and bowing—a disarming spectacle. Would not the gentlemen consent to intrust the letter to them? It would be immediately delivered; since His Excellency would have it forthwith, why make trouble over a mere formality? What did it matter who took it to him? But Mr. Astell hardened his heart to these blandishments. It was precisely to circumvent the Co-Hong that he had been sent to the gate. The new policy for which Lord Napier stood would be fatally prejudiced were he to cede the letter to these smirking seductors. He stoutly refused. The crowd hooted. The police made a show of using their whips.

Another mandarin was now seen approaching. From his retinue it seemed he was really of high rank or had been made to appear so by those who had sent him. Mr. Astell immediately offered him the letter. This notability went so far as to look at it, though he did not touch it. When he saw the character for 'letter' written on the envelope, instead of that for 'petition', he appeared quite astonished and assured Mr. Astell that on that ground alone, though without prejudice to other grounds, it was his duty to refuse to transmit it to the Viceroy. To do so would be a shocking indiscretion and he was sure they had no desire to see him suffer for their error. Their best course, their only course, was to return at once, and he offered this advice with the friendliest feelings.

While this farcical palaver was in progress, the Tartar General's Adjutant put in an appearance. We have already made his acquaintance at the English factory, but on that occasion he was eclipsed by his senior officers. Now among the men-of-straw mandarins, who had been deputed to keep off the Barbarians, he seemed a person of exalted quality. At last, thought poor Astell, they are giving way; this man will take the letter: and he confidently offered it to him. But the Adjutant pretended he had not understood. Whereupon Astell offered it a second time. The Adjutant declined it with such splendid politeness that Astell could not think he had seriously refused, and again, for the third time, pressed it upon him. Whereupon, with a perceptible stiffening of manner, he made his refusal unmistakably clear.

At this awkward moment Howqua—for the old fellow was among the Hong merchants present—Howqua, frail, delicate, smiling his whimsical smile, made a suggestion, after a whispered conversation with the Adjutant. 'Gentlemen,' he said, with all the insinuating charm of which he was master, 'His Honour is infinitely distressed that you should have had to come all this distance in vain. There are obstacles—and I am sure you appreciate them as much as he does—in the way of him personally handling this petition. But I can take it from you and, together, he and I, we will lay it before the Viceroy.' As he said this his face was as open as a child's. But we must remember that he was a very clever man.

However, the trap was sufficiently evident. After a moment's reflection Mr. Astell saw that the proposal was not the compromise it purported to be. If he handed the letter to Howqua in the presence of the mandarins and crowd, there would be a hundred witnesses to proclaim that the Barbarians had been brought to heel and forced to make their plaint through the Co-Hong. He declined the offer and the situation relapsed again into deadlock. The Adjutant was seen to whisper with the others and shortly afterwards they withdrew to confer, informing the British they would soon be back. They were not away very long and on return told Mr. Astell with finality that the letter could not be received. Three hours had now elapsed since the arrival at the gate. Astell had done his best. There was nothing more he could do. Formally offering the letter once more and being as formally refused, he wished the Adjutant good-day and returned to the factory.

The Chinese had won. They had made it clear in their manner that they had no intention of submitting to the new order of things which the Barbarian Eye had attempted to spring on them.

(V)

Laboriously Vile

The Viceroy, Lu, whose subordinates had made him, no doubt, a full report, not only about what had happened on 27 July at the Petition Gate, but of everything they had been able to learn about Napier, decided in accordance with old practice to put the screw on the Hong merchants, and on 28 July addressed a stiff Edict to them. He begins by reminding them that their duty is to admonish and guide the Barbarians, who, though they come from beyond the bounds of civilization, can yet be taught to obey civilized law. One of the most established of rules, he goes on, is that a traveller from devildom, no matter who he may be, must obtain from the Chinese customs at Macao a red permit before he can enter the Celestial Regions, and that such a permit is not issued without reference to the Emperor, if the applicant is unknown or his business unusual. In the present instance a Barbarian Eye called Lord Napier (he represented Napier by two ideographs which meant laboriously vile) came up without a permit. For not preventing this, the customs officials concerned would have to stand their trial. 'But out of tender consideration for the said Barbarian Eye, being a newcomer', he continues, 'and unacquainted with the laws and regulations of the Great Pure Realm, I will not strictly investigate.' As soon as ever his business is finished, however, Laboriously Vile must go back to Macao nor presume to return without a permit. It is your duty, he tells the Hong merchants, to see to this.

133

Referring to the attempt the previous day to communicate with him by letter, he points out that Laboriously Vile, though apparently an official and not a merchant, has come on business connected with commerce. But, he says, the petty affairs of commerce are no concern of civil officers. The merchants themselves manage them under established rules. Should there be a proposal to change any such rules, the Co-Hong may petition his office, when the case will be sent up for the Emperor's orders. The Barbarian Eye may have had proposals of that nature; if so, he should have followed the procedure and submitted them through the proper channel. That he did not do so shows that the Hong merchants have neglected their duty by failing to instruct him.

He then formally tells them that they must make sure that Napier does not do this again. 'If the said Barbarian Eye throws in private letters, I, the Viceroy, will not receive or look at them.' And he sums up: 'Nations have their laws; it is so everywhere. Even England has its laws; how much more the Heavenly Realm! Under its shelter are the four seas. Subject to its soothing care are ten thousand kingdoms. The said Barbarian Eye, having come a myriad leagues over the sea, must be a man well versed in the principles of high dignity. I, the Viceroy, looking up will administer the imperial wish by cherishing with tenderness men from a distance. Assuredly, I will not treat slightingly the Outside Barbarians. But the national laws are extremely strict. Let the said Barbarian Eye be more careful in future.'

He concludes with a threat: 'When this order reaches the Hong merchants, let them enjoin it upon the said Laboriously Vile, that he may know it thoroughly. If they with diligence explain it clearly, opening and guiding his understanding, he assuredly cannot but obey. Should he oppose and disobey, it will be because the Hong merchants have mismanaged the affair. In that case I shall be obliged to report against them and the laws shall instantly be put in full force.' This last phrase was a euphemism for the infliction of capital punishment.

The Edict is more reasonable than its tone suggests. Lu had, in fact, no authority to recognize Napier. It was his duty to maintain the existing regulations. He had no more power to change, modify, or repeal them, without reference to the government from which they emanated, than any official in any country. They had been drawn up originally to keep the Barbarians at arm's length. Napier's attempt to get to close quarters struck at their very root. What a bother, the Viceroy seems to say, that he has managed to slip in! How to get rid of him without unpleasantness? Unpleasantness led to uproar, uproar to accusations. The Emperor would hear. That meant an investigation. One could not tell where that would end. There were many things which would not bear looking into. The Hong merchants must get him away quickly. He would squeeze them till they did.

On the same day Napier received the Hong merchants in a body and had a long desultory conversation with them. The Edict was not yet in their hands and the object of their case was to soothe his Lordship after the refusal of his letter on the previous day. They held out hopes that it might be accepted after all if the Viceroy's designation were made rather more ample and the word 'petition' substituted for 'letter'. Howqua, in making this latter proposal, did not say so straight out, but it was to this that his labyrinthine circumlocution amounted. While yielding readily on the first point, Napier was firm in regard to the second. So the Hong merchants departed with no more than an amended style. It had been a barren day for both sides.

On the morning of the 29th Napier received a note from Howqua to say he was coming to call at one o'clock. When Dr. Morrison was translating it, he noticed that his Lordship's name was not written with the two ideographs which he had selected to express its sound in the letter to the Viceroy, but by two others, which he saw meant 'laboriously vile'. He felt it his duty to tell Napier of this affront. In 1796 when Lord Macartney's attention was drawn to the flag flying on the houseboat in which he was travelling to Peking and he was told that the characters inscribed thereon signified 'Barbarian envoys bringing tribute', he thought it politic to take no notice. But that was over forty years back and the battle of Trafalgar had taken place in the interval. So, at one o'clock when Howqua presented himself and had explained the object of his call, which was to say that the superscription 'petition' was unavoidable, Napier taxed him with the matter of the name. Whether it had not occurred to Howqua that the Barbarian Eye might discover the meaning of the transliteration or whether his secretary had copied it from the Viceroy's Edict without saying anything to him, we cannot know, but he showed no signs of confusion. On being asked abruptly to explain his reason for such a gratuitous insult, he replied that he had been 'so instructed by the pilot'. Pilot! exclaimed Napier, when this delphic remark was translated to him. What pilot? What does he mean? What has a pilot to do with it? But Howqua said no more. He knew the value in a crisis of the inconsequential remark, and smiling mysteriously bowed himself out.

(vi)

Napier is ordered to go

If Napier was unable to serve his letter on the Viceroy, that personage was in no happier case about getting his orders conveyed to Napier. On 31 July, armed with no less than three Edicts, Howqua called at the English factory, but Napier would not let him read them out. We have already examined the Edict of the 28th. On the 30th Lu had issued a second Edict and on the 31st a third. They exhibit his increasing impatience and irritation. The most important point in that of the 30th is his peremptory order that Napier leave at once, permission to finish his business, accorded by the Edict of the 28th, being cancelled. After angrily accusing the Hong merchants of dilatoriness and, even, connivance, he directs them to go to the English factory and compel Napier to depart. I cannot have him, he says, loitering about here. If he refuses to go, you will be punished. And he concludes: 'Say not that you were not forewarned. Tremble hereat! A Special Order.' In the Edict of the 31st he reinforces his authority by quoting a letter he had received on the 25th from the Hoppo. About midnight on the 15th, wrote that worthy of Napier's arrival, four English devils were observed landing and clandestinely entering the factory of their nation. Such a thing could only have happened through the connivance of the Hong merchants, they being solely responsible for the movements of the Barbarians. This unjust accusation suited the Viceroy and he uses it to underline again his determination to punish, that is to squeeze, the Hong merchants if they failed to get rid of the obnoxious Eye. 'These are the orders,' he concludes. 'Tremble hereat! Intensely tremble.'

There can be no doubt that the Hong merchants did tremble intensely and we can picture their state of mind when they called in the afternoon of the 31st and were refused permission to convey the orders.

The position of affairs, therefore, at the end of July 1834 amounted to this: The Viceroy had received no official intimation of Napier's object in coming to Canton, while Napier for his part did not yet know that the Viceroy had issued orders for his expulsion. In his despatch to Lord Palmerston

dated 9 August, he argues that the Viceroy would eventually
be forced to accept his letter, for without it his report to the
Emperor would be incomplete. He proposed, therefore, to do
no more for the moment than wait. He had now indirectly
learnt, he says, that the Viceroy wanted him to return to
Macao, for Howqua, forbidden to convey any orders, had
attempted during a call the previous day to get round the
difficulty by hinting that Macao was a much pleasanter
place than Canton in August. At the end of the despatch,
feeling perhaps that his mission so far had been singularly
unsuccessful and that he was defying those whom Palmerston had urged him to placate, he writes that he could not
have acted otherwise without compromising the honour of
the British nation; that the British merchants were solidly
behind him; and he believed that events would justify him
in the end. On this optimistic note he concludes.

That he might be outmanoeuvred by the Viceroy never
entered his head, because his contempt for him and the
whole Chinese nation clouded his intelligence. In fact, his
position was precarious. England no doubt was very powerful, but at the moment she was not poised to make that
power felt in China. Given time she could concentrate ships
and men and force her will, but in August 1834 Napier had
nothing at his back. The attitude he had adopted was no
better than bluff. And the Viceroy was to call his bluff.

The realities of the situation were simple and obvious. A
large body of British merchants traded by permission at a
Chinese city eighty miles from the open sea. They had no
arms, no troops, no warships. They were wholly in the
power of the Chinese Government. Their stay and the existence of the tea trade depended on the continuance of that
permission. They could be expelled at a word. The trade
could be suspended. Even were the suspension short, losses
would be sustained. This weapon of suspension had been
used with success by the Chinese on a number of previous
occasions to bring the British to reason. That Napier did not

perceive they would use it again is strange, as it is that he did not realize he was without the means to resist it.

Yet there is an explanation. Half the trade, as we know, was outside the Bogue: the opium trade radiated from Lintin Island up the coast and it was carried on by armed ships beyond the power of the Chinese to suppress. Jardine and Matheson had a greater share in that trade than any other firm. Their commitments in the legal trade were subordinate. The Chinese Government therefore could not hurt them by closing the port of Canton. If that port were shut, their rivals lost, not they. It had long been their considered view that only force would oblige the Emperor to trade freely with the west. If the whole country were opened to trade, they knew they were better situated than any other firm to profit by it, either in addition to or in place of their present smuggling. A period of disturbance suited them, partly because it tended to raise prices and also for the reason that, their organization being superior to that of any other firm, they could ride a storm in which others foundered. Napier's flouting of the rules and regulations therefore fell in conveniently with their ideas. They would support, even push, him in his intractable attitude. The more he was insulted, the more the Crown which he represented was humiliated, the easier it would be later on to persuade Parliament to sanction the use of force, which they did not doubt could soon open the whole China market. Their share of that market would admittedly be large; their firm would grow enormously rich. Yet it was so wide a market that everybody could find room. Wealth would flow to England as never before. That, they argued, was the ultimate justification of their policy. They were looking to the supremacy of their own firm in China, but they were also looking to the supremacy of the British nation in the world.

So subtle and so bold an assessment of the potentialities, founded as it was upon long personal experience of China, was far over poor Napier's head. His experience had been of mountain sheep and of ships. The complexities of a Far Eastern imbroglio was beyond his grasp. He had been given inconsistent orders and when he tried to obey them was confounded by the result and looked for guidance. The advice he got from Jardine was fatal to him personally but in the end it solved the China question.

(vii)

Napier becomes heated

Howqua and his colleagues, having failed to serve the Viceroy's orders direct, and their hints that Napier would be more comfortable in Macao having had no effect, now tried an indirect method and sent the Edicts to Jardine, being pretty sure he would pass them on. Their covering letter contains some phrases which heighten the comedy. 'A respectful notification' it begins, and describes the contents of the Edicts in the following euphemism: 'We now send you His Excellency's several orders of cherishing and showing tenderness.' They ask for sympathy in their own predicament, declaring with touching candour that if the Edicts are not served, the Viceroy will 'inflict punishment which it will be impossible for us to bear'.

As they anticipated, Jardine immediately took the Edicts to Napier. They could not fail, he knew, to stiffen the noble lord and make him the more ready to fall in with the views of the forward section of the British community.

We are able to gauge the effect their reading had, for on

the 14th August, three days later, Napier addressed a long despatch to Lord Palmerston, utterly different in tone from his despatch of the 9th. It shows him voicing views far more boisterous than those he entertained on landing, views so similar to Jardine's that we seem to hear the *ipsissima verba* of the Old Rat with the Iron Head.

He opens by declaring that the Edicts prove that the Chinese Government has not the smallest disposition to modify old regulations and extend trade (a deduction so obvious as to be hardly worth making). But though its attitude appears firm, it is in reality a weak Government. He has been ordered out of Canton and has defied the order, yet the Viceroy has not deported him. 'Suppose a Chinaman, or any other man, were to land under similar circumstances at Whitehall, your Lordship would not allow him to "loiter" as they have permitted me'. Such a Government is imbecile, he cries; it does not deserve to be approached under the forms prescribed for civilized peoples. Its weakness and imbecility arise from its unpopularity. It has not the Chinese people behind it, because it is a foreign tyranny. The people wish to trade with Britain, would be glad to see all the ports opened and a commercial treaty made, but their masters stand between them and this happy prospect.

We may pause here for an instant. It was precisely because the Ch'ing Dynasty did not feel secure that it desired to keep foreign trade confined to the extreme corner of the empire. Napier's way of putting this fact obscures its reasonableness from the Chinese Government's point of view. And he is too optimistic about the Chinese people or over-simplifies the problem. It was not going to be easy to divide them from their Government. And he over-simplifies the matter of his expulsion. The authorities at Canton were not without their plans, but they first had tried indirect methods, as causing less noise; the less noise the safer has always been an axiom of oriental administration.

To return to the despatch. The time is close when this

weak Government should be confronted with an ultimatum, says Napier. Give Britons the same privilege in China which every Chinaman, Pagan, Turk or Christian, sits down to in Britain, that is what should be demanded of the Emperor. Such a demand will not lead to war but to concessions. If, however, the Emperor remains obdurate, then tell his subjects your reasonable intentions and the benefits which will accrue to them. 'Disclaim every view of conquest; disturb not the passage of their vessels or the tranquillity of their towns; only destroy their forts and batteries along the coasts, and on the river sides, without interfering with the people. Three or four frigates or brigs, with a few steady British troops, not sepoys, would settle the thing in a space of time inconceivably short.'

So he wrote, in spite of the direction of the Sign Manual: 'Do cautiously abstain from making any appeal for the protection of Our military or naval forces.' And he had come to this, or Jardine had brought him to it, after a residence of only three weeks in China.

The Americans and all other nations trading here will benefit equally with Great Britain, he continues. 'Such an undertaking would be worthy the greatness and the power of England, as well from its disinterestedness towards other nations as from the brilliant consequences which must naturally ensue.' And he promises his Lordship that 'the exploit is to be performed with a facility unknown even in the capture of a paltry West Indian Island.' Feeling he may be accused of exceeding his instructions, he hastens to add that, of course, his remarks are to be regarded as no more than suggestions. 'Your Lordship may rely on my forbearance towards a Government, which is too contemptible to be viewed in any other light than that of pity or derision.'

While Napier was composing his despatch, the Viceroy had acted. He told the Hong merchants to take preliminary steps for the stoppage of trade. This, he calculated, would create a schism among the British merchants, and it did. Those firms which were unconnected with the opium traffic without the river were hit, while the rest were not. As a result, though Jardine and his like continued to back Napier in his refusal to leave the city, the others began to waver, murmuring that His Majesty's Commission, on which such high hopes had been set and whose arrival was to herald a new day for the free merchants, had only precipitated a crisis and exposed to loss those whom it had been sent out to protect. This put Napier in a difficult position. In a postscript to his despatch, dated 17 August, he announces the stoppage and says 'Now there are two things to be considered —the honour of His Majesty's Commission, and the interest of the merchants. I conceive my duty to be to sustain them both, but not one at the expense of the other.' Having been completely won over, however, by Jardine, he was angry with the malcontents, merchants who 'care not one straw about the dignity of the Crown or the presence of a Superintendent'. Yet he is afraid to do anything which may endanger the Grey administration's majority in the House and declares: 'If after a fair trial of all justifiable means, I find the merchants are likely to suffer, I must retire to Macao, rather than bring the cities of London, Liverpool and Glasgow upon your Lordship's shoulders.' He closes the postscript by imploring him not to allow such people to interfere with the forward policy sketched in the body of the despatch.

There is something rather shrill about the tone of this state paper, as if Napier were beginning to lose his head. It was received in London on 31 January, 1835, by which time the little drama at Canton had been played out. Lord Grey's Whig Cabinet had fallen in July 1834, and Peel had formed a Tory Ministry in November with the Duke of Wellington as Foreign Secretary. The Duke's reply, dated 2 February 1835, which did not reach the addressee, may be quoted here as showing how Lord Napier had failed to convince the Cabinet that his actions, so much ahead of orders, were justified by events. The aged Duke was brief and stiff. He referred Napier to those articles of his commission that urged caution, and delivered the following *obiter dictum*: 'It is not by force and violence that His Majesty intends to establish a commercial intercourse between his subjects and China; but by the other conciliatory measures so strongly inculcated in all the instructions which you have received.' Had Napier fallen less under the influence of Jardine and his party, had he been able to remain cool and to treat the Viceroy's Edicts less as insults than as routine declarations of policy, he would not have made the mistake of thinking that Parliament would support him, though it must be confessed that his instructions were confusing. Nevertheless, if one thing is clear from their general tenor, it is that he should not precipitate a collision. He did not remain cool, however; rather, he became more and more heated, till he found himself in an untenable position.

(viii)

The Victory of the Chairs

Before the drama closed in, there was to be a short interval when Napier thought he had intimidated the Viceroy. Having come to believe that a show of force would suffice to humble his antagonists, he was now delighted to find himself unexpectedly able to dispose of two frigates; his spirits rose and he began to see his way.

The frigate on which he had come out, the *Andromache*, had not remained at the Bogue. Soon after he landed from

144

A STREET IN CANTON
from a painting by Thomas Allom

THE EMPEROR TAO KUANG REVIEWING HIS GUARD INSIDE
THE FORBIDDEN CITY OF PEKING
from a painting by Thomas Allom

his cutter at Canton, she was ordered to cruise for a week outside the estuary in the vicinity of the Ladrones, lest the presence of a man-of-war at the river mouth be misconstrued. She returned on 17 August to her former position, accompanied by the *Imogene*, a frigate from Indian waters, with Admiralty orders to call at Macao and relieve the *Andromache*, which was to sail for home with despatches. For the moment both frigates swung by Chuenpee fort. This circumstance, wrote Napier on hearing the news, 'I may be able to turn to good account.'

And another circumstance also raised his spirits. This was the appearance a few days later of three Imperial emissaries from Peking, the most prominent of them being the President of the Censorate. We have not a copy of their instructions, but it appears they were not directly connected with the present pass but had been sent to investigate specific charges, made at Peking against the Hoppo and other officials, though a general power of inspection was included. Napier saw in the arrival of these grandees from Court an opportunity to circumvent the Viceroy. If he could win their ear, it might open a way even to the Emperor. The Viceroy, sure to be nervous of what they might think or pretend to think of the way he had handled the situation, would be anxious to keep the facts from them. That gave a lever: a threat to complain might be enough to make the Viceroy more amenable. But as we shall see, neither the frigates nor the emissaries sufficed to save his Lordship.

The state papers show clearly the course of events. Unlike most documents of the sort, they are full of colour. On 18 August, the day after the arrival of the frigates but before he knew of it, the Viceroy issued another Edict. This document is a résumé of the situation from the Chinese point of view. It may have been drawn up for the benefit of the emissaries, and has a certain mellowness of tone, a sweet reasonableness calculated to present the writer in the light of a man seeking every way to reprove and soothe.

It begins with a classical quotation, for a tag was considered as elegant and gentlemanly among the Confucian bureaucracy as in the Georgian Houses of Parliament. 'When you enter the frontiers, enquire respecting the prohibitions. When you enter a country enquire into its laws.' Laboriously Vile, however, had entered China like a burglar, surely an indecorous act for a man who claimed to be an official?

The Viceroy then relates how he had admonished the Eye for his trespass and ordered him to report at once through the Co-Hong. This was not slighting an Outside Barbarian, but a kindly effort to acquaint him with the law. Yet the order was disregarded. Could the Viceroy be blamed for invoking the rule—'obey and remain, disobey and depart?'

The Hong merchants, he goes on, rightly indignant at the Eye's perverse disposition, demanded a stoppage of trade. As China had no need of western commodities, a stoppage was a matter of indifference to her, but to the Barbarians was a very serious blow. Without tea (and rhubarb) they could not live.

Sympathy for the English in such a predicament, and the reflection that her chieftain had hitherto been reverentially submissive, moved his Excellency to declare with feeling: 'I, the Viceroy, looking up and embodying the sacred Emperor's divine command to nurse and cherish tenderly, as one, both those within and those without, feel that I cannot bring my mind to bear it. In commiseration I grant temporary indulgence and delay.' Let the Co-Hong again admonish the Eye.

In all my service, he continues, I have never treated a man contrary to propriety. Far less will I maltreat those who have braved the perils of a myriad leagues of sea in the hope of making here a little money. But there are limits; a nation's dignity cannot be sacrificed; there are eternal principles; there is right and wrong. The said Barbarian is of reasonable intelligence; his speech, it is said, is placid and slow. If he applies himself with perseverance, he may yet distinguish right from wrong. Let him not be led by those about him; there are men among them who would delude him. (This allusion here, of course, is to the Iron-headed Old Rat.) He must rouse from these deceptions, and repent his errors, obey the Edicts, answer through the Hong, abandon obstinacy and reverentially submit.

Howqua and his shaking co-adjutors were told to enjoin the above effusion on Lord Napier and then file it. As with the former Edicts, they sent a copy to Jardine, that being the only way they could bring it to his Lordship's notice.

Three days later, 21 August, Napier wrote to Earl Grey. (He could not know, of course, that his ministry had fallen in July.) The letter begins by repeating what was said to Lord Palmerston, that the time had now come to *extort* a commercial treaty, even though trade should suffer momentarily and there be an uproar in consequence. The Chinese Government is described as 'being in the extreme degree of mental imbecility and moral degradation, dreaming themselves to be the only people on earth, and being entirely ignorant of the theory and practice of international law'.

Napier then makes a point, which, though quite true and showing his better grasp of realities, is curiously frank for a diplomatic despatch. The stoppage, which is already partly in operation, he says, is not really of great importance, because if the Viceroy does not lift the embargo 'the smugglers will do it for him', meaning that since half the trade was already a smuggling trade no doubt most of the other half would soon become so. This raising of the veil for an instant emphasises the comedy underlying the whole altercation.

But Napier's sense of humour—if he had any—was in no way tickled. As if he had made no admission of the feebleness of his moral position, he repeats his incitements and in righteous anger urges 'His Majesty's Government to assert our ancient rights of commerce'. The two angles being here so closely juxtaposed in the despatch, it is curious that he did not pause and reflect that English law had never recognized the smuggling of goods into a foreign country as an 'ancient right of commerce'. We are left with the impression that the noble lord was becoming very confused.

The rest of the despatch can only be called bellicose. Its details follow so clearly the merchant's letter quoted at the beginning of this chapter that one sees at once the source of the ideas. He asks that forces be sent from India, both naval and military, in time to operate in September 1835. Peking should be warned of their approach and, by the threat of it, obliged to make a commercial treaty. The seizure of the island of Hongkong is advocated. The writer's opinion of the Celestial forces is expressed thus: 'You read of a standing army of above 1,000,000 of men to defend the empire: it is an absurdity; they could only muster a few hundred wretched creatures last year at this city to send against a rebellion; and one half of them were utterly incapable of taking the field . . . What can an army of bows and arrows, and pikes, and shields do against a handful of British veterans? . . . The batteries at the Bogue are contemptible; and not a man to be seen within them.'

Feeble though the Chinese forces were, Napier was to yield to them within the month.

On the evening of the next day, 22 August, he received news which led him to think that the presence of the frigates, though outside the Bogue, was having its effect. Howqua and Mowqua were announced. They came in smiling. His Excellency, they declared, had directed three mandarins of high rank to call the following morning at 11 a.m. Would the Chief Superintendent agree to receive them? Napier was overjoyed. No mandarin of any kind had come near him so far. Of course, he told Howqua, and he would receive them in state in the main hall of the English factory.

What induced the Viceroy to unbend and make this move, we cannot be sure. Not the frigates, judging by what happened afterwards. We might ascribe it to a necessity of acquiring more information, if we knew that the emissaries had been cross-examining him. That they already had begun to squeeze him, we do know. There is a letter from Jardine which is here to the point. Referring to the Senior Censor who was their chief, he writes: 'It became necessary to bring him over. The arguments now may be inferred from the following circumstances: he brought no money with him; he had none to receive from them; but when he left Canton he carried away so much money with him in gold that his emissaries in purchasing it raised the price of gold . . . before they had procured all they required . . . by $3\frac{3}{4}$ per cent.' It was calculated afterwards that this indicated a squeeze of a hundred thousand pounds sterling. With work of this kind in progress behind the scenes, it is risky to posit what moves the Viceroy was reduced to, yet one feels the sending of the mandarins to have been in some way connected with his efforts to put himself right with the Censor. The real purport of many of the papers quoted is hardly to be disentangled without personal experience of the Orient. Such experience suggests in this case that the Viceroy had particular reasons for exposing the mandarins sent to call on Napier to risk of failure and loss of face, and saw a profit to himself in their discomfiture. He may have desired to procure their dismissal, perhaps in lieu of his own. One cannot be sure, except that it was certainly a tenebrous affair.

The next morning at 9 a.m. the Hong interpreters, a class of men known as linguists, arrived at the English factory with servants carrying ceremonial chairs. Before anyone noticed what they were doing, they took the chairs to the state reception room, called the hall, and there arranged three of them facing south, the quarter of happy augury towards which authority always faces in China, with two rows of four chairs at right angles to them and facing east and west. When this was done, they announced that the three mandarins would take the chairs facing south and the

Hong merchants the others. They were unable to answer the question where Lord Napier and his colleagues would sit, but presumed they would stand.

Mr. Astell, the secretary, hastened to inform his Lordship that a monstrous and calculated insult was intended. Napier immediately came to the hall, was astounded when he saw the chairs and became incensed on noticing further that one row was so placed that its occupants would have their backs to the portrait of George IV. The late Governor, Chu, had so sat down, as was well known, and remembered still with indignation, though he had later expressed regret, saying it was done inadvertently. How disingenuous had been his regret was now apparent. They were scheming to do it again.

Napier then gave his orders. A table was fetched. He would sit at it facing south with a mandarin on either hand. Mr. Astell would sit at the other side of it, facing north, with one mandarin on his right and the Second Superintendent on his left. The Hong merchants would sit in a row a little back from the table and directly face the portrait. By this arrangement no one had his back to King George.

When the chairs were in their new position, Howqua, accompanied as usual by Mowqua, arrived and was shown up. As soon as he saw the chairs, he appeared much disturbed and intimated that were the present arrangement retained he and his fellow merchants would be blamed and squeezed. He was sure that for a trifling matter such as the position of a few chairs his Lordship would not see an old friend of British commerce victimised. Had he not said only the other day how much he disliked the Manchu domination and sympathized with his Lordship's aspirations for open trade? His Lordship was of placid temper and slow to wrath: the Viceroy himself had admitted as much. His Lordship would therefore hear him with patience when he urged that the chairs be restored to their original position. After all, his Lordship was now resident in China. By the usages of that country, mandarins of his visitors' rank always sat facing south on such occasions as the present or else they would abdicate their rightful authority. The order of the chairs, no doubt, was what obtained in England when one official was receiving another, but here things were different and he must ask his Lordship to consider again before he inflicted what would be taken for a deliberate affront, for which, as he had already remarked, the Co-Hong would have to pay.

But Napier was not moved by this pleading to concede the smallest modification, and as it was by now eleven o'clock, the hour fixed for the visit, he took his seat at the table, being in full dress.

There followed a wait of two hours and a quarter, Napier becoming more and more impatient and angry. The mandarins were not late; throughout the East a personage of rank is never late; he just does not arrive until two hours after the time fixed; for him to be punctual would be to compromise his dignity, though when visiting a superior in rank he must not be content with punctuality but arrive some hours early, in the case of Imperial Audience six hours early. That the mandarins should have kept Lord Napier waiting for two hours and a quarter was therefore in order, for they considered him their inferior.

As the clocks were striking the quarter after one, the mandarins were ushered into the hall. The two Superintendents were seated, but rose, bowed, and requested their visitors to take the chairs set for them. It was an anxious moment. Would they do so or make objection? Whatever may be said against the Chinese senior official of that date, at least he had perfect manners when you met him and an instinctive feeling for the close connection between manners and dignity. For the mandarins when confronted with the chairs to have shown the smallest sign of surprise or vexation would have been a breach of manners, a blow to dignity and so, a loss of face. With a pleasant face they seated them-

selves, smiling, and even protesting that the honour was too
great. Lord Napier, however, ascribed their amenability to
the frigates or the emissaries, the Viceroy's desire to settle
or their own contemptible characters, and opened the proceedings by asking Howqua, through Dr. Morrison who was
seated behind him, whether he had not been directed by
them to give notice of their intention of calling at eleven
o'clock. For once the millionaire was off his guard or perhaps
he could not conceive of the rudeness behind the question.
He replied without hesitation in the affirmative. On getting
this answer, Lord Napier proceeded to rebuke the mandarins for having kept him waiting over two hours. 'It is an
insult to His Britannic Majesty', he said severely, glancing
at the portrait of his late Majesty, George IV, 'which cannot be overlooked a second time. Whereas on previous
occasions you have had only to deal with the servants of a
private company of merchants, you must understand hence-
forth that your communications will be held with the
officers appointed by His Britannic Majesty, who are by
no means inclined to submit to such indignities.' In this
last his Lordship was anticipating too hopefully, for in
fact no further official communication was ever to be held
with him.

To his reproof the mandarins made no reply. That they
felt the occasion to be highly disagreeable cannot be doubted,
but training and tradition enabled them to disguise their
feelings and deprive him of the satisfaction of witnessing
their upset.

Continuing to conduct the meeting, Lord Napier now
asked the senior mandarin, who was Prefect of that quarter
of the city in which the Factories were situated, to be good
enough to state the object of the visit. The Prefect replied
that the Viceroy had ordered him to ascertain the cause of
his Lordship's arrival, the nature of his business, and when
he proposed to go.

In reply to the first question Napier drew their attention

to the Edict of 16 January 1831, in which the then Viceroy had addressed the Select Committee of the Company through the Co-Hong and asked them, in view of their impending dissolution, to write to England and suggest that a competent head to the free merchants be appointed to manage the commerce as heretofore in conjunction with the Co-Hong. In response to that request, said Napier, I was appointed. Here is the Sign Manual setting up my commission. As to the nature of my duties, these are set out in my letter to the Viceroy, which his men refused to take delivery of at the gate and which I invite you now to deliver to his Excellency or open and read, if you prefer. The reply to the third question is that I shall go to Macao when it suits my convenience.

The Prefect replied that the late Viceroy's Edict had asked for a person of the status of merchant, so that the old system could be continued. Instead, the King of England had sent an official, granted him certain powers and given him instructions to change the system. The system had been formulated by the Emperor. If the King of England desired to change it, he should have written to the Viceroy, explaining wherein he desired alteration, when His Imperial Majesty's orders would have been sought. Had he been bearer of such a letter, his Lordship would have been asked to remain at Macao pending instructions from the capital. If the Emperor had agreed to the proposed amendments, then he could have taken up his residence in Canton. As it was, the King of England through ignorance of the correct procedure had sent no letter but only his Lordship who, with no less ignorance, had thought that by entering Canton without a pass and claiming as a right privileges which the Emperor, not only had not granted, but had never been asked to grant, he could change overnight regulations which had been in force for centuries.

To this lucid statement of the Chinese point of view Lord Napier had no more convincing reply than that it would have been incompatible with his dignity for the King of England to address a letter to the Viceroy.

After some desultory argument the Prefect returned to his original point. He was not authorized to take delivery of the letter to the Viceroy, he said, for that would be contrary to the rules, but if his Lordship would inform him of its contents, he would be much obliged, for it was principally to obtain this information that the Viceroy had sent him. To this Napier replied that official matters of such importance could not be communicated by word of mouth.

This ended the call. The mandarins had been told not to take delivery of the letter and they had failed to obtain a statement of its contents; they had also failed to convince Lord Napier that his procedure was irregular and that he had no *locus standi*. But their manner showed no trace of annoyance or pique. They accepted Napier's invitation to partake of refreshments and over their wine appeared to be in high spirits. The noble Lord was surprised at their easy geniality and put it down to the firm line he had taken and not to their determination to maintain face to the end. When they hinted, still playing their rôle, that they might be waiting again on him shortly, he believed them, thinking that the Viceroy would yet yield to avoid resort to force, and when they announced their departure there was quite a little scene of compliments and farewells.

As soon as they were gone, Napier composed a memorandum which he sent to London a few days later. The tone throughout is of a man who has gained a victory. If indeed he had, then this victory of the chairs was his Lordship's only victory in China.

The Viceroy Acts

It was one of Napier's beliefs that Chinese opinion was on his side. He reiterates in his despatches that the population favoured a commercial treaty, but was refused it by its Manchu overlords. If he could turn that wish into an active opposition to the Viceroy's policy, he would be able to exercise strong pressure. With this object, on 26 August, three days after the meeting with the mandarins, he drew up a proclamation and had it affixed at street corners. It gave a summary of events to date and spoke of 'the ignorance and obstinacy' of the Viceroy, and of the 'thousands of industrious Chinese who must suffer ruin and discomfort through the perversity of their government' in stopping the trade.

When the Viceroy found himself publicly libelled in his own city, he was extremely angry. Such an open attempt to tamper with the loyalty of the people had never actually happened before, though it had long been held that the Barbarians had a special propensity for stirring up trouble. Accordingly he felt obliged to counter the proclamation by one of his own, though it was not issued over his signature. Its phrasing was violent and direct, unlike the official language of the Edicts. 'A lawless foreign slave, named Laboriously Vile, has issued a notice. We do not know how such a barbarian dog can have the audacity to call himself an Eye. Were he so in fact, though a savage from beyond the pale, his sense of propriety would have restrained him from such an outrage. It is a capital offence to incite the people against their rulers and we would be justified in obtaining a mandate for his decapitation and the exposure of his head as a warning to traitors.'

This notice was posted up on the 28 or 29 August and was followed by an Edict, dated 2 September, signed by both the Viceroy and the Governor. Like the previous Edicts it began by a summary of the circumstances, now become so familiar. Coming to the visit of the mandarins, the Viceroy says he sent them to find out whether the Barbarian Eye had not some confidential reason for refusing to submit his letter through the Co-Hong, there being perhaps something in it which it would have been inexpedient for the Hong merchants to see or, on the contrary, perhaps they had read his letter and being afraid to communicate its contents pretended they had not received it, or, again, their instructions to him had not been sufficiently plain, for the barbarian mind was slow and dull. But nothing had come, said the Edict, of this condescension on his Excellency's side.

We may take this as expressing at least part of the object in sending the mandarins, but it would be a mistake to exclude the additional or private considerations which may have prompted the Viceroy. A Chinese of Lu's finesse and position in the administration would never have acted in quite so innocent a way. In fact, the Prefect was dismissed the following day. It is impossible not to see in this dismissal a pointer to internal stresses of which we do not know the details. The Viceroy, involved in smuggling and other malpractices, had to deceive the Court and buy off its inspectors. He was spied upon by his colleagues and subordinates, any one of whom might petition against him if opportunity offered. It may well be that he sent the Prefect so that he should fail, his failure being used in some subtle manner to discredit him with the Imperial Envoys. Whatever was the fact, Lu now seems to have seen his way clear to open

156

measures, a course which Chinese officials always postponed till the last on the principle of the less noise the better. What he did is revealed in the last paragraph of the Edict.

'The Barbarian Eye,' he says, 'has listened to what was told him as if entangled in a net. He is indeed stupid, blinded, ignorant. To make him see reason has been impossible, so misled and extravagant a man is he. There can be no quiet while he remains here. I therefore formally close the trade until he goes.'

A partial stoppage had been operating since 16 August. It was now made complete. The British merchants were to be isolated. Their brokers, agents, their interpreters and boatmen, their servants, porters, were all withdrawn. Shopkeepers were forbidden to sell them provisions and a cordon of soldiers was drawn round the Factories on the landward side. It was permissible for anyone who so desired to leave Canton for Whampoa and Macao, but no Englishman from those places was allowed to enter. Death was the penalty for any Chinese who disobeyed the orders. The Edict concluded: 'The said Barbarian Eye, Laboriously Vile, has cut himself off from the Celestial Empire. It is not at all what we, the Viceroy and Governor, could have desired. The barbarian merchants of all other nations are permitted to trade as usual. They need have no suspicion nor any anxiety. Let all with trembling awe obey. Oppose not. A special Edict.'

The Battle of the Bogue

The American, Hunter, in his book already quoted, has a story that the terms of the 2 September Edict were not conveyed to Napier by Jardine as previous Edicts had been, but were brought to his attention in a more startling way. On the afternoon of 4 September the noble Lord was dining in the English factory with Sir George Robinson, the Third Superintendent, and others, when twenty Chinese soldiers arrived at the gate and hung up a board on which the Edict was pasted. Which done, they mounted guard at the gate. The Chinese servants of the Factory, who had watched these proceedings with growing concern, and deduced from the demeanour of the soldiers, which in accordance with Chinese military practice was made to appear as ferocious as possible by melodramatic poses, exclamations and the like, that a threatening situation had suddenly arisen, rushed upstairs and intruding with a minimum of ceremony upon his Lordship and the gentlemen with him, who were in the middle of the pudding course, declared in a sort of screaming voice that an Edict was swinging on the gate and that a company of Chinese soldiers were preparing to enter and put all to the sword.

Napier immediately rose from table, and descending the staircase with Sir George and the rest crossed the garden to the gate and examined the placard. Being made acquainted with its contents, he ordered it to be removed at once and in a peremptory manner told the soldiers to go home, with which order they complied, though with very bad grace, daring even, it appears, to gesticulate and take a pose or two, using the while opprobrious epithets, though these did not so much express their sentiments as exhibit the front a soldier should take under the rules of military science and dramatic art, which two arts, according to British notions, the Chinese tended to confound.

With his Lordship upstairs again and finishing his pudding, the conversation not unnaturally centred upon the interruption. We do not know for a fact that Jardine was present, though it is on record that during the previous two days he had been acting for Napier in some feelers through the Hong merchants, negotiations which had come to nothing at 7 p.m. the evening before. Indeed, the publication on 4 September of the 2 September Edict immediately followed this last failure to reach an accommodation. It is highly probable, therefore, that Jardine was there, or that, if he was not there from the first, he was asked after the posting of the Edict to come over from his own dining room in the Creek factory, which was only a few paces away. At this stage Napier was making no decisions without him and his influence over the other two Superintendents seems to have been equally strong. The decision now to be taken was so exactly in accordance with his known predilection for a vigorous forward policy, that we may safely assume that it was he who pressed for it. As we have said, the frigates *Andromache* and *Imogene* were anchored at Chuenpee without the Bogue, under the command of Captain Blackwood of the *Imogene*. It was decided over the dinner table that Sir George Robinson should take a letter the next morning to the captain, directing him to enter the river and come up to Whampoa. If the Bogue batteries tried to stop him, he was to silence them, though not to fire first; and after passing the Bogue he was to send ahead by cutter to the English factory a guard of twelve marines under Lieutenant Reed, with two midshipmen and a sergeant. It was alleged officially afterwards that the reason for so drastic a step as ordering two men-of-war to burst into a port belonging to a Power with which Britain was at peace, was the danger to the life and property of the British merchants in Canton, as disclosed by the threatening attitude of the Viceroy and his colleagues. That may very well have been Napier's reason or his main reason; he may have thought there really was danger. The Viceroy had openly declared that he deserved to be executed. The British community unquestionably was powerless. There was nothing to prevent the Viceroy arresting him or any of them and putting them to death. But with the frigates at their very door, the authorities would pause, Napier believed, before they proceeded to extremes. We have seen how for some time he had viewed the frigates as an instrument of pressure. Now they would be used for protection in case of danger. Should that not develop, their presence at Whampoa, only thirteen miles from the city, would exert more pressure than at Chuenpee. In either case the move would be beneficial. But though, no doubt, Napier had this double consideration at the back of his mind, it was the threatened danger which alone enabled him to take a step which his instructions explicitly forbade save in circumstances the most critical.

But if this was Napier's view of the situation, it cannot possibly have been Jardine's, whose long experience of the country will have told him that the lives and property of the British residents were in no danger whatever. It was not the first time that the Canton authorities had stopped the trade in order to gain a point in dispute; it had happened again and again, was the stock weapon for keeping the Barbarians in order, and never failed to bring them to heel, nor had ever been accompanied by loss of life or property. In Hunter's book the complete security, in which the Barbarians—it amused him so to refer to himself—lived and did business, is insisted on more than once. If there were any arrests or punishments, it was always the Chinese who suffered, never

WILLIAM JARDINE
from a painting by George Chinnery

JAMES MATHESON
from a painting by George Chinnery

the British. When Chinese troops showed themselves, their chief duty was to protect foreigners from an excited rabble. So well known was all this that, in a letter addressed later in the month by the agents of the Honourable Company at Macao to the Court of Directors in London on the subject of these events, they went out of their way to emphasise that in their opinion the Company's treasury, which was still located in the English factory at Canton pending closure of accounts, did not require the protection of frigates, for it ran not the smallest danger of being broken into and despoiled; they were not consulted, they said, about the sending in of the warships; had they been, they would have declared it wholly unnecessary.

Jardine certainly was aware of this and cannot have had any apprehensions. Yet he advised Napier to send for the frigates and, if he did not put the idea of danger into Napier's mind, assuredly he said nothing to dispel it. We already know why he took this line. He disapproved of Parliament's Chinese policy. His ideas were those of the new manufacturing interest. He wanted to see the world opened to British manufacturers. He believed that England by supplying China could dominate China. If the navy showed itself, agreement would follow. The present situation he viewed from that angle. When the frigates reached Whampoa, one of two things would happen, either of which might be deemed satisfactory. They would intimidate the Viceroy and force him to make a settlement granting Napier's demands or they would not suffice to intimidate him, in which case Napier would have to withdraw. But if he withdrew it would be a slap in the face for Britain and the navy, a slap which the manufacturing interest could use to rouse Parliament and cause it to send, not two frigates, but a fleet. 'Mr. Jardine was a gentleman of great strength of character,' wrote Hunter. That he was so can be in no doubt.

Napier's order dated 5 September was delivered by Sir George Robinson to Captain Blackwood the same day at 9 p.m. He had brought a pilot with him, one of Jardine's clipper captains. The marines were immediately despatched and landed at Canton next morning, a very smart piece of work, the distance being nearly fifty miles each way. The frigates, however, could not weigh, for there was a flat calm. On the 6th, there being still insufficient wind for them, Captain Elliot, the Master Attendant, arrived from Macao on the *Louisa* cutter. On 7 September a light breeze from the westward enabled the frigates to start at 12.30 p.m. They entered the Bogue mouth and began laboriously to beat up past the first two forts, whose position, with that of the other forts, is described in Chapter Two, Section iii. No opposition, save a wide ball or two, was met at this stage, and the two men-of-war, the *Louisa* cutter following, tacked their way towards the two inner forts, four miles up. At 1 p.m., as they neared them, the wind shifted suddenly due north, an awkward circumstance. At the moment the *Imogene* was tacking towards Wantong fort on the western side and the *Andromache* towards Anunghoi fort on the eastern side. The change in the wind slowed both vessels so much that when abreast the forts at the end of their tack, they had little way. Had the guns in the forts been well laid both ships must have been sunk before they could extricate themselves. They each carried 28 guns and so each fort was threatened by only 14 guns. The exact number of guns in the forts is not on record, but appears to have totalled for both about sixty. In short, each fort should have been in a position to bring some 30 guns of heavy calibre and in stone casemates to bear against 16 guns, at most 32 pounders protected only by wooden bulwarks. When the Chinese saw their opportunity they opened fire without preliminary parley. It was 1.16 p.m. The frigates immediately returned them a broadside. The action continued in this way until 2.5 p.m., the frigates passing from one tack to another and slowly working up the river. Yet excellent though their targets were, the Chinese gunners hit them infrequently, causing no serious damage and killing nobody. For their part, the frigates were unable to silence the forts. The *Louisa* cutter manoeuvring in their wake, as best she could, also drew the fire of the batteries, as if the Chinese gunners were provoked to waste their shot on an unarmed vessel by the sight of Captain Elliot calmly sitting on deck under an umbrella.

The wind, such as it was, finally enabled the frigates with the help of the flood tide to clear the two forts of Wantong and Anunghoi, but then dropped altogether. At 2.15 p.m. it became necessary to anchor. On examining the damage, they found that the *Imogene* had received two shots in the larboard bends, one passing through; a larboard main chain plate was shot through, and a ball had cut the larboard second deck hammock netting and grazed the mainmast. One main shroud and half a dozen ropes of minor importance were shot away. A rating was wounded by a splinter.

The *Andromache* had received even less damage. For the rest of the 7th, and till 2.11 p.m. on 9th no progress was made. At that hour a light breeze from the south enabled them at last to get under way. In line ahead they stood towards the remaining fort on Tiger Island which commanded the exit. At 2.20 its batteries opened upon them at 200 yards range. Here they could use their united larboard broadsides, which heavily punished and silenced the Tiger batteries, many 32 pound shot entering the embrasures or shattering the parapet. At this point two seamen were killed and five wounded on the frigates. At 2.55 p.m. the Battle of the Bogue was over. The frigates were through into the river, but with continuing calms did not reach Whampoa till 7.15 p.m. on 11 September. One of their officers, a Lieutenant Skinner, was an artist and made two drawings of the action which were afterwards published as coloured mezzotints by Ackermann and Company. The prints, excellent of their kind, show the fight at the top of the narrows and again at Tiger Island. In the first, on an almost unruffled water, the frigates are seen discharging their broadsides at the end of their starboard and larboard tacks. The *Louisa*, about the size of a fishing smack, is in the wake of the *Andromache*. The rocky and precipitous sides of the defile tower about them. On the water level are the Wantong and Anunghoi forts, heavy stone structures in tiers of casemates. In the second print, under a splendid sky of cloud and on the same glassy water, the frigates in line ahead are bombarding the Tiger fort at the base of the high bluff which forms the island. The Battle of the Bogue is one of the least known of our naval exploits. It can hardly be called a naval victory of note, though one is sure that Lieutenant Reed and his twelve marines were disappointed at not being there. Its importance lies rather in what it led to, for it may be described as the first clash in the first war ever waged between China and the West.

(xi)

The Frigates are Trapped

Between 5 September when Napier sent his letter to Captain Blackwood and 11 September when the frigates anchored in Whampoa Reach, there was a lull at Canton. Though deprived of servants and supplies, the British residents, as on former occasions, remained perfectly safe. The inconveniences they suffered were, moreover, less real than might appear, for not only had they a stock of provisions on hand, but fresh eggs, vegetables, fowls and bread were procurable by a little bribery. The future, however, was less secure. Since Napier was set against going and had taken the provocative course of calling up the frigates, the crisis was bound to intensify. No one could tell whether the Viceroy or his Lordship would be the first to draw in his horns.

Napier had not been feeling well for some days. The average noon temperature in Canton during the month of September is 83 degrees Fahrenheit, the night temperature 76 degrees. There are days when 88 degrees are registered. Napier had arrived on 25 July. June, July, August and September not only are the four hottest months in the year, but also the wettest. Damp heat is trying to the nerves and induces fevers. One of these fevers his Lordship now contracted. The symptoms were intermittent, a rise, a fall, followed by another rise of his temperature. He might have handed over his duties to the Second Superintendent, Mr. Davis, but was loath to do so in the middle of a crisis. Mr. Davis, too, was elderly and quite undistinguished, and as an old Company man had little authority with the new merchants. So instead of staying in bed and taking such remedies as his personal surgeon, Dr. Colledge, prescribed, he remained on his feet and continued the struggle, fortified in his belief that the arrival of the frigates would cause Lu to bend.

During these days between the 5th and 11th of September the rift of opinion among the merchants became more evident. Jardine's party had a considerable majority. We know its policy, for it had become Napier's. Dent and Company, the most important firm after Jardine and Matheson, headed the opposition: Dent himself had a personal animosity for Jardine. That Napier's policy would lead to the ruin of the China trade, that a Superintendent was too expensive a luxury in such circumstances and that the Commission would be well advised to withdraw, these were the views he put about, and in the uncomfortable circumstances of the stoppage those supporting him increased in number. It is alleged that he even intrigued with the Chinese, assuring them he could procure Napier's departure. Beyond doubt this split encouraged the Viceroy.

On 8 September, the day the frigates lay becalmed between the north end of the Bogue and the Tiger fort, Napier addressed a letter to the Viceroy through a Chamber of Commerce newly constituted by Jardine's party. The fever was on him and the tone of his letter is highly irritable, almost hysterical. After claiming contrary to the historical facts that for two hundred years there had been personal intercourse between the Viceroy and British subjects, he denounces the present Viceroy's tyrannous behaviour. Then referring to what had happened at the Bogue the previous day he says in a menacing way: 'It is a very serious offence to fire upon or otherwise insult the British flag . . . I recommend the Viceroy and the Governor to take warning in time; they have opened the preliminaries of war.' And he goes on emotionally: 'I will lose no time in sending this true statement to His Imperial Majesty the Emperor at Pekin . . . His Majesty will not permit such folly, wickedness and cruelty, as they have been guilty of since my arrival here, to go unpunished.' And he concludes, mimicking in atrocious taste the Edicts addressed by the Viceroy to the Hong merchants: 'Therefore tremble Viceroy Loo, intensely tremble!'

The letter also contained a veiled threat that the *Imogene* and the *Andromache* would fight, for it included this sentence: 'The Hong merchants are already aware that there are two frigates now in the river, bearing very heavy guns for the express purpose of protecting the British trade, and I would warn them again and again, that if any disagreeable consequences shall ensue from the said Edicts, they themselves, with the Viceroy and the Governor, are responsible for the whole.'

It is clear that Napier believed that this threat would result in the capitulation of the Canton Government. But in this he was wholly mistaken. On 11 September, the day the frigates arrived at Whampoa, the Viceroy issued an Edict which disappointingly revealed that he was resolved to meet force with force. The first part of the document is temperate and dignified. It states clearly and with cogency the Chinese case, with which we are already so familiar that to recapitulate it would be otiose. Then he says: 'The said Barbarian Eye has not learned to arouse from his previous errors, but has further called to him many persons, bringing in boats military weapons which have been moved into the barbarian factories . . . He has again opposed the laws by commanding the ships of war to push forward into the inner river; and in allowing the barbarian forces to fire guns, attacking and wounding our soldiers and alarming our resident population. This being so far out of the bounds of reason renders it still more unintelligible what it is he wishes to do.'

If it is the protection of the British merchants that he has in mind, goes on the Viceroy with bitter sarcasm, how could two small warships protect those who live on land and wholly within the power of the Chinese military forces? And what does he want to protect them from? Have they not always lived in security? The armed forces of the province, he continues, are marshalled and ready. They can be set in motion by a sign from him. Yet even now, late as it is, 'if the said Barbarian Eye will speedily repent of his errors, withdraw the ships of war and remain obedient to the old rules, I will yet give him some slight indulgence.' This is his last chance, and if he does not grasp it, the Celestial troops will drive him out.

In this way he called Lord Napier's bluff. For bluff it was, his Lordship knowing well that the frigates could effect nothing if the Canton Government stood firm.

As soon as it had been reported that the frigates had forced the Bogue, Lu immediately took a number of counter measures. On the 10th and 11th, while the war-ships were slowly beating up the river, he made the following arrangements designed to neutralize them. The river between Whampoa and Canton was blocked by sinking twelve barges loaded with stones in the channel, by drawing cables across and by staking it. These obstructions closed it entirely for the frigates, and made it difficult, if not impossible, for their boats to bring up an armed landing party. A fleet of war-junks guarded the block and cruised on the lookout for armed boats. To prevent a landing opposite Whampoa, stockades were erected and guns mounted along the bank. A hundred fireboats were got ready, to be loosed on the frigates, if necessary. And preparations to block the second bar with great stones were made, the effect of which would be to box up the frigates in a stretch of some 20 miles of river.

These measures were complete, or nearly so, when the *Imogene* and *Andromache* let go their anchors at Whampoa on 11 September. The ships had been rendered harmless. They could neither go on nor go back; nor could their crews fight their way to Canton. They had sailed right into China and were as completely in Lu's power as if he had already captured them. But he did not want to take the last step which would give him physical possession. To do so would cause a tremendous hullaballoo. When diplomacy can gain an issue it is idiotic to use force. Thanks to the frigates having placed themselves in his power, he was now in a position to oblige Napier either to leave or to lose the frigates. He was convinced Napier would elect to go, that he would go quietly, that the frigates would go quietly. Perhaps the Emperor would be very angry with him over the bursting of the Bogue, but if the affair were ended neatly in this way punishment would be mitigated. Therefore, as we have already seen, he wrote on the day of the frigates' arrival: 'If the said Barbarian Eye will speedily repent of his errors, withdraw the ships of war and remain obedient to the old rules, I will yet give him some slight indulgence.'

Napier's Discomfiture and Death

When it was made known to Lord Napier that the frigates, on which he had depended to frighten the Viceroy into an accommodation, had been rendered impotent, that all communication between him and them was interrupted, and that they themselves were cut off from the outer sea and dangerously open to attack by fireboats, he saw that the game was up: he must withdraw and it only remained to make the withdrawal as dignified as possible. Jardine, who was in constant attendance, offered to mediate and immediately began a series of conferences with the Hong merchants.

Harassed by the mortifying situation in which he found himself, Napier was no longer able to fight against the fever and retired to bed, lying in the palatial but stuffy bedroom once occupied by the President of the Company's Select Committee. Dr. Colledge viewed his condition with apprehension and declared it to be imperative, apart from all other considerations, for him to leave Canton at once for the sea breezes of Macao. This brought a new element upon the scene. If it could be made to appear that he was only leaving for reasons of health and not because the Viceroy had manoeuvred him into such a position that he had no option but to go, appearances would be kept up, the honour of Britain would be less tarnished, the Crown suffer less humiliation. Furthermore, should the Viceroy permit him to embark on one of the frigates and sail out of the river, colours flying, such a complexion could be put on the affair as largely to disguise its melancholy actualities. Napier from his bed tried to achieve these objects, but he was not successful for the very reason, in reverse, which had prompted them: the Viceroy had his own face to consider. He had lost face by the storming of the Bogue and if he were to rehabilitate himself must now cause Napier to depart in such a manner that there could afterwards be no doubt of his departure being forced. Had he ordered his arrest, he would have demonstrated this beyond question, but it was never his policy to push any matter to extremes, when he could equally effect his end by finesse.

On 14 September, three days after the arrival of the warships, Napier thought it expedient to inform the British community that he was about to go and gave it as his reason that 'having used every effort to establish His Majesty's Commission at Canton, he did not feel authorised, at present, by the continued maintenance of his claims, to occasion the further interruption of the trade of the port.' This letter was received with a good deal of satisfaction by one section, at least, of the merchants, as we may guess, for these gentlemen all along had held that the Commission was a superfluity with which they could dispense. Even those in favour of a strong policy had no high opinion of it, and declared that not until His Majesty's Government was resolved to back its demand for open trade with adequate forces would anything be effected.

Four days later, the 19th, an agreement was reached with the Hong merchants. The meeting was at their Council Hall at the top of Old China Street. There were present Jardine, Dr. Colledge, Howqua and Mowqua. The terms were simple. Napier engaged to order the frigates to return to Lintin and himself to apply for a red permit authorising him to go down to Macao by private boat; the neglect of which formality for coming up had been the start of all the trouble. In offering these terms, which gave the Viceroy all the face he wanted, Dr. Colledge, who was acting for his Lordship on this occasion asked that: 'His Majesty's ships be not obliged to submit to any ostentatious display on the part of the Chinese Government', meaning that the Viceroy should waive any inclinations he might have to humiliate the ships by some public demonstration of his victory.

Howqua knew the terms would be acceptable and was profoundly relieved. 'Mr. Colledge,' he said, 'your proposition is of a responsible nature and from my knowledge of your character I know you intend honestly to carry it out. Shake hands with me and Mowqua and let Mr. Jardine do likewise.' 'We all joined hands,' wrote Dr. Colledge in his account of the affair published two days later in the *Canton Register*, Jardine's newspaper.

Howqua and Mowqua then left to see the Viceroy, and returned late that evening to say that His Excellency had accepted the terms and undertook that no insult should be offered the frigates as they passed through the Bogue. Not, however, until 10.30 p.m. on the day following, the 20th, was formal permission given Napier to leave, though the sun was near setting on the 21st before the red permit was actually issued.

Napier had hoped that the *Louisa* cutter would be allowed to come up and take him off. But the Viceroy had not acceded to this. Napier must go in a Chinese boat and under guard; only thus could His Excellency's face be adequately secured.

The start was made soon after the arrival of the permit. Napier, though very weak, was slightly better. Some days earlier he had moved from his stuffy bedroom to a much airier apartment which Mr. Innes, whom we last met smuggling opium on the coast, readily placed at his disposal. Here he got some sleep, but his temperature still remained above normal. Yet he was now able to walk, though with assistance, as far as the English factory's wharf, where the Chinese boat was waiting, a houseboat, comfortable enough and properly supplied. The course to Macao was to be by the inner route through the creeks, much shorter than going by the Bogue, three and a half days generally sufficing for the passage. Dr. Colledge anticipated that the quiet and fresher air of this little cruise would help to restore his Lordship. What happened was far different. Napier was to arrive a dying man.

When they embarked—the sun had already set—there was no sign of any police escort nor had they been told they were to travel under surveillance. But presently Dr. Colledge became aware in the darkness of armed boats and knew they were being convoyed. That meant they were no longer masters of their own movements. Their boat had turned down the Macao passage, a reach opposite Canton and at right angles to the main stream to Whampoa. When about eight miles on, and near that well-known landmark on the east bank, the pagoda fort, the guard ships anchored, obliging Napier's boat to do the same. The lights of Canton were still visible twinkling down the reach. There his Lordship was forced to spend the night, instead of proceeding quietly on his journey. It was noisy and very hot, and the halt did him no good. When dawn broke they had a view of the convoying vessels, eight armed boats, two transports full of soldiers, and another boat with a civil mandarin, who was in charge of the squadron. The pace set by the escort was very slow. During the whole of the 22nd and the 23rd they crawled south, and it was not till midnight on the latter day that they reached Heang-shan, a little creek-port some twenty miles from Macao. Here they were detained until 1 p.m. on the 25th. Heang-shan had a custom-house, where passes were checked and countersigned. The official in charge declared himself to be without instructions and withheld permission to proceed. The noise in the roadstead was distracting; gongs sounded, crackers exploded. When Napier's temperature rose, Dr. Colledge was much alarmed. He had not come well provided with medicines and could do little to alleviate his patient's symptoms. On the morning of the 25th he sent a linguist to the mandarin in charge to say the detention was an outrage and that if it continued he could not be responsible for what might happen. The linguist failed to get any positive reply. 'Provoked at length beyond all endurance by this cruel display of power,' wrote Dr. Colledge in his account of the journey, 'I requested the linguist to accompany me to the mandarin's boat, which he did without any kind of reluctance; and on the linguist's sending up my name, an interview was immediately afforded me. Through him I most fully described Lord Napier's sufferings, and the danger of delay under such circumstances. The mandarin replied that he must consult with the Heang-shan authorities before he could promise to release us, but that he would lose no time in representing my statement. No further communication took place until 1 o'clock p.m. when this said mandarin, accompanied by two others of inferior rank to himself, came to us and handed me the Heang-shan pass.' It would be idle to seek the precise reason for the delay or to speculate whether the Viceroy had anything to do with it, but anyone who has himself been the victim of official procrastination will suspect it was a matter of red tape.

The twenty miles to Macao took another eighteen hours, for not until the morning of 26 September was his Lordship landed, 'altogether in a worse state than he had ever been since the commencement of his illness.' They carried him to the airy house on the hill where Lady Napier and her two daughters—the Chinese records say three daughters—awaited him. Though, 'surrounded by the unremitting attention of his affectionate family,' and in spite of every comfort, the fresh sea air, and the best medical skill of the place, his fever showed no signs of abating. No diagnosis exists so that one cannot tell what manner of fever it was, whether malarial or otherwise. There are many tropical fevers and even today their causes and cure are not wholly elucidated. The most baffling are those when the patient continues day and night for weeks with a temperature between 101 and 102 degrees. This appears to have been the nature of Lord Napier's long fever. He remained conscious and derived much comfort from devotional exercises, in which he was assisted by the Reverend Mr. Bridgman, whom he had learned to esteem as a preacher when attending public worship at the little church in the English factory. The frequent ringing of the Macao bells, however, disturbed him, which the Portuguese ecclesiastical authorities, at his request, considerately discontinued. On Wednesday 8 October, though very feeble and clearly drawing near his end, he was aroused by the forts on the ridge saluting a ship direct from Portugal. The identity of her flag being disputed by those about him, he was distinctly heard to say: 'If it is the Portuguese arms between white and blue, then it is the Donna Maria's new flag.' These were his last recorded words. His two great interests had been sheep and ships. He lingered two days longer and expired on the night of 11 October.

Late as it was, and tired though he must have been, Dr. Colledge sat down at once and addressed Howqua and Mowqua. 'Gentlemen,' he wrote, 'it is my painful duty to report to you the demise of His Majesty's Chief Superintendent of British commerce, the Right Honourable Lord Napier, this day at 10 o'clock and 20 minutes p.m., and to request that you will cause this sad event to be made known to His Excellency, the Viceroy of Canton.'

To which, in due course, he got the answer: 'A respectful communication. We the other day received your letter informing us of the death of your honourable subaltern officer, Laboriously Vile, and have reported the fact to His Excellency, the Viceroy. We have now received his Edict in reply, a copy of which we append for your perusal. This is the task we impose and for this purpose we write; and presenting compliments are etcetera:' This epistle they signed with their real, not their pidgin, names, Wu Shao-yung and

Lu Wan-kin. The Viceroy's Edict was extremely brief. 'Lu, Viceroy of the Two Kuangs, to the Hong merchants. Your report has been authenticated and the contents noted. Await a proclamation by the Hoppo.'

Sometimes the baldest documents are more revealing than a narrative finished with deliberate art.

The funeral took place on 15 October at 10 a.m. and was attended by all the British and Portuguese notabilities. As the long procession moved along the ridge to the cemetery, minute guns were fired in the road by the *Andromache*, which, with the *Imogene*, had passed through the Bogue without incident, similar guns being also fired at Whampoa and at the opium isle of Lintin.

Leading was a Guard of Honour, composed of Portuguese coloured troops. Then came Dr. Colledge, with two British seamen holding aloft the Union Jack. The pall-bearers were the captains of the two frigates, the Governor of Macao with two other officers of His Most Faithful Majesty's, and Captain Elliot, the Master Attendant. Immediately behind the bier were Lady Napier and her daughters. After them went Mr. Davis and Sir George Robinson, the Second and Third Superintendents, who had been largely displaced as his late Lordship's advisers, by the man now walking at their heels, William Jardine, on whose left was the Reverend E. C. Bridgman. Then followed a number of officers of His Majesty's navy and of His Most Faithful Majesty's army and navy. At the rear, heading the main body of merchants, went opium runner James Innes and opium magnate James Matheson.

This list of names, with their order, is also revealing. It tells so much more than it was intended to do.

The funeral sermon was not preached until the following Sunday week, when the Reverend Bridgman delivered it at Canton. A sermon of 1834 is unlikely in 1946 to reward the reader, yet we may dip into this one with profit, for it is integral with the age, far more than would be a sermon today. 'Short and precarious is human life,' began the reverend gentleman to his little congregation of merchants in tail coats and cravats. Death, in fact, had been very busy among them that month. Not only had Napier died but also a young merchant, recently out from home, and Dr. Morrison, the interpreter. Death in life, that was the theme of the discourse.

Before developing it, however, the preacher sketched Napier's character and antecedents. Descended from the John Napier who discovered logarithms in the reign of James I, he was the son of the eighth lord. 'His parents were both exemplary, and he enjoyed in the home of his youth the best example, both moral and religious.' Ready, aye ready, was the motto of the family. From 1827, when he left the navy for good, until 1834, when he was appointed Chief Superintendent, he devoted himself to his estate of Thirlestone, coming to London only when Parliament was sitting. He belonged to the Presbyterian Church and his reading was chiefly mathematics and the Bible. The intellectual and moral improvement of mankind was a subject which often occupied his thoughts. On his appointment as Chief Superintendent it was natural therefore for him to hope that a free and well regulated intercourse with China would be followed 'by the overthrow of idolatry and the complete triumph of pure Christianity'.

We have observed before that this pious aspiration was not confined to those who, like him, were noted for a careful observance of religious forms, but was widely shared by the public in general.

As Mr. Bridgman had ministered to his Lordship during his fatal illness, he was able to say how edifying was his death. 'In the last hours of his life it was pleasing to observe with what readiness and confidence his mind turned to the only true source of support and consolation.'

The sermon then reverts to its main theme of the transitoriness of earthly glory. It was short for the period, not

PROBABLY A PORTRAIT OF MOWQUA
from a painting by George Chinnery

THE PRIVATE HOUSE OF ONE OF THE HONG MERCHANTS NEAR CANTON
from a painting by Thomas Allom

taking more than an hour to deliver. Though a funeral oration, which is a form of the panegyric, we may conclude what was said to have been largely true. Napier was a man of many good qualities, but was also a strait-laced Presbyterian at a time when the Presbyterians were a narrow sect. In his heart he considered the Chinese ignorant heathens and, when he discovered that they saw him as an unlettered barbarian, was disconcerted and thrown off his balance, having no saving grace of humour or liking for paradox as had merchants like Hunter, who found it all very funny.

(xiii)

What the Dragon said

To see this drama out, we must now listen to what the Dragon said. His style, it will be recalled, was Glorious Rectitude and we saw him last bowing in supplication to Heaven.

Napier had been under the impression that the Viceroy had not reported to Court his arrival. This was incorrect; Lu had done so. He could hardly have done otherwise with Imperial Commissioners on the spot. As it was, to prevent them reporting adversely, we know the enormous squeeze he had had to pay. This enabled him to submit an account of Napier's first doings, which threw no unfavourable light upon himself. The storming of the Bogue necessitated a further despatch, which was sent off on 15 September, four days after the frigates anchored at Whampoa. Normally, the journey from Canton to Peking took three months by river and canal, but by express messenger, using relays of horses and galloping 150 miles a day, the distance could be covered in a fortnight.

Lu's despatch which was signed also by the Tartar General, the Governor and the Hoppo, was carried by such a messenger. In it, the irruption through the Bogue was ascribed to the negligence of subordinates. The Admiral-in-Chief had, under instructions, deputed a certain Captain Kao to guard the Bogue entrance and patrol the adjoining waters, but the frigates had given the Chinese squadron the slip. After thus laying the blame on Captain Kao, the despatch described the measures taken to trap and make impotent the British warships.

The Emperor, however, refused to accept this excuse. He was very angry and immediately indited the following Mandate with his Vermilion Brush: 'It seems that all the forts have been erected in vain. They cannot even beat back two barbarian ships! It is ridiculous, detestable! If our forces can do no better than this, no wonder the Barbarians only sneer at them. Our further pleasure shall be given. Respect this.'

The papers were then forwarded to the Board of War for necessary action. This body drew up a Mandate for the Imperial Seal, which, with the Supreme Mandate in Vermilion, was sent by express to Canton and was received there on 19 October, eight days after Napier's death. Their contents were certainly disagreeable, but as the Viceroy had had a triumph in the meanwhile he will have read them without extreme perturbation.

The punishments awarded were these: Captain Kao to be degraded from his rank and ordered to wear the cangue in front of his men at the Bogue mouth until further orders; the Admiral-in-Chief to be degraded; the Viceroy, Lu, for not taking better preventive measures, to lose his title of Guardian of the Heir Apparent, to have his decoration, the

Peacock Feather, plucked out publicly, and be degraded though temporarily retained as acting Viceroy. The Mandate ended with these words: 'Should the Viceroy truly arrange the matter speedily, and end it with security and propriety, he may yet receive some little indulgence and slight diminution of his sentence. If he continue to involve himself in errors, and cause future misfortunes, he must be acted with according to martial law, when no indulgence will be shown. Tremble fearfully hereat. Be attentive hereto. Respect this.'

The Tartar General, the Governor and the Hoppo were not punished, but in a supplementary Mandate the Dragon admonished them. The line they were all to take was also clearly laid down. 'It is absolutely requisite to make the said Barbarian Eye to tremble and quake before His Celestial Majesty, and penitently arouse to reverential submission. When once he is brought under, a trifling indulgence may be accorded him. But if he do not arouse, but remain perverse as before, then set in motion the machinery of expulsion and destruction.'

These extracts show that the policy of the Court was identical, even down to the phraseology used to express it, with that which the authorities at Canton had pursued.

Immediately after Napier's expulsion on 21 September, Lu, with Ha, the Tartar General, and the Governor, had sent off a despatch describing the happy ending of the affair. Of all the documents in this correspondence it is, perhaps, the most picturesque: 'A reverent memorial forwarded by express messenger, whereon Your Majesty's servants, looking upward, entreat that the Sacred Glance be cast,' it begins.

In composing it, Lu had two courses open to him. He might either write up the Napier affair as an effort to subvert the system governing relations between the Middle Kingdom and the outside Barbarians, and declare the entry of the frigates, defeated by his energetic measures, to have been an attempt to bring force to bear for that end, or he

179

might write it down. He chose the latter course, even if this meant representing himself in a less heroic light, because he thought it safer to pretend that nothing particular had happened, than, by laying stress on his own masterly steering, to give room for the inference that he had allowed a serious situation to arise.

His argument, therefore, went like this: A Barbarian Eye, named Laboriously Vile, having presumed without a red permit to enter the city, presented an improperly addressed letter, and continued, in spite of admonition, to be obstinate and perverse, until it became necessary to stop the trade. The Eye then called in his frigates, but when these saw 'in the passage before them spars ranged out across and around, with guns and muskets as if it were a forest, and soldiers encamped on every place on shore, their force compactly joined, their array alarming, and perceiving boats full of firewood and straw, they remained subdued nor dared advance a step.'

The bringing in of the frigates, 'though in no way a heavy offence against the laws,' was yet a breach of the port regulations. It also caused damage, some of the rafters and tiles at the Bogue fort being shaken and cracked. It was clearly impossible to overlook such conduct altogether, and when Laboriously Vile, much frightened by the dangers to which his frigates were exposed, begged to be allowed to leave the city, the Hong merchants were deputed to ask him what he meant by his impertinences. To their questions he replied in a most contrite manner, declaring that the frigates had entered the Bogue by mistake, their captains, as strangers, having lost their way. This excuse, of course, was merely the stupid prevarication a Barbarian might be expected to employ; nevertheless it indicated repentance. On further questioning and reproof, Laboriously Vile broke down, begged for forgiveness, said he would pay for any damage to the tiles and rafters, and renewed his entreaties for permission to depart.

After careful consideration it was decided to grant this indulgence. Although the Eye had entertained absurd visionary fancies, he had shown no real disregard for the laws. To have exterminated him would, in the circumstances, have been too harsh. Nor was there precedent for such severity. The Everlasting Lord had always cherished virtuously those coming from afar, soothing them and, to the utmost limit, extending to them justice and benevolence. When contumacious, they were corrected; if submissive, they were pardoned. Never were extreme measures taken against them. Laboriously Vile, moreover, was a harmless, half-witted sort of fellow. The barbarian merchants to a man deplored his lack of propriety. He had no support whatever in that quarter.

Accordingly it was resolved to treat him with mildness. He was sent to Macao under guard and commanded to remain there until a Mandate was received. On the same day the frigates were driven out of the river. A few days later the trade was re-opened.

Such was the version of Lord Napier's mission which Lu concocted for the Sacred Glance. It found favour, as he had anticipated. The Government's policy was to maintain a strict aloofness, but to do so with the least possible friction. Lu's despatch showed that he had acted in this sense, and with success. A Mandate in reply was drafted, and sealed on 7 October. Lu must have read it with relief. After the lengthy resumé of events customary in Chinese state documents, it declared: 'The said Viceroy and his colleagues, have acted in this affair with skill and correctness. Though at the beginning they failed to take adequate preventive measures, for which failure they have been duly punished, yet they were able in the end to settle the thing well and securely, without loss of national dignity and without shedding blood. We hereby declare that We are highly pleased. His title and decoration are restored to Lu. But he cannot be freed wholly from blame on account of his neglect to take precautions and must continue for the present degraded from official rank, though retained in office.' Proceedings against the Admiral were closed and Captain Kao had his cangue taken off. The Mandate ends with the usual paternal admonition, the Canton officials being directed 'to review their bad habits and with contrition to eradicate them one by one'.

(xiv)

Conclusions from the Misadventures

The conclusion drawn by the leading merchants at Canton from Lord Napier's misadventures was that the belief, long held, that China could be persuaded by argument to enter into modern trade relations with the West, had finally been shown to be without foundation.

But the alternative policy, now become practicable, of forcing China to make a trade treaty, was complicated by the existence of the drug traffic. Britain's case before the world would be overwhelming were it not for that. How would opinion, both at home and abroad, view force used to push opium smuggling, for so a war would be represented? On the other hand, if nothing were done, there was danger of the whole trade, legitimate and other, degenerating into a vast smuggling racket with its centre at Lintin, not only a disgraceful and, indeed, unsound way of doing business, but one which was certain to lead to armed clashes of all sorts.

The position was paradoxical. The smuggling firms were making fortunes, but they were not content to let things be.

A firm like Jardine and Matheson was organized to carry opium, but its organization would enable it to carry ordinary goods with equal efficiency. A treaty that opened all China to commerce would in the end be a safer and more profitable business.

And besides business instinct, there was a further reason which prompted the principal merchants to advocate the use of force. To trade in a noxious drug was not characteristic of British commerce. The wares of England had always been noted for the soundness of their workmanship and the excellence of their material; and her merchants for their solidity, their caution and their honesty. An exception to this had been the slave trade, which public opinion had ended a few years earlier. That so reputable a community should in China have fifty per cent of its capital sunk in opium smuggling was a rôle that did not really suit it. Therein lies the psychological explanation of the resolve to force a commercial treaty on China: the merchants wanted to rehabilitate themselves.

So, immediately after the death of Lord Napier, Jardine's party addressed a petition to His Majesty King William IV. There were sixty-four signatures. They declared that had Lord Napier been supported by the requisite armed force, he would not have been obliged to bow to insult and retire disgraced nor would they now have the dismal prospect of having to continue to trade as heretofore, exposed to the persecutions of the Chinese authorities. Accordingly, they begged His Majesty to send a Plenipotentiary of rank in a ship of the line, attended by two frigates and some sloops, with orders to demand an open trade. The demand should be backed by a direct threat to the capital, the ships being ordered to land troops in its vicinity. That was the way to talk to the Chinese, said the petitioners, the only way, and the safe way too, for they would give in at once: 'We are confident that resort even to such strong measures as these, so far from being likely to lead to more serious warfare . . .

would be the surest course for avoiding the danger of such a collision.'

The Duke of Wellington, Foreign Secretary in the short-lived Grey administration of November to April 1834-35 received the merchants' petition and the other papers relating to Napier's failure and death. The old war-horse, however, was in no way aroused. That the tea trade, which paid substantial duties, should not be disturbed seemed to him of paramount importance. He did not feel that the treatment of Lord Napier amounted to a national insult. He had no inclination for the adventure sketched in the merchants' letter. It is doubtful whether he understood all the bearings of a complicated situation. In the Memorandum which he made on 24 March, 1835 he jots down points of fact, as if feeling his way to a defined attitude, but can only arrive at the summing up: 'That which we require now is, not to lose the enjoyment of what we have got.' James Matheson, who had gone home with Lady Napier and her girls in the hope of stirring the Government to action, was disgusted. He wrote to Jardine, that the Iron Duke was 'a cold blooded fellow . . . a strenuous advocate for submissiveness and servility.' Nor did British policy towards China change at once when Lord Melbourne formed a Whig ministry on 10 April, 1835, with Palmerston as his Foreign Secretary. Matheson had pinned his hopes on the new ministry, but it was no less pacific nor was there any sign of indignation in the country. 'The fact is, Jardine,' he wrote sarcastically at this time, 'the people appear to be so comfortable in this magnificent country, so entirely satisfied in all their desires, that so long as domestic affairs, including markets go right, they cannot really be brought to think of us outlanders . . . Lord Palmerston means to do nothing.'

Chapter IV

FOREIGN MUD

British Opinion of the Chinese Armed Forces

Already there is hint of the possibility of war. The British do not want war, but they do want an arrangement. The Chinese do not want war, but they have no intention of coming to any arrangement. What would happen should there be war? A section of the British merchants, believing that a threat would suffice, declared there would be no campaign. The subject was so topical that the *Chinese Repository* devotes a long article to its discussion in its issue of August 1836. In a missionary owned journal of the sort, a pacific tone was *de rigueur*, and the author of the article—his identity is not revealed—begins by saying that the object of war is now become to end war and he cites in this connection some kind of an early machine-gun, the invention of a Mr. Toplis and named the Pacificator because it was so deadly a weapon, being capable of propelling 'a stream of balls to a radius extent of near two miles,' so that no soldiers would face it and there could be no more fighting. However, as Mr. Toplis's gun was not yet in use, the author proceeds to estimate what fight the Chinese land and sea forces could put up against British arms as they actually existed.

The Chinese army, he says, differs little in 1836 from what it was in 1275, the date given for the Chinese invention of gunpowder. The Jesuits of the seventeenth and eighteenth centuries certainly cast good cannon for the Emperors, but for some reason these were not copied, and the cannon generally in use burst so often that they were more dangerous to their gunners than to the enemy. If they did not burst, it was because the powder was of the lowest grade, as was evidenced when the *Andromache* and *Imogene* forced the Bogue in 1834, it being then observed that many of the balls bounced off the ships' wooden bulwarks, if they reached as far, which few did, even at point-blank range, the majority falling short or even dropping down out of the mouth of the guns. The powder, he declares, was supplied by a local contractor (and anyone with experience of local contractors in the Orient knows what that means). This accounted for the frigates losing only two men, though three hundred pieces of cannon were mounted in the Bogue forts and the men-of-war had to tack up in the face of a northerly breeze with the tide against them at the narrowest part. Yet the Bogue, says the writer, is the most powerfully fortified place in all China.

The troops stationed in Canton itself were a stage army, he goes on. You can see them any day if you stroll up to the Petition Gate. This is held by 'a coolie-looking man, armed with a pair of breeches, a fan, and perhaps a rattan whip.' Should you be accompanied by other foreigners and give the impression that you want to present a petition, the guard turns out. They straggle up one by one, 'undressed, unarmed, unprepared and half asleep.' Presently an officer loiters into view, 'generally the largest man that can be found.' The guardsmen are told to put on their uniforms, which have been brought and deposited in a pile. When dressed, they look more imposing, for on their chests and backs is boldly embroidered in black on gold the ideograph for courage. Their swords, however, were so rusty that they drew them with difficulty. These are the regular troops, explains the writer, and are not in great numbers, as often alleged, for in emergency, when extra soldiers are required, they are hired by the day. To impress Lord Napier the authorities pressed into service 'discarded cowkeepers, broken down tailors, shoemakers and other riffraff', who were dressed in imitation tiger-skins and taught to shout war-cries.

The writer then quotes from a Chinese drill-book, which a Jesuit had translated into French:

On frappe un coup sur le tambour; les soldats tournent comme s'ils vouloient s'ouvrir un passage de ce côté, et poussent un grand cri.

On frappe deux coups sur le tambour; les soldats se tournent à gauche, et fixent la vue sur les étendards qui sont déployés, et poussent un grand cri.

On frappe cinq coups sur le tambour; chaque soldat, ayant le corps ramassé sous son bouclier, dont il est entièrement couvert, fait un pas en avant en se roulant sur ce même bouclier, qui lui sert de point d'appui, comme il feroit sur une roue, et après le tour entier il se relève tout de suite, et se trouve debout dans la disposition d'attaquer, et pousse un grand cri.

(This intimidating somersault gave the Sung one of their most notable victories over the Tartars, notes the Jesuit.)

There is a great deal more in the same vein, 'frappe le tambour et pousser de grands cris' being the invariable refrain throughout, and causing the contributor to the *Depository* to exclaim with Corporal Trim to Uncle Toby: 'Ah, your Honour, one good thrust of the bayonet were worth it all!'

In point of fact the text book (it is contained in Vol. 7 of *Memoires concernant les Chinois*, Paris, 1782) does not consist entirely of stage tactics, but contains a number of aphorisms even of value today. For instance:

'In ancient times those experienced in war never fought a campaign which they knew they could not win. Before going into battle they tried to humiliate, fatigue and mortify the enemy in a thousand ways.'

And again:

'Have spies everywhere, and take it for granted that the enemy has his. When you discover them, be sure not to put them to death, for they can be most useful to you if you see to it that false statements as to your proposed marches, actions etc., reach their ears, and, through them, those of the enemy.'

The point here to be seized is that the *Depository* is reflecting the amused contempt which in the eighteen-thirties was the current attitude to all things Chinese. With the decline of the dynasty all her ideas were become oddly puerile, 'a collection of pompous, trite, meaningless commonplaces,' as the contributor puts it. But, of course, the merchants resident in Canton saw a stratum of Chinese society very different from that which the Jesuits had described so flatteringly at Peking. The pidgin English, a Viceroy who was himself a smuggler, the Bogue forts, the fanciful language of the Edicts, the Hong merchants, so rich, so amiable, so squeezed, so crooked, so honest, so grovelling—all this was both funny and contemptible.

The Chinese navy was no less a subject for hilarity. The contributor to the *Depository* words it thus: 'What terms can convey an adequate idea of the monstrous burlesque which the imperial navy presents to our astonished gaze? Powerless beyond the power of description to ridicule or portray, yet set forth with all the braggadocio and pretence for which the Chinese are so famous, the marine of this vast empire presents a state of things unparalleled among even the most savage states or islands that we know of: we query much whether a couple of New Zealand war canoes would not be an overmatch for all that could be brought against them. It has been seen that more than once a whole imperial fleet has kow-towed to a single unarmed merchant-man, manned by Lascars; and the miserable equivocations, to which admirals and governors of large provinces have had recourse to get rid of so formidable a visitor, are as well known as the valour with which they have fired at the ship, when sailing away four or five miles from them.' And he describes in detail the Chinese warships, 'large unwieldy-looking masses of timber, with mat sails, wooden anchors, rattan cables, a considerable sheer, flat upright stems . . . with large goggle eyes in the bows.' And he concludes: 'To convey to the mind of a stranger the ridiculous excess of the inutility of the naval establishment of China would, we are well aware, be impossible. Helplessness and cowardice are the chief, we may say the only, points.'

His summary of the situation as a whole is no less trenchant, and coincides with that expressed in the petition sent home by the merchants: 'It seems indeed strange that the whole fabric does not fall asunder of itself: of this we are convinced, that at the first vigorous and well directed blow by a foreign power, it will totter to its base.' He hastens to disclaim any desire for war, declaring it in fact to be extremely unlikely, for the Chinese would give in before any hard blows were struck. But if things are allowed to go on as they are and no commercial treaty is vouchsafed by the deluded Court, a risk is being run. 'Is it wise to wait till quarrels of a murderous nature spring out of misunderstandings?' And he ends with these words, which reflect with much clarity the changed attitude towards China which followed the Napoleonic Wars and England's realization of her new power: 'Of what may constitute, in the eyes of kings and ministers, the just grounds of war, we cannot judge, but that a nation nursing itself, like the Chinese, in solitary, sulky grandeur, and treating as inferiors all other nations, most far its superiors in civilization, resources, courage, arts and arms, seems to us so much of an anomaly that we cannot contemplate its long duration when the scales have fallen from the eyes of the "barbarian" nations, who for so many years have in ignorance bowed the knee to a power which, as to efficient strength, is no more than the shadow of a shade.'

Just as the British were debating the relative military strength of the two nations, so were the Chinese pondering the matter. Their information, however, was very limited. Though they had had to do with a few frigates and had felt the force of their guns, they had never seen any British soldiers. They knew nothing of the Napoleonic Wars nor of the resources, arms or organization of modern armies. Even the most intelligent of them were victims of their own fanciful estimation of China as the hub of the universe. We possess what one of them thought to be a cool and objective assessment of the case. This is a memorial to the Throne written in 1839 by Lin Tsê-hsü, of whom, as Commissioner Lin, we shall hear a great deal more. After explaining that the right way to manage the British was with a mixture of leniency and rigour, the first to soothe and the second to put them in awe, he gives his estimate of their strength: 'Now here is the reason why people are dazzled by the name of England. Because her vessels are sturdy and her cannons fierce, they call her powerful. Because she is extravagant and squanders lavishly, they call her wealthy, yet they do not know that the warships of the said Barbarians are very heavy, taking water to the depth of tens of feet. These vessels are successful only on the outer seas; it is their speciality to break the waves and sail under great winds. If we refrain from fighting with them on the sea, they have no opportunity to take advantage of their skill. Once in harbour their vessels become unwieldy. One, Laboriously Vile, ventured to enter the Bogue. Soon he was struck with fear and returned to Macao to die there. This is clear proof of what I wrote above. As to their soldiers, they do not know how to use fists and swords. Also, their legs are firmly bound with cloth and in consequence it is very inconvenient for them to stretch. Should they land it is apparent that they can do little harm. Therefore, what is called their power can be controlled without difficulty.'

Lin was an intelligent man, a Mandarin of the First Rank, who had held a Governor-Generalship. But he was writing of something about which he knew nothing. He was founding his opinion on the Napier episode, which had turned the way it did because the force which might have backed it was not used. What that force was 'and how it could be used was outside his information.

(ii)

The Affair of the Strangling

After the death of Lord Napier in October 1834, his powers devolved upon his second in command, Sir Francis Davis, who made Macao his headquarters. He had no idea what to do, and decided to do nothing until he received instructions from London. These he could not hope to get until the bad news reached the Cabinet and a new policy was devised, drafted and despatched. All that might take eight months or so. He remained accordingly 'in a state of absolute silence and acquiescence,' as he wrote to Lord Palmerston. The legitimate trade had been re-opened; the ships were lading tea at Whampoa as usual; the illegitimate trade was in full swing at Lintin. There was, indeed, noth-

THE FRIGATES ANDROMACHE AND IMOGENE FORCING THE BOGUE

from a painting by Thomas Allom

VIEW OF WHAMPOA
from an aquatint by W. J. Huggins

ing for him to do except sign manifests, pay rolls and such like. This silence might even cause the Chinese to feel uneasy, he thought, and induce them, perhaps, to make advances. But, in fact, they were the reverse of uneasy. They interpreted the lack of noise to subservience. The Emperor's letters were not anxious but triumphant, when he replied to the reports of his officers at Canton. Far from making advances he thought the moment opportune to strike a blow at the drug trade and re-issued the standing orders that opium smuggling must be stopped.

The proclamations to that effect which were regularly posted up at the beginning of each season caused laughter, for no action was taken to give effect to them, but this time the Viceroy began to take some measures of repression, as if he guessed that the Court was likely to call for a detailed report of what he had done and not be put off by the usual fiction that he had driven the smugglers out to sea. Nevertheless, what measures he took were more for show than in earnest, for he had no intention seriously of hurting his own pocket. The drug trade continued, time slipped by. London remained mute. Though in due course, Davis, and his successor, Sir George Robinson, were told to press for the direct communication with the Viceroy, which had been Napier's object in coming out, the Melbourne administration did not afford either of these Superintendents the power to do so. Sir George in November 1835 actually moved his headquarters to Lintin Island and so was residing at the opium emporium. But he had no instructions to interfere with it and sat there, as idle and useless as his predecessor, watching the clippers transferring the chests to the receiving hulks, and these in turn delivering consignments both to the Chinese boatmen whose employers in Canton had paid in advance and to the British ships which went trading to the several ports on the coast northwards. He was a respectable man, the old East India Company type, and acted on the tenet which the Honourable Company had always maintained that though it might cause to be grown, might buy up and auction all the opium in India, it would have nothing to do with its distribution in China. The close spectacle of the smuggling, however, was not agreeable to Robinson. He eventually wrote to Lord Palmerston in February 1836 that if desired he was well placed to take measures against it. But the British Government had not sent out Lord Napier to discourage smugglers, but to improve the amenities of the legitimate traders, nor had it in any way changed its view in that regard. Sir George continued to watch the clippers come and go under his windows, drew his pay of £6,000 a year and occupied himself as best he could with trifling routine. In December 1836 he retired, his place being taken by Captain Charles Elliot, R.N., whom we have already met as Lord Napier's Master Attendant.

The Viceroy had been right in his first apprehension that the orders from Court directing him to suppress the opium traffic presaged the beginnings of a more energetic policy. In point of fact, the traffic had been under urgent discussion at Peking for some time, a number of memorials having been received.

The submission of memorials to advocate a reform or to deplore an evil had for millenniums been a normal procedure in China. The Board of Censors was maintained for that purpose, though any official was entitled to submit his views: the Government of the empire was less an autocracy than a bureaucracy, each member of which had the right to advise without prejudice. This liberal custom was one of those which had added to the admiration in which China was held in Europe during the eighteenth century. There is an essay, contributed in 1738 to the *Gentleman's Magazine* by no less a personage than Samuel Johnson, in which the Doctor eulogises this practice and contrasts it by implication with the state of things in England, a country which prided itself on being the fountain of free speech. As an admirable and little known example of his style, I will quote from it for the pleasure of the language. 'The student of Chinese history,' it runs, 'will meet with honest Ministers, who, however incredible it may seem, have been seen more than once in that Monarchy, and have adventured to admonish more than once the Emperors of any Deviation from the Laws of their Country, or any error in their Conduct, that has endangered either their own Safety, or the Happiness of their People. He will read of Emperors, who, when they have been address'd in this Manner, have neither storm'd, nor threaten'd nor kick'd their Ministers, nor thought it majestick to be obstinate in the Wrong; but have, with a Greatness of Mind worthy of a *Chinese* Monarch, brought their Actions willingly to the Test of Reason, Law and Morality, and scorn'd to exert their Power in defence of that which they could not support by Argument.'

This is, no doubt, a flattering view of the Chinese Government, but it was true at certain epochs and always represented the theory of Confucian rule. The eighteen-thirties, when the Ch'ing Dynasty was in decline and the bureaucracy had become increasingly corrupt, was hardly a time when one would have looked to see ideals put in practice. Nevertheless, this was what happened, to the vast surprise of the British residents, whose contempt for China was as great as had been their ancestors' admiration.

The memorials submitted by high officials on the subject of opium between 1836 and 1838 were numerous and the views expressed various. It was agreed by all that the widespread smoking of the drug must be stopped, both because the health and honesty of the people were being undermined and because a great quantity of silver was leaving the country. In the view of Chinese economists this drain of silver would, if it were allowed to continue and increase, affect the financial stability of the country by unduly raising the price of silver ingots in relation to copper coin. This view, as expressed, may not have been sound, but it was certainly true to say that the silver so exported would have been better employed on productive enterprises. For a farmer to use his savings to buy opium instead of employing them to improve his farm, or a trader to utilize his profits in the like way instead of seeking to extend his business, was clearly certain to lead to impoverishment. Though this economic aspect of the question has a prominent part in the memorials, the deleterious effect of opium on health and moral probity was not given less stress. 'It will mean the end of the life of the people and the destruction of the soul of the nation,' wrote the Censor Yuan Yü-Lin in November, 1836.

But if the spread of the opium habit was grave, how was it to be stopped? The orders forbidding the import of the drug were disobeyed. The Barbarians continued to offer it on the coast in increasing quantities and the officials whose duty it was to prevent its importation sided with the smugglers and let it in.

This brought the memorialists face to face with the great weakness of the Ch'ing administration, its corruption. We have given several examples of how the mandarins at Canton and along the coast were enriching themselves by an almost open patronage of the drug trade. While the discussions how to suppress it were in progress at Peking, the Viceroy of Canton and all his subordinates were making hay, though with despatches arriving from Court by every post urging them to active measures of suppression, they were obliged to give an appearance of strictness. Thus the Viceroy ordered his river police to pursue relentlessly and seize all smugglers in the river. The police carried out his orders with such thoroughness that presently there was not a smug-boat in commission, and the men arrested were put to death by strangling. Nevertheless the smuggling went on just the same, if it can be called smuggling when the Viceroy himself now chartered a fleet of boats and brought the drug up under his own flag. Some British merchants, also, stepped into the breach and in their own boats, which were armed, boldly carried opium through the Bogue to Whampoa. The

situation would have been farcical, had it not been for the
Viceroy strangling smugglers for what he was doing himself, a fact that caused the British opium magnates to view
the Chinese bureaucracy with increased contempt and to be
certain that no Canton functionary, whatever his protestations, would ever take serious measures to diminish a trade
so profitable to himself; a view which was in error, as the
near future was to prove.

With the Viceroy actually sending his own boats to the
Lintin hulks or receiving ships to take delivery of and distri-
bute the contraband drug, it would have been reasonable to
suppose that as the adjutant and partner of the Barbarians he
would have unbent to them somewhat. But, of course, he
dared not do this, for the Court was watching and he had to
be able to report that he was discouraging them. Indeed, to
cover his tracks, he pretended to stiffen and demanded that
nine of the leading British opium dealers, including Jardine,
should leave the country, though when they made no move
to comply he did not attempt to force them.

His obliquity and finesse are well illustrated by the following. It was his habit from time to time, when he thought it
prudent to impress the Court with his thoroughness, to
apprehend an opium cutter which belonged to the British.
Thus, on 3rd December, 1838, his officers seized a small
consignment which was being rowed away by coolies from
the *Thomas Perkins*, anchored at Whampoa. The coolies
explained that they had been hired by Innes, the merchant,
whose connection with the opium trade has already been
mentioned. The Governor, the Viceroy's colleague, in his
summing up of the case against Innes and another merchant
called Talbot, who was the consignee of the *Thomas Perkins'*
cargo, said: 'For men out of the pale of civilization, who
transgress the laws, the Celestial Dynasty has decreed severe
penalties. But I, the Governor, looking up and imitating the
profound benevolence of the Great Emperor towards people
from afar, have only required the hatches of the said ship to

be closed and together with the foreigners to be driven out of port, in my great leniency forbearing to make deep investigation. This is an act of favour beyond the laws. The said foreigners are fortunate in escaping the net. Will they not, then, reform and reproach themselves.' But he ordered the coolies to be strangled.

Bearing firmly in mind that the last thing the Viceroy wanted was for the British to stop offering opium, though it is possible that he may have found inconvenient their carriage in their own boats of the drug inside the river, let us now consider what he did a few days later on the 12th of the month.

At eleven o'clock that morning a Chinese magistrate with his servants and guards, and two executioners leading a man, entered the square in front of the Factories. When he reached a spot near the American Factory, he halted, descended from his sedan, gave orders for his tent to be erected and for a cross, which his men had been carrying, to be fixed in the ground. It was at this point that some Europeans idling in the square realized what was happening: an execution was about to take place; the man held by the magistrate's henchmen would, as soon as the preparations were complete, be tied to the cross; his neck would be attached to the upright arm by a cord, which would be tightened by inserting at the back of the cross a stick into the cord's loop and twisting it round, thereby strangling the man.

Word was immediately passed to the Factories that the Chinese were about to execute a man on the premises, and a crowd of British merchants came flooding out of the British Factory, which adjoined the square on the east side. At their head was the American, William Hunter. Hunter went up to the magistrate and protested against the square being used as an execution ground.

The magistrate replied that he was acting under the Viceroy's orders, that the man to be executed was an opium-

198

den keeper (not one of Innes' coolies who had been arrested on the 3rd) and the execution was to take place in the square as a warning to the Barbarians who had dealt with him.

Hunter pointed out that the square was private property, having been leased to the foreign merchants as a place for recreation. To which the magistrate replied that it was part of the Emperor's dominions and might be used for whatever purpose local authority deemed proper. A wrangle ensued, the merchants declaring that to turn the only place they had for promenade into execution dock was a gross insult and an affront to their feelings, the magistrate that if they had not indulged in smuggling foreign mud they would have been spared both insult and affront; let them watch the miserable end of a fellow mortal whom they had led into temptation and resolve in the future to be of good behaviour. As he lectured them, he drank cups of tea and smoked a number of small pipes, which were handed to him in succession by his respectful servitors. His clerks looked on with careful smiles, giving him the silent support of their admiration, which minor officials know so well how to offer their chief. His sedan-bearers were happy; the occasion was doubly agreeable—a pleasant strangling to watch and a neat snubbing to listen to. As for the executioners and the unfortunate victim, the former waited patiently to be given the word and the latter, the fatal rope already on his neck, peered in a daze, which was partly due to his ill-treatment in prison and partly to the opium they had given him, less out of mercy than to avoid an improper scene at the last.

Much exasperated by the magistrate's cool insolence, Hunter and the rest declared that come what might they would not allow the execution to take place. The American consul had lowered his flag and a party of British sailors, who had just landed at the steps from the *Orwell* (Captain Larkins) that lay at Whampoa, clustered round, their rough hearts moved to pity for the den-keeper's plight. Indeed, we may suppose that this was now the feeling that dominated the merchants. Everything in their English nature told them that it would be cowardly to abandon to his fate an unfortunate who was no more guilty than themselves. The sailors, their simple minds prompt to the suggestion that throbbed in the air like a spoken command, suddenly made a rush, seized the cross, broke it to pieces and began to belabour with the bits the executioners and the guard. Others tore down the tent, upset the chairs, the table, and scattered the teacups on the ground. They were about to set on the magistrate himself, when the merchants intervened to save him. In the confusion, the guards, who had kept their heads, dragged the prisoner away and prevented his rescue. The magistrate scrambled into his sedan and was carried off, striving all he could to maintain his face. Rather ragged, but determined, the procession reformed further back and, under the magistrate's orders, went to the street behind the Factories, and there in due form did to death the den-keeper.

But the affair was not yet over. A mob, said to have numbered several thousands, and drawn from the most disreputable quarters of Canton, thronged into the square. The merchants, at the rabble's intrusion, had retired into the Factories, but now the cry was raised: 'Clear the square!' A party of the younger and more boisterous sallied out and violently set on the Chinese with sticks. The mob became enraged. Stones and brickbats were snatched up. There was an ugly shout, a sinister clapping of hands. The ragamuffins swelled to eight thousand, while many more came racing in from Hog Lane, took the offensive and drove the odd hundred British and others back into their factories. A concerted attack was then made on these buildings; showers of stones were flung through the windows, the railings were pulled up and battering rams were mounted against the doors.

Thus matters stood at three o'clock. The Chinese, screaming and howling like madmen, seemed about to break in and exterminate the Europeans. The city police were nowhere in evidence. They appeared to have abandoned the foreign devils to their fate.

At this grave posture of events it occurred to somebody that Howqua was the person to whom they must turn, dear Howqua, the senior Hong merchant, so gentlemanly, so amusing with his pidgin, so rich, so fatherly, so human, so slippery, who was always admonishing them with his deprecating smile, who only the previous week had written to his charges: 'Ask yourselves, gentlemen, whether in my place you could be at ease, for there are surely some reasonable men among you.' But how to get in touch with him was the question, for every exit from the Factories was blocked. Finally, Hunter and an American called Nye volunteered to make the passage. They climbed along the roofs until they managed to get down into a shop in Hog Lane. Thence they reached the main street behind the factories and made their way to Howqua's office. They found the old gentleman in an agitated state. News had reached him of the crowd in the square, and, though he did not know that the riot was dangerously increased, he was painfully aware that, whatever the damage, he and his colleagues would have to foot the bill. As soon as he was apprised of the seriousness of the case, he bestirred himself and sent an urgent message to the city's chief magistrate, asking that the police should immediately be despatched. Some little time elapsed, but at last was heard the sound of gongs, announcing the approach of an armed posse. When it was sighted by the crowd, there was a stampede to the outlets. The officers drew their whips and laid about them. Some of the rabble were so terrified that they jumped into the river to swim for it, where several were drowned, the sampan-men paying not the slightest attention to their cries for help. The Chief Magistrate himself had arrived in his sedan and directed his myrmidons to seize three or four of the more prominent rioters, who were flung to the ground and flogged severely. This settled the matter. Calm descended. The magistrate had a chair brought and called for tea. The merchants began to venture out of the Factories. His Honour assured them they had nothing more to fear, that a guard would be posted with lanterns all night. The sun set and he took his departure. Though several of the merchants had been hurt, no fatal casualties had occurred. It was a moderate riot, declared the *Chinese Repository* in its account of the affair, 'compared with what is often exhibited in that line on the other side of the globe.'

Of the official obliquities inherent in this episode mention has already been made, but before leaving it a further elucidation may be offered. It shows how safe the European residents at Canton thought themselves. They had no arms except a few fowling pieces and depended entirely upon the protection of the Chinese police. During the hundred odd years they had been there, they had never before been attacked by the mob. As Jardine, in a diary entry describing the event, admits, there would have been no riot on this occasion had the Europeans not first started to use violence. That they should have provoked the mob shows not only what contempt they felt for anything it might do, but also how certain they were that the Chinese authorities would side with them. So sure of their own safety did they feel that, as the same diary entry shows, they declined to make use of protection offered by their ships' crews at Whampoa. Captain Elliot, the new superintendent, was at Whampoa that day and on the news being received there of the riot sent a hundred armed sailors, who arrived at 10 p.m. when all was over. But the merchants, confident that the Chinese police would prevent any recurrence of trouble, sent the sailors back, after giving them supper.

Returning now to the conferences on the opium traffic, which were taking place at this time in Peking, it will be easy to appreciate the chief difficulty which confronted the memorialists, namely the monstrous corruption of the mandarinate at Canton. How could the opium traffic be stopped when those persons whose duty was to suppress it, battened on it themselves and disguised their malversations with such astuteness? The answer was given by Lin Tsê-hsü, the Governor-General of Hu-Kuang. He presented three memorials, in July, September and October 1838, and the drift of them was that the traffic could be stopped provided that the laws against smokers and distributors of opium were applied with the rigour which he had used in his own jurisdiction of Hu-Kuang. The people there were called upon to surrender their pipes and stocks, and when they did so no proceedings were taken. Where they persisted the death penalty was inflicted. Enormous quantities of the drug were seized. The officials who had shielded traffickers and addicts were frightened into reforming themselves. If this could be done in Hu-Kuang it could be done everywhere.

The Emperor had no private reason for refusing to listen to such memorials. Unlike his officials, he was no beneficiary from the drug traffic. On the contrary, the system of smuggling which had grown up at Lintin was ruining the income he derived from the Canton Customs. Not only was there no profit to him in opium, but he had become unnerved by the argument that silver was leaving the country in such quantities that price levels would soon be upset and some kind of a financial crisis would supervene, the very indefiniteness of its nature making it all the more alarming. He and his Council were therefore disposed to give the memorialists all their attention, for the problem was far more than the mere rescue from a bad habit of about two per cent of the population, that being approximately the figures for smokers. And there was a further point which also influenced them. As has frequently been insisted, the policy of the Ch'ing had been to restrict foreigners to Canton, where they could be watched, it being held dangerous, for a variety of reasons, to allow them to trade at more ports. But the opium traffic, being illegitimate, was uncontrolled; the foreigners were putting in at a number of ports; their clippers were taking soundings all up the coast. All this was highly undesirable, running counter, as it did, to the fundamental policy of China towards the West.

When, therefore, Lin Tsê-hsü came forward with his tried proposals for putting an end to the opium traffic, the Emperor decided to make use of him. He was well known as an honest official. We should conceive of him as old-fashioned, only tolerably well informed, more enthusiastic than practical, and inspired by those ancient Confucian ideals of conduct which the Chinese classics held up to admiration.

In December 1838 the Emperor sent for him and had nineteen interviews with him. The problem, of course, was more than a matter of internal administration. It involved the Barbarians. The policy had always been to soothe. But the suppression of opium would mean irritating them. Would it irritate them unbearably? And if so, were they strong enough to be dangerous? Lin's opinion of the British Navy has already been quoted. He did not think there was any danger. But could the opium which was not on shore in Chinese possession be seized? It was useless to empty the pool if it were to be refilled immediately by fresh importations. How could the authorities get at the chests on the receiving ships at Lintin, on board the clippers along the coast? The preventive police were not equipped to put out to sea, or should they attempt to, fights would ensue which there was small chance of winning. To this conundrum Lin had an answer: all could be accomplished by pressure; the Europeans at Canton were wholly in the power of the Empire; by adopting towards them a less indulgent attitude, by threatening, if necessary by surrounding the factories and detaining the inmates, as had been done in the time of Laboriously Vile, but more thoroughly than then, they could be overawed and frightened into delivering up the whole store of their opium, both at Lintin and afloat; and to prevent the next year's crop being offered, they could be forced to enter into a written undertaking to deal in opium no more on pain of trial before the Chinese Courts and, on conviction, of strangling; and it could be made impossible for British men-of-war to enter the river to rescue them, though, in fact, since the British Government had never given open support to the drug traffic, there was not the smallest risk that any warships would make the attempt.

The Emperor was satisfied that these views were sound and, since Lin was largely their author and was possessed of both the honesty and resolution to give effect to them, he was appointed on 31 December 1838 Imperial Commissioner to Canton with full authority to inspect the offices of the Viceroy, the Governor and the other officials, and to give all orders that he might deem necessary for the eradication of the opium traffic for ever.

It is reported that, when the Viceroy read this posting in the *Gazette,* he fell into a swoon which lasted an hour.

We know why he swooned: his carrying of the forbidden drug in his own boats. But there were further reasons for his faint. We may be quite sure that he had also taken advantage of the stringent orders from Court and had accepted heavy bribes, from those rich enough to pay, to refrain from punishing them. And there was even a third reason for his losing consciousness: in a corrupt administration guilty officials seek to rehabilitate themselves by informing against each other, particularly the lesser upon the greater, for there is then always the chance that by causing your chief to be dismissed you yourself may succeed to his appointment. The Viceroy, therefore, knew that he was surrounded by dreadful perils from which he could hardly hope to emerge with his fortune.

Captain Elliot's Difficult Position

As the crisis had developed Elliot had sought to find the right path through the maze of events. On taking over his duties at Macao as Chief Superintendent his first step was to apply to the Viceroy for leave to go to Canton, for the passive attitude of his predecessors had yielded no results whatever. Knowing that his application would be returned unless worded in accordance with the rules, he framed it as a petition from an inferior to a superior, thereby abandoning the pretension to equality which had been one of the chief objects of the Napier mission. He did this on his own responsibility and without the British Government's concurrence. The Viceroy was pleased. 'The phraseology and subject-matter of the Barbarian's address are reverential and submissive,' he wrote to the Hong merchants, giving permission for Elliot to come up. This was a reversion to the previous state of things; Elliot could now be regarded by the Chinese authorities as no more than the *taipan* or headman of the British merchants, the person with whom the Hong had to deal.

If we study the correspondence which passed between him and Lord Palmerston, we find surprisingly little of moment. Palmerston did not approve of his having petitioned the Viceroy and told him not to do it again, but he did not tell him how he was to avoid the consequences, which would certainly have been the refusal to receive his letters. In fact, the British Government made no adequate statement of policy at this time; Palmerston was feeling his way. Elliot was not let know that he might count on armed support nor was he given authority to interfere with the drug traffic. He was expected, it seems, to see that the legitimate trade in tea went on smoothly, but to shut his eyes, as his predecessors had done, to smuggling. This meant that he was to ignore the main elements of a situation which was becoming increasingly explosive. One can hardly imagine a more difficult situation for a man in an executive position; there was no clear principle on which he could act.

In result he followed a vacillating policy, which pleased nobody. He was not sufficiently subservient for the Viceroy's liking. Hoping further to ingratiate himself and his nation with that functionary, he took the opportunity afforded by the rescue of certain Chinese by English seamen in April 1837 to write him a letter describing the episode and dilating upon the happy consequences which might be expected from the warmth which the rescue would engender between the two nations. For this attempted geniality he was heavily snubbed. The Governor, in a letter to the Hong merchants instructing them to admonish him, pointed out—what had been stated by Chinese authority very very often—that the British merchants were allowed to trade at Canton solely on account of the all-pervading goodness and cherishing kindness of the Great Emperor towards those whose wretched lot it was to be born outside the pale of civilization. 'How can there be', he exclaims, 'what the Barbarian superintendent is impertinent enough to term "bonds of peace and good-will" between the Occupant of the Dragon Seat and the ministering servants to whom he distributes his bounty? The superintendent,' he goes on with stage haughtiness, 'has omitted the respectful expression, "Celestial Empire" and has absurdly used such expressions as "your honourable country". Not only is this deplorably disrespectful, but the ideas that animate it are ludicrous in the extreme.' The said Barbarian, he allows in mitigation, is new to the place and for that reason his solecisms can be viewed indulgently, though not so indulgently that he repeat them, to prevent which the Hong merchants should scrutinize any further communication from him, and if they notice, 'anything, as in this case, inconsistent with propriety or any crude or loose phraseology, they are to return the petition to him at once.'

In regard to the drug traffic, Captain Elliot viewed with alarm the new departure of carrying opium into the river by British cutters. When only the Chinese landed the drug, the importers were able to keep in the background; it was almost possible for them to claim they were not smuggling at all but merely selling a commodity to Chinese buyers. And the Crown's representative could take up the attitude of the late Company and allege that his business was to oversee the tea trade and that he had no hand in or responsibility for the other. But with British boats engaged in direct smuggling close to the provincial capital, it was impossible for Elliot to maintain such an attitude. He was further alarmed because the preventive police from time to time attempted to seize such boats, as we have seen in the case of Innes. Sooner or later one of these encounters would lead to a serious affray. Chinese would be killed, perhaps, and a demand made for the surrender of the British responsible. It was a cardinal principle never to surrender an Englishman to Chinese justice. The old case of the *Lady Hughes* was not forgotten. When, on 12 December, 1838, the riot, far worse than he anticipated, occurred following the attempted strangling opposite the Factories, he felt obliged to take action. Summoning the merchants he declared to them in a heartfelt manner that the open smuggling by British cutters was the cause of what had happened on the twelfth, that the British name was being degraded, the legitimate trader endangered, and that he had no alternative but to order the cutters out of the river.

As we know, this was an incomplete reading of events.

AN OPIUM SALOON AT CANTON
from a painting by Thomas Allom

THE GARDEN OF THE EAST INDIA CO. HOUSE AT MACAO
from a drawing by George Chinnery

The Central Government was concerned to extirpate the whole traffic, not merely the riverine carriage of opium. His order for that to cease was only a palliative and one wholly insufficient to stay the course of events. It pleased no one; the Chinese were unsatisfied, and the British merchants felt that a Crown authority, by taking a stand against opium smuggling, though only in part, thereby admitted the wrongfulness of the whole, an admission which might be highly embarrassing in the future if, as was rumoured, the Court was determined to go to extremes. Indeed, this order of Elliot's helped to convince Lin he need not fear the active wrath of the British Government if he destroyed the traffic, for just as that Government in the past had been loath openly to associate itself with it, so now would it shrink from coming out in its defence. This was the posture of affairs when Lin was appointed on the 31st of December, 1838. Two more months were to elapse before he reached Canton to take over his office. The British smuggling boats did not leave the river, for Elliot, as he had previously complained, had in fact, no way of controlling those engaged in the drug traffic. As the two months went by, he became more and more agitated. Though others refused to believe the Chinese were serious, he was certain of it and had no clear idea how the crisis would turn nor how it could be met. In a letter to Lord Palmerston, written five weeks before Lin's arrival, he describes a long conversation he had on the subject with Howqua, whom age, experience and character had elevated, as it were, to the position of an ambassador. Howqua said that Lin would force the British to give up smuggling opium by stopping the legitimate trade; to which Elliot replied that the British Government would regard that act as unjust and hostile. 'Such is the present sinister aspect of circumstances,' he wrote to Palmerston.

Lin demands the Surrender of all Opium

The rank and file of the English in Canton, who now numbered some two hundred with the influx of new firms after the close of the monopoly, were a happy-go-lucky set of people, who thought the Chinese authorities a joke and put their Edicts in the wastepaper basket, but were fond of the Hong merchants whom they often dined with and with whom they had grown intimate in the half serious sort of way that the English get intimate with Orientals. So they were not in the least alarmed at the prospect of Lin's arrival. He would not differ from the many Chinese officials of whom they had experience. He would make a show of severity, satisfy the Court, squeeze the Hong and depart a rich man.

Hunter and two friends decided to go out and see Lin arrive. It was a Sunday morning, and half past eight o'clock, the 10th of March 1839. In a holiday mood they went on board a small schooner lying off the Factories, for the Commissioner was to enter the city by water. The river presented its usual appearance. The season's tea crop had been bought and already mostly sent down to the ships at Whampoa. Business was being wound up preparatory to the annual migration to Macao. The water was crowded with craft of all kinds; the factory flags streamed out in the morning breeze. The scene was one with which generations of Englishmen had been familiar: the splendid light, the colour, the cries, the hurrying, the jostling, all were there.

Presently the river police began to hustle the various craft close to the shores. A hush fell as a procession of mandarin boats was seen approaching. In the principal one under an umbrella was seated a large corpulent man with a heavy black moustache and a long straggling beard. This could be no other than Commissioner Lin himself. He was soberly though richly dressed, appeared about sixty, and his expression was very firm, almost harsh for a Chinese. He looked neither to right nor left as he was rowed in the utter silence past the schooner, where Hunter and his friends were straining their eyes. Behind came a string of gay boats with the Viceroy, the Governor and other high officials on board, their crews in new uniforms, white trimmed with red, and wearing conical hats of rattan. Further along the front the Commissioner landed, entered his sedan and was escorted by lictors into the city. The three Barbarians hastened back to the British factory to tell their companions what they had seen. In spite of themselves they were impressed; Lin's appearance was so forbidding.

The Commissioner had his plans ready and without delay began to unfold them. But before detailing what he did, it will much clarify the whole field to describe what he might have done. For a century and a half foreign merchants had conducted their business in China under the difficulties which have frequently been described in this book. They were unable to develop it in a modern way by buying and selling wherever the market was suitable, and because they were so restricted had been obliged to purchase tea with silver. This disability had called the opium traffic into existence, for in a wide view that traffic was the only way to hand of financing the tea trade. The line that Lin might have taken, had he been so empowered by the Emperor, would have been to send for Captain Elliot and inform him that if the British Government ceased to offer opium for sale the Chinese Government would remove the age-old restrictions on the legitimate trade, abolish the Hong system, open the ports, allow foreigners to travel into the interior and buy and sell all products freely. An offer of that kind would have been accepted by the British Government. The freeing of the legitimate trade would have led to its enormous expansion and to the making of huge profits on the basis of an exchange of commodities. The finance provided by the sale of opium would no longer have been required, and though, no doubt, prohibition of the growth of the poppy in India would have been difficult and the abolition of the Calcutta sales of opium have embarrassed the revenue of the Indian Government for a time, these drawbacks would have seemed small compared with the splendid prospects of an unlimited China trade.

But his Government was afraid to direct Lin to attempt to negotiate any such bargain. The reasons for its fear have already been given. British colonial expansion seemed a most alarming phenomenon. The recent entry of the British into Burma and Malaya argued that they were solidly on the move into further Asia. Moreover, the momentum of their march eastwards would be increased if their merchants prepared the way for them by undermining the political structure of China with all sorts of novel ideas. Britain was, from the Chinese point of view, as revolutionary a state as later, to Britain, was to be communist Russia. The Emperor dared not offer the bargain described. The *status quo* must remain, but the traffic must go. And to get the British to relinquish it meant force. China had a trump card to nullify British seapower. Lin's plan was to play that card.

Again and again during the previous century and a half, whenever the Barbarians gave trouble, the Hong had been forbidden to deliver tea, the hatches of the ships at Whampoa had been sealed, all labour called off, until the Barbarians saw reason. The East India Company had always been very nervous of this lever, and it had been enough to cause Napier to give in. But Lin proposed to go much further than
212

stopping the tea trade. Its stoppage had turned on the fact that the foreign community in Canton was entirely in the power of the Chinese. Without men or weapons or armed ships nearer than Whampoa, thirteen miles away by river, and these only a handful and not regular forces, the merchants could not resist. The Chinese had always been careful not to push their advantage so far as to aggravate them beyond endurance or put them in fear of their lives. The stoppages were short and were followed by kindly admonishment and indulgent soothing. The Chinese might have been much more unpleasant, but they had held their hand. This time they would not hold their hand but take full advantage of the weakness and isolation of their charges and put them in fear of their bodily safety. In point of fact, they had not the alternative, since the trade for that year was just completed. There is one thing the British never forgive and that is being frightened. How rash, then, of the Chinese to plan frightening a race which, though without material resources on the spot, had the power and resolution to bring them from the other side of the globe!

Eight days after Lin's arrival, the 18th of March, a Mr. Thom was called to Howqua's house to translate an Edict addressed to the foreigners. It began: 'I, Lin, Imperial High Commissioner of the Court of Heaven, President of the Board of War and Viceroy of Hu-Kuang, issue these my commands to the Barbarians of every nation.' After detailing the enormous favours bestowed upon the foreign merchants by the Emperor and the monstrous ingratitude these same had shown by seducing and deluding the sons of the Middle Kingdom by selling them opium, he comes slowly to his point: 'Let the Barbarians deliver to me every particle of opium on board their store-ships. There must not be the smallest atom concealed or withheld. And at the same time let the said Barbarians enter into a bond never hereafter to bring opium in their ships and to submit, should any be brought, to the extreme penalty of the law against the parties involved.'

If they obey these orders, he continues, and thereby manifest their contrition, he will memorialize the Dragon Seat, imploring that they be pardoned their past errors and, as a mark of extraordinary favour, be granted in some measure an Imperial benefaction.

If they do not obey, the army and the navy will be used to force them, and all trade will be permanently closed.

Three days were given for compliance. And Lin ends with these words: 'Do not indulge in idle expectations, or seek to postpone matters, deferring to repent until its lateness renders it ineffectual. A special Edict!'

Along with the above for delivery to the Europeans, the Hong merchants also received, while on their knees before the Commissioner, an Edict addressed to themselves. In it, they were lectured for being too friendly with the Barbarians and for trying to shield them, and commanded to acquire an earnest severity of deportment, to abandon their contumacious disposition, and to act with energy and loftiness of tone by a brisk insistence that the opium be surrendered. If they persisted in their perverted inclinations, then 'I, the High Commissioner, will forthwith solicit the Imperial death-warrant and select for execution one or two of the most unworthy of you. Never say that you did not receive early notice! A special Edict!'

So the business opened, Lin coming into the field at full gallop. Elliot was at Macao and so the British in Canton had no chief on the spot to advise them. Jardine had retired from his firm on 30 January 1839 and sailed for England, his place being taken by Matheson who had returned. But neither Jardine nor Matheson commanded the support of the whole British community, which was split into two factions, as we have seen.

Lin increases the Pressure

The publication of these two Edicts of 18 March caused much excitement, but the merchants who had been in the country the longest and had been accustomed to Edicts of which nothing came, hastened to reassure those who asked nervously what would happen. Nothing will happen probably, they said, and what can happen? The season is over, so the Chinese cannot stop the trade. Nor can they get at the opium, as it is at Lintin or aboard clippers up the coast. The amount at Canton in stock is very small. As a precaution, however, Matheson sent word down to Lintin that what opium the firm had on board their receiving ship, *Hercules*, was to be loaded on clippers and sent up the coast; he could afford to take no risks, for his firm was handling at the time such an uncomfortably large percentage of the total cargoes imported.

The next day, 19 March, Lin fired his second shot. He issued an Edict through the Hoppo forbidding all foreigners to leave for Macao, as they were preparing to do, an order that amounted to their detention in Canton. This had never happened before. Word of it was immediately sent off to Elliot.

Nothing transpired on the 20th except a great deal of talk. The 21st was the last of the three days' grace granted by the Commissioner; compliance with his orders must be shown by that day. At 10 a.m. a meeting of the Chamber of Commerce was convened. After a long and animated discussion, it was decided to temporize. A letter was sent to the Hong merchants stating that the Commissioner's orders involved such complicated interests that it had been found necessary to appoint a committee to report; a definitive reply would be submitted on the following Wednesday, the 27th. This letter was conveyed by a deputation to the Hong merchants, who immediately carried it to the Commissioner.

As the day wore on, ominous signs that Lin was putting on the screw were noticed. All business was brought to a standstill by the shutting of the customs office; the river was closed, normal communication with the ships at Whampoa being cut off by armed junks patrolling up and down; and troops were reported to be assembling in the suburbs. With increasing anxiety the Europeans awaited the return of the Hong merchants. At last, at 10 p.m., they appeared and the Chamber was hastily summoned. On being asked what had happened at the Commissioner's office, Howqua said: 'We took the words of your letter to him, and he gave them to the Prefect to examine. On hearing them read, he exclaimed that you were trifling with us, but that you should not trifle with him. If the opium were not immediately delivered up, he said he would go to the Council Hall of the Hong tomorrow at 10 o'clock, and then he would show what he would do.'

As he spoke, Howqua appeared very agitated, and Mowqua, the second Hong merchant, who was with him, honest stout Mowqua whom some of the British preferred to Howqua, sat visibly trembling. 'If,' said he, 'no opium is given up assuredly two of us will be strangled tomorrow morning.'

The British were much affected by the terror of these men whom they knew so intimately, with whom they had joked for so many years, who had been so honest in their business dealings and whom so often in the past they had seen victimized by their rapacious masters. A few, among them Matheson, suspected a trick, thinking the Commissioner had ordered the Hong merchants to play on their feelings. But the majority, calling to mind the preparations to confine them more closely, were afflicted by the risk and dared not assume that Lin's threats were empty. Certain individuals, unable to bear the thought of Howqua and Mowqua coming to harm, offered a certain number of chests. The Hong merchants were moved. 'You shall not be the losers,' they declared; 'we shall make it up to you afterwards.' This encouraged further offers and at last a total of 1037 chests was reached, representing a value of £140,000 composed in part of chests belonging to the Hong merchants themselves, for like everyone from the Viceroy downwards they also had their share in the traffic.

Next morning, 22 March, Howqua and his colleagues went to Commissioner Lin with the offer of the 1037 chests. Their reception was bad. 'This is merely a fraction of the opium,' he said angrily, and refused to accept it. 'There are tens of thousands of chests and I have demanded them all. Do you think my words are only air?'

The Hong merchants humbled themselves. His Excellency had ordered them in his Edict to show a brisk insistence and an earnest severity of deportment. They had endeavoured to do so and had already succeeded in obtaining over a thousand chests. 'Go and tell the Barbarian, Dent, that I want to see him,' said Lin. 'Why, he alone has six thousand chests and I shall get them out of him!'

They departed on their errand. Mr. Dent was one of the oldest residents in Canton. His firm handled more opium than any other except Jardine and Matheson's. It was late in the day before the Hong merchants saw Mr. Dent. He expressed his willingness to go, though it meant entering the walled city and placing himself wholly in Lin's power. But he was one of those old China hands whose contempt for the Chinese was so great and his affection for them so warm —a curious combination but quite usual among Englishmen with long experience of the Orient—that he could not imagine them doing him harm. However, when his friends protested that it would be only common prudence to apply for a safe-conduct and further information about the Commissioner's intentions, he asked the Hong merchants to return in the morning, when he would go, if all were in order.

At 10 a.m. next day, Saturday 23 March, Howqua and Mowqua reappeared at his house. They presented a melancholy spectacle. The buttons of rank had gone from their caps and they wore iron chains round their necks, the chains that criminals wore when on the way to execution. Mr. Dent, they said sorrowfully, you have brought us to this. Last night when we had to report to His Excellency that you had not obeyed his order to come, he degraded us from our ranks and bound on us these chains which you now see. And he threatened us again that should you not go to him this morning he would take the lives of two of our number. Howqua's son has already been thrown into prison, as has Gowqua, the third of our body.

This they said in pidgin, that language so droll that even a tale as doleful as theirs sounded ridiculous. And among those present were a few who did not believe it, holding that old Howqua and stout Mowqua had got themselves up as disgraced officials in order to move the Barbarians' hearts, more especially as Mr. Dent was known to be a very soft hearted man. But others held it to be no histrionics, that their guise was no masquerade and that their life was really in the balance. What the exact truth is cannot be determined, though there can be no doubt that the Hong merchants were delicately placed.

Everything chivalrous in Mr. Dent's nature prompted him to go forthwith to the Commissioner. But when he made this plain, his friends urgently begged him not to do so. Lin would imprison him in the city and perhaps by torture force him to surrender his opium and sign the bond to be of good behaviour. The Commissioner would then send separately for Matheson and the other well known importers of the drug, constraining them in turn to disgorge. Dent must not go without a safe-conduct from Lin himself. Dent's brother was so violently alarmed that he protested with vehemence: 'If you let him go, I will lay his death at your door.'

When the Hong merchants perceived that Dent would not go or would go only if his safety were guaranteed, they confessed that they dared not carry such an answer back. It was then that John Inglis, a partner of Dent and Company, volunteered to go and tell the Commissioner. The Hong merchants were very grateful. Soon afterwards he set out with three other Englishmen who could speak some Chinese. They were conducted into the city where in a temple dedicated to the Queen of Heaven they had an interview with four senior officials. These asked indignantly how Dent dared to disobey the High Commissioner's summons, and when they were told that it was feared he would be detained, they replied that come he must next morning or Commissioner Lin would have him dragged from his house. Inglis and his companions were dismissed with this message. At midnight the Hong merchants were again with Mr. Dent, urging compliance with the Commissioner's order. A missionary who was present here interposed, reminding Howqua that the next day was the Sabbath, the foreigner's day for religious worship. The old gentleman seemed delighted at the suggestion and was sure that a day's grace would be sanctioned. Application was promptly made to the Prefect who was in the vicinity and he gave answer that Mr. Dent need not present himself till ten o'clock on Monday, 25 March.

On Sunday the whole community went twice to church. That the texts of the two sermons preached should have been 'What is our life?' and 'We must all appear before the judgment throne of Christ' is indicative of the rising alarm that prevailed.

But at 6 p.m. Captain Elliot unexpectedly arrived from Macao and as the Crown's representative took charge of the situation. What he had been doing during the crisis and how he managed to get through the blockade are described in the next part.

(vi)

Captain Elliot to the Rescue

It will clarify the narrative to recapitulate here what was Captain Elliot's legal position. On his becoming Chief Superintendent he inherited the instructions which had been issued to Lord Napier under the Sign Manual of 1833 and these had not since been modified. According to them it was his duty to protect the interests of the British merchants at Canton and to mediate between them and the officers of the Chinese Government, with whom he should pursue a cautious policy nor ask for naval help except in the case of grave necessity arising, and he should shut his eyes to the opium traffic. During the two and a half years of his holding this office, he had pursued an ineffective course, as was inevitable under the circumstances, hoisting his flag some-times in Canton, sometimes in Macao, never recognized by the Chinese as more than head of the merchants nor himself enjoying the merchants' united support. Jardine and his set always thought him a fool because his experience of China was so much less than theirs and because they considered him too subservient to the Viceroy. Moreover recently, when alarmed by the Court's drive against opium he had forbidden British cutters to carry the drug into the river, they held that he had exceeded his instructions, since he had no authority to interfere in any way with the traffic. But though he was neither popular nor well respected, he was of course recognized as the representative of the Crown, and his authority in general was not disputed. His difficulty, however, had always been to know what to do in complexities which Napier had found insoluble and which since then had grown even more baffling. Palmerston had spared little time to correspond with him and, four months' journey from his chief, he was obliged, as the man on the spot, to assume all sorts of responsibilities without being sure in advance of the support he would get. Now in March 1839 he was to have to shoulder responsibilities of a most trying kind, and though personally courageous he had not the steady nerve and aplomb required.

Copies of the two violent Edicts of 18 March and the news of the detention of the British did not reach him at Macao till 22 March, the day after that on which the period of grace expired. Realizing at once that the long expected crisis had arrived, he acted without a moment's delay. First, he wrote to the Governor of Canton, declaring that the late events had destroyed all confidence in the just and moderate disposition of the provincial authorities and demanding to know whether it was their object to make war upon the British nation. To Lord Palmerston he reported this action, declaring his belief that a firm tone and attitude would check the rash spirit of the mandarins. Next he ordered all British merchantmen without the river to assemble in the anchorage between the mainland and the Island of Hongkong, on which at that time were only a few fishing villages. The ships were to be put in a posture of defence in case the Chinese attacked them with fireboats, and were to serve as a refuge to which those free to do so could retire and to which they could send their property. The only ship of war in Chinese waters was the H.M.S. *Larne*, and that was but an 18 gun sloop. Her Commander, Captain Blake, R.N., was ordered to take charge of the fleet of merchant ships. The previous year, 1838, Rear-Admiral Sir Frederick Maitland in H.M.S. *Wellesley*, a ship of the line, had called at Macao in pursuance of instructions from the Admiralty to show the flag, and had gone as far as the Bogue's entrance, but he had left in September. The naval force at Elliot's disposal was thus very small, far too weak to make a sally into the river and rescue the British confined in Canton.

In giving these orders Elliot was fully aware of their embarrassing implications. He was asking the British Navy to protect the smuggling fleet, for some of the ships directed to Hongkong and put under Captain Blake's orders were opium clippers. But his first duty, as he conceived, was the safety of British life and property. If he were afterwards blamed for an action which made the British Government seem openly to back the drug traffic, he would claim that the preservation of British lives took precedence over anything else.

Having made these arrangements Captain Elliot now held it to be his bounden duty to go to Canton and place himself at the head of the British there, or else some desperate calamity would ensue. To go there in the *Larne* would mean a fight at the Bogue and, if he got through, a running fight all up the fifty miles of river against the numerous armed junks which the Chinese had assembled. Accordingly he set out in his own cutter on 23 March. Before leaving he sent a message to Captain Blake to say that should he learn of the situation in Canton having reached a pass sufficiently alarming, he was to adopt such immediate steps as might be necessary.

On Sunday the 24th Captain Elliot passed through the Bogue unmolested and at 4 p.m. was at Whampoa. There he heard that all communication had been cut with Canton for forty-eight hours. Resolved, however, to get through, he put on his uniform, entered the *Larne*'s gig, which he had towed up, and with ensign and pennant flying and his passport and identity papers in his hand called on the senior man-

SELF-PORTRAIT OF GEORGE CHINNERY

A EUROPEAN HOUSE ON THE RIDGE AT MACAO
from a drawing by George Chinnery

darin of the place. To this official he explained that his sole object was peace and the protection of his countrymen, and earnestly begged him to issue orders forbidding guard boats to fire on him. The mandarin was either impotent or unwilling to issue any such order, and Elliot, disregarding his efforts to dissuade him, embarked again on his cutter and pushed on. When within four miles of the Factories he was stopped by armed boats. To their commanders he made similar representations and they did not prevent him from transferring to the gig and proceeding on his way. At a point further on and not far from the landing-steps, a number of boats made as if to cut him off. But, he wrote afterwards to Palmerston, 'the admirable steadiness of the four people of the *Larne* and a commanding favourable breeze enabled me to baffle the attempts to obstruct me and at about 6 p.m. I pushed into those stairs, to the great relief of my distressed countrymen, many of whom had watched the latter part of my approach with feelings of keenest solicitude.'

On entering the garden of the British Factory he noticed that the flag was not flying and immediately had hoisted the gig's ensign, 'for I well knew, my Lord,' he wrote, 'that there is a sense of support in that honoured flag, fly where it will, that none can feel but men who look upon it in some such dismal strait as ours.'

(vii)

Lin succeeds in frightening Elliot

But was he really in a dismal strait? It was true that Lin, after demanding the opium and threatening to use armed force to get it, had forbidden the British to leave Canton and had taken police measures to see they obeyed him; and he had also asked Mr. Dent, the second largest importer of opium, to go and see him. But did that amount to more than legal pressure? Were the British in fact in bodily danger? They were certainly not in any danger if they complied with his demands. But if they did not, were they in danger? Would he, for instance, have seized the leading smugglers one by one, thrown them into prison, subjected them to maltreatment, even to torture, until they sent orders for their clippers to bring in the whole season's importation and until they signed a bond promising never to deal in opium again on pain of submitting themselves to Chinese law?

It is only necessary to pose these questions to be able to perceive that Lin conceived of a gradual pressure: he was not suddenly going to overrun the Factories with an armed rabble and deal in a brutal manner with those in his power. And inasmuch as his method was diplomatic by nature, it would enable the British to counter with diplomacy, to bargain, to threaten on their side, and to make offers, as for instance to curtail the drug traffic in return for concessions in the legitimate trade. In short, it is doubtful whether the situation was as alarming as it seemed to Captain Elliot. There were expedients of all sorts yet to be tried. We have seen that a number of experienced persons there present were disinclined to a panicky view. A perusal of the minutes of evidence taken before the Select Committee on China Trade the following year in London supports the cooler estimate. Mr. Inglis, Dent's partner, and other witnesses then testified that a bargain could have been made had the matter been handled with skill and nerve. But Elliot felt it was a dismal strait and he was in command. It must be admitted that to be detained in the power of a foreign state, when you have broken the laws of that state, is an unnerving experience. It seems that Elliot, who had started from Macao with the idea that a little firmness would soon cause the Chinese to abate their claims, became increasingly agitated as he approached the scene of action; he dramatized both his own courage and the plight of those he came to rescue.

After he had heartened himself by looking up at the flag of old England, he hastened to enquire for the latest news. When he heard that next morning Dent was due to go into the city to meet Lin, he declared that never would he allow such a thing; they must all stand together united to the last nor let one of their members be a scapegoat for the rest. And walking immediately across to the Factory nearby leased by Dent and Company, he insisted with a kind of heroic indignation on saving the astonished gentleman. 'I took him under my arm and brought him to this Hall, where by God's gracious mercy he still remains,' he wrote to Palmerston emotionally.

Then he assembled the whole community in the Hall, adjured them to be firm and calm, and explained how he had ordered the ships to Hongkong for safety. Hardly had he finished before it was announced that every servant in the Factories had been withdrawn by Lin's orders and that supplies of food and water had been cut off. Was it the Commissioner's intention, then, to starve them into submission? Or after weakening them by famine would he attack them? The gongs of the troops occupying Thirteen Factory Street could be heard in the darkness; the square also was occupied by troops; and from the windows they could see men with drawn swords in their hands patrolling right up to the portico of the Hall. Information was also brought in that the river was more closely blocked than before, an arc of boats filled with soldiers being drawn across the whole frontage of the Factories. By the time Elliot got to bed, at a late hour, these carefully adjusted moves had had the effect which Lin calculated they would have and had convinced the Superintendent that, as he phrased it, 'the safety of a great mass of human life hung upon my determination.'

He had already by his actions at Macao assumed a certain responsibility for the drug traffic. He must now assume the whole responsibility, and without instructions from home, indeed against the tenor of the instructions he had, he must engage the Crown in the open recognition of the illegal trade by the admission that the opium in the hands of the British was a property of which it took legal cognisance, for if he declared that he had no control over the drug traffic, the ruin and death of his countrymen would afterwards be laid at his door. And having come to this decision, he applied it in a manner which was extraordinary.

(viii)

Elliot surrenders the Opium

During the two following days, the 25th and 26th, it became clear that, although the Chinese took further precautions to prevent the British either escaping or sending messages for help to their ships at Whampoa, there was not the smallest risk of starvation. Not only were the Factories stocked with stores of flour and salt beef, but the faithful Hong merchants came secretly to the rescue with fresh food. Representing to Lin that breaches of the peace might occur if soldiery ignorant of European customs guarded the doors of the Factories, they induced him to allow them to place their own servants as guards. These men conveyed into the Factories at night, in rolls of bedding, blankets or the like, a quantity of provisions of every sort. The only inconvenience suffered was the absence of servants, but judging from William Hunter's account this was found amusing for a change. Cooking, washing up, drawing water, lighting fires, the merchants enjoyed themselves as if on a picnic.

But neither the jokes and laughter of his companions nor the clandestine good nature of the Hong merchants changed Elliot's decision and on the 27th he revealed it to the community in a public notice. Constrained, he said, by paramount motives affecting the safety of the lives and liberty of the foreigners forcibly detained in Canton, he now required all Her Majesty's subjects to surrender to the Crown the opium under their control for delivery to Commissioner Lin. If they did so, he, as the Crown's representative, guaranteed that they would be indemnified later on. In reporting this momentous step to Palmerston he explained that he had taken it, not only to save the lives of his country-men, but also because 'the forced and separate surrender to the Chinese of all this immensely valuable property by individual merchants, without security of indemnity, must have led to some desperate commercial convulsion in India and England, which might have embarrassed the Queen's Government in an incalculable degree'.

The British read this demand to surrender their opium to the Crown on promise of payment with much complacency. It was good business. During the previous months it had become increasingly difficult to sell opium; the price had fallen and they had considerable stocks in hand. With the arrival of the following year's crop in the autumn, they would be starting the next season heavily overstocked. And if Lin destroyed the opium to be handed over to him, so much the better, for that would send up the price for the new crop. It occurred to one or two to wonder whether Elliot was em-powered to make this purchase, which, as the bill would have to be met by the British taxpayer, should in the ordinary way have been sanctioned by Parliament. But as Elliot did not discuss with the Chamber of Commerce his correspondence with Lord Palmerston, they did not know what might not have passed between him and the Cabinet. Nor were they at all inclined to question their Chief Superintendent's authority in a matter when its exercise was so satisfactory to them. On receipt, therefore, of the public notice they immediately intimated their desire to comply with it.

Elliot's first step towards effecting the delivery was to ask the merchants to send him their books. Adding up the import entries, he calculated there should be some 20,000 chests in stock and without consulting the owners whether this figure was in fact correct, he wrote to Lin stating that he was ready to surrender that amount and that he believed it to be the whole.

We do not know whether the Commissioner was surprised. Elliot had only been in Canton six days; he had not tried to bargain and in one jump had offered to give up ten times more than had the British merchants, both surprising acts to Chinese ways of thinking. But if Lin was not surprised and put down his success to the fear he had inspired, he was certainly gratified. In his reply he said: 'The real sincerity and faithfulness shown are worthy of praise.' He ordered that the chests be collected from the receiving ships, stores at Whampoa, and the clippers at sea, and landed at Chuenpee, whither he would go personally to take delivery. As to the dozen or so American, Dutch and French merchants at Canton, though Elliot could not oblige them to obey him, he was told to use his influence to see that they followed the example of the British. And Lin ended: 'This is the day and time for reformation; if embraced, the enjoyment of unending advantages will be the result.' And acting on the tried Chinese maxim of first to awe and then to soothe, he sent to the Factories a quantity of food, though, thanks to the Hong merchants, there was no instant need. As for those worthy gentlemen, they were astonished at Elliot's naïve compliance. Matheson writing to Jardine in

England records that they said: 'What for he pay so large? No wantee so much. Six, seven thousand so would be enough.'

Lin sent off an express to the Emperor, with instructions to travel 130 miles a day. He detailed the glad news and, intent on soothing, asked His Majesty's sanction to the grant to each individual, who delivered up a chest, of five catties of tea (6½ lbs) 'to reward his sense of obedience and to strengthen his determination to repent and improve himself.'

(ix)

The Destruction of the Opium

Pending the delivery of the opium, which would take some time to collect, the foreign community was kept in detention as before. To encourage them to hurry the surrender, Lin promised that, on a quarter of the twenty thousand chests being landed at Chuenpee, the servants would be allowed back, after a half, the passage boats could ply to Whampoa and Macao, after three-quarters, the trade would be re-opened, and the *status quo ante* would be restored when the whole had come in.

Meanwhile the merchants were instructed to sign the bond by which they engaged never to deal in opium again and to submit to be tried for their lives should they do so. They complied, but the large importers like Jardine and Matheson did so with the fullest mental reservations. Indeed, Matheson at the moment was organizing the Coast Trade from a new base, Manila, having taken the precaution to send Jardine's nephew there just before the blockade began. In fact, even had they wished it, the imprisoned merchants had no way of intimating to buyers in India that they should not bid in the forthcoming sales at Calcutta, which the Government was due to hold in the usual way. It was becoming clear, moreover, that the community would not be living in Canton in future. As soon as permission to depart was granted, they would go to Macao nor return with the winter season. They could not expose themselves in general to a repetition of what was happening nor individual members to the risk of arrest and strangulation. They would have to abandon Canton and trade as best they could from Lintin, Macao or some other place until the reaction of the Home Government was known. Most people believed that the British nation would now be forced to demonstrate its real power in Chinese waters and that that demonstration would suffice to solve the problems of the future. So, not unduly agitated, they waited in Canton until the opium was surrendered and Lin was pleased to let them go.

On 10 April the Commissioner and his staff went to the Bogue to receive the opium which was beginning to come in at Chuenpee. On their way down the river they passed through the fleet of merchantmen at Whampoa, twenty-nine in number, which, though loaded with the season's teas, had been kept waiting all this time for their papers. Highly irritated as many of the commanders were at the delay and the confinement of their countrymen in the Factories, they might easily have captured His Excellency and all his retinue. But Elliot had issued the strictest orders for them to keep the peace, and as they watched the carved and beflagged mandarin boats row by, they did no more than shake their fists.

By the 16th ten thousand chests had been delivered at Chuenpee, and Lin kept his promise about the servants and the passage boats. He was now confronted with the problem of how to dispose of the opium. At first he had thought of sending it to Peking in proof of his zeal and honesty, for it was predicted by his enemies that he would sell it privately and make his fortune, a view shared by many of the British community. The difficulties of sending twenty thousand chests to the capital were many and the risk that on the way much of it would be stolen was great. On reflection he decided to destroy it all at Chuenpee. But it was not easy to destroy so much opium. Were he to try and burn it, there would remain a residue which would supply tens of thousands with enough for a smoke, indifferent indeed, but better than nothing. Accordingly he devised a method of dissolving it in water. There has come down to us an eye witness account of how this was done, for a Mr. King, reputed to be the only foreign merchant who had never smuggled opium, and that for conscience' sake, was allowed to go to Chuenpee and watch the process. After disembarking at the place, he and his wife and Captain Benson, the commander of the vessel on which he had come, were conducted by Lu, a captain, to the scene of operations, which was on the bank of a creek. They saw an area surrounded by a bamboo fence in which were three trenches, 150 feet long, 75 feet broad and 7 feet deep, flagged with stone and lined with timber. The process of destruction was this: the trenches were first filled with water piped from a stream to the depth of two feet. Planks were then put across and coolies emptied baskets of opium into the trenches, while other coolies standing in the water mixed the opium thoroughly with it. After this more coolies arrived with salt and lime, tipped them into the mixture, which was further churned. After a time this caused the opium to decompose, when it was drained off by a sluice into the creek. Mr. King observed the extreme care which was taken to avoid any leakage of opium. Overseers were posted at various points to watch the five hundred workmen employed. Entry into the enclosure was by ticket and on leaving it everyone was searched. While he was there, one man was caught with a small quantity of the drug and instantly decapitated.

At the conclusion of the inspection, Mr. King was informed that Commissioner Lin would receive him in his pavilion on the east side of the enclosure, a large and commodious wooden building. He was taken to the hall of audience, about twenty feet square and a little elevated, and open on the west side so as to command a full view of the trenches. The floor was covered with carpets and on the walls were paintings and specimens of calligraphy. Lin was discovered on a broad chair between two tables with his chiefs of staff seated to right and left. Lesser officials were standing, dressed in light summer silks, silk boots and straw hats crowned with the appropriate button of their rank. Mr. King had never in all his residence in China seen such a crowd of dignitaries; no merchant had ever been received by mandarins of such rank. The extraordinary favour he owed to his reputation as a non-smuggler, and he took it as a very particular compliment. Before entering the hall he had been asked by his conductor, Captain Lu, whether he would make the kowtow and his refusal to do so had been taken in good part. So now he advanced towards the Commissioner hat in hand and standing directly before him made a grave bow, though Captain Lu prostrated himself on the ground.

A long conversation ensued, chiefly about the prospects of the legitimate trade, which Mr. King, as being interested in that alone, was most anxious to see restored to its former tranquillity. Lin was bland and vivacious, without a trace of the fanatic sternness with which he was credited. He looked young for his age, was short, rather stout, with a smooth full round face, a slender black beard and a keen dark eye. His voice was clear, his words distinct. His expression was more that of a thinker than a man of action. Once he laughed outright when Mr. King, on being asked which of the Hong merchants was the most straightforward, was unable to name one. And he frowned, as if the information was unpalatable, when told about the steamships which were just beginning to be used in the British navy as gunboats. It may be that even in the hour of his triumph he was not entirely free from anxiety.

Lin admonishes Queen Victoria

Though Lin had destroyed the 1838-39 opium crop and extracted from the firms in Canton an undertaking to import no more, he was well aware that as long as opium was grown in India efforts would be made to sell it in China. He must try to persuade the British Crown to stop the trade at its source. Accordingly, at this time, he addressed two letters to Queen Victoria, then a young woman of twenty. These curious epistles are preserved in the *Chinese Repository*, and as the second is largely a repetition of the first they may be taken together.

Chinese despatches are more like leisurely essays than official documents. Lin begins by stating the assumption that, though England is twenty thousand miles from China, in certain fundamentals she resembles her, there being in both countries the same distinction between benefit and injury and the same respect for the way of Heaven. The British have certainly received benefits from China; rhubarb, tea, raw silk, are these not the very essentials of life? Nor did the Court of Heaven begrudge them, for it was acting in accordance with the immemorial principle that even those in the farthest confines are human and, so, qualified to benefit by the Sacred Bounty.

But how was this incomparable benevolence received? With ingratitude, with the basest return. A tribe of depraved and barbarous pirates had brought for sale a deadly poison, the which seduced the simple folk, to the destruction of their persons and the draining of their purses. 'We have reflected', he goes on, 'that this noxious article is the clandestine manufacture of artful schemers under the dominion of your honourable nation. Doubtless, you, the honourable chieftainess, have not commanded the growing and sale thereof.'

In assuming the innocence of the Queen's Government and ascribing the drug traffic to the state of inefficiency normal in the administration of a barbarous country, Lin is too generous, for in fact the Cabinet had for long been fully informed. In 1832 a Parliamentary Committee had reported at length on this item of the Indian revenue, the House had debated it and, in adopting the Committee's recommendation 'that it does not seem advisable to abandon so important a source of revenue as the E.I. Co's monopoly of opium in Bengal,' had taken responsibility for the traffic's continuance. Nor in public opinion generally did any stigma attach to those immediately engaged in it; to cite one instance, Jardine on his arrival home in 1839 was soon afterwards returned as a Member of Parliament. But Lin was poorly informed or, it may be, that he desired to save Queen Victoria's face and make it easier for her to comply with his bidding.

He goes on: 'we have heard that in your honourable barbarian country the people are not permitted to inhale the drug. If it is admittedly so deleterious, how can to seek profit by exposing others to its malific power be reconciled with the decrees of Heaven?'

He then admonishes the Queen, declaring that the Son of Heaven is too just to pronounce severe punishment without first affording opportunity for repentance. Let the Queen, therefore, order all opium within her dominions to be destroyed, as he has destroyed all within the Celestial Kingdom. 'You should immediately', he directs, 'have the plant plucked up by the very root. Cause the land there to be hoed up afresh, sow the five grains and if any man dare again to plant a single poppy, visit his crime with condign punishment. Then not only will the people of the Celestial Kingdom be delivered from an intolerable evil, but your own barbarian subjects, albeit forbidden to indulge, will be safeguarded against falling a prey to temptation. There will result for each the enjoyment of felicity.'

And he ends: 'On receipt of this letter, let your reply be speedy, advertising us of the measures you propose to adopt. Do not by false embellishments evade or procrastinate. Earnestly reflect hereon. Earnestly obey. And thus displaying a devout sense of duty and a clear apprehension of celestial principles, you will have the approbation of the great sages and Heaven will ward away from you all calamities.'

This Confucian epistle—it does not seem to have ever reached the royal addressee—rests on the old assumption that Queen Victoria was a tributary sovereign, as were the Georges to whom similar Imperial Edicts had been sent. Indeed, Lin refers to this in the course of the letter, writing: 'You, Queen, sit upon a throne occupied through successive generations by rulers who have been styled respectful and obedient. Looking over the public documents accompanying the tribute sent by your predecessors on various occasions, we find the following: "Those of my people arriving at the Middle Kingdom to trade gratefully acknowledge the Emperor's kindness and justice." ' That kings of the confines had so excellent a sense of propriety was pleasing and His Majesty bestowed on them redoubled proofs of his urbanity. The advantages that England had derived from his condescension had enabled it to become a flourishing kingdom.

All this sounds very odd. That the Chinese should have continued until 1839 the masquerade of the Son of Heaven as Universal Monarch shows an ignorance of reality, a lack of humour and a pedantic conservatism that would almost pass belief did we not reflect that they continued the masquerade into the twentieth century, and that the Japanese reposed faith in a similar make-believe till yesterday.

But reflecting on this letter one is surprised to perceive that, while old-fashioned in one way, it was, for 1839, new fashioned in another; in fact, it happened to express the latest notions of the reforming West. Humanitarianism, which had just had a great triumph with the abolition in 1833 of slavery in the British dominions, was proof of the advancing civilization of England. It had been carried forward a great bound by Wilberforce, and Raffles had given its principles effect overseas, for besides the foundation of Singapore, the key of the Empire's expansion eastwards, he had demonstrated while Governor of Bencoolen in Java that the British had duties towards subject races which transcended the making of business profits. In course of time the view that you should not seek your advantage by causing detriment to other peoples became generally the accepted policy of the empire and it is no exaggeration to say that England's extraordinary position in the world is due as much to her humanitarian practice as to the courage of her soldiers and the enterprise of her merchants.

Lin's contention, therefore, that the sale of opium to China was inhumane and offended conscience was one which, had his letter been generally read in England, would have been acknowledged by a select few as a true statement. And those few would have included, not only men interested in the humanitarian movement, but also thinkers able to perceive that in the long run the British would lose their reputation, one of their most valuable assets overseas, if they persisted in the drug traffic.

The ramifications of the opium question are thus seen to have been very wide. It was ardently discussed in many circles, but the only arguments which could be given for the continuance of the traffic were the practical ones, that its discontinuance was impossible until some other ways of raising revenue in India and of financing the tea trade in China could be found. It was excused, of course, on the ground that the Chinese officials facilitated the entry of the drug and that opium killed no more people in China than did drink in England. But the first argument lost its validity when Lin showed that his Government was taking energetic measures to suppress it, and the second, though you find it repeated to this day by arm-chair historians, was never one which those who have come face to face with the effects of the drug in China have expounded with conviction, for opium is incontestibly a most debilitating and warping poison.

So, it came to this, that though excuses, both practical and other, were made, it was not, nor could it be, denied, that the traffic was disreputable. Nevertheless, the British would not support the idea of being forced into its abandonment by the sort of methods employed by Lin. They would rather fight for a bad reason than bow before the attempted intimidation of a people for whom they had come to have nothing but an amused contempt. That is the root of the matter. Lin handled the British wrongly. His Government could have made a settlement by which, in return for a free trade, the opium traffic would have been gradually brought under control. But instead, it authorized its special Commissioner to try and frighten, to make vain threats to, to seek to browbeat, the proudest, stiffest, most powerful nation in the world.

Chapter V

SLIDING INTO WAR

Lin's Descent upon Macao

By 21 May, 1839, the twenty thousand chests had been delivered for destruction. Lin accordingly reopened the Port of Canton. The foreign merchants were permitted to proceed to Macao, if they so desired; and the ships at Whampoa were given their papers and departed with the season's teas. The only penalty he imposed was that sixteen merchants notoriously concerned with the drug traffic were informed that they would never be allowed to enter Canton again. Among these were Dent and Matheson, who between them had surrendered more than half the total number of chests.

But if Lin hoped that he would be able to report to the Emperor that he had completed his mission by restoring, after its purgation, the even tenor of the trade, he was mistaken. Elliot determined to evacuate the Canton Factories until he received instructions from London, which could hardly reach him until February or March, 1840. He was not going to allow the British community to put its head again into the lion's mouth. Both it and its ships should remain outside the river, if possible at Macao, or, if not, in the anchorage between Hongkong Island and the mainland at Kow-loon. This did not mean, however, that when the season came round again for shipping tea no business was to be done. It was understood that the Americans intended to remain at Canton. The trade would be done through them as commission agents.

The letters which Elliot now sent to Palmerston display his considered, though no calmer, opinion on what had occurred. In one of them he writes of Lin: 'This rash man is hastening on in a career of violence, which will react upon this empire (China) in a terrible manner,' a remark which shows that he anticipated that the British Government would not swallow the affront of the forcible seizure of British property, which he denounced as 'the most shameless violence which one nation has ever yet dared to perpetrate against another'. And he urges upon Palmerston a 'powerful intervention'. He is careful, however, to hold no brief for the opium traffic. He is clearly ashamed of it, writing that it is 'discreditable to the character of the Christian nations, under whose flag it is carried on', and that it will become 'plain buccaneering'. He uses this expression because the destruction of the twenty thousand chests had enormously enhanced the demand, the price having jumped from five hundred dollars per chest to double that amount in some localities, so that, with the prospect of so much gain, smuggling was renewed with violence and desperation. The big firms had their clippers, more heavily armed than before, everywhere on the coast, and plenty of opium was got ashore, handled by formidable gangs of ruffians. All this, so shameful and so ominous for the future, could have been prevented, declares Elliot, had Commissioner Lin at the start taken him into his confidence and opened discussions, instead of blindly rushing upon the merchants with dark menaces. The British Government must take charge of affairs in the China seas, or anarchy and ruin will supervene. And he also writes to Lord Aukland, Governor-General of India, asking him to send ships for the protection of British subjects, pending the general measures to be decided on by the home government. Simultaneously, the merchants also addressed Palmerston, urging him to indemnify them as soon as possible for their losses and to take the most vigorous action against the Chinese.

During June and July 1839 the British resided in Macao, as they had always been accustomed to do at that season, but now everyone was anxious and felt insecure, for it was impossible to tell what steps Lin would take when he realized that the drug traffic, which he had thought destroyed, had revived and was flourishing again.

On 7 July an awkward event had occurred. A number of English and American ships were at anchor in Hongkong road. Some sailors went ashore, and because they were drunk and quarrelsome, they fell to blows with villagers on the eastern side of the anchorage. At the end of the affray a Chinaman was left dead on the ground. The authorities at Canton had always insisted that when a Chinese was killed by a foreigner, the latter must be handed over to them for execution, but since the deplorable case of the gunner of the *Lady Hughes* this had been resisted, and fortunately such cases had been extremely few. Elliot knew that the Chinese would now demand the culprit and as to hand him over was out of the question, he made great efforts to hush up the affair, offering at once the substantial sum of £300 to the family of the deceased, an additional £125 for tips to the mandarins, and £25 for a general distribution in the village. But it was no good. Lin got wind of what had happened. His success over the opium had led him to think that he could force the British to recognize the Chinese criminal courts. Moreover, by this time he had heard of the revival of the drug traffic and planned to use the matter of the affray as a device to bring the British to heel. He, therefore, demanded peremptorily that the guilty seaman be delivered up. Meanwhile, Elliot put six of the rioters on trial before a court convened on board one of the merchantmen. A certain Thomas Tidder, a boatswain, was accused of murder, but the jury held there was no evidence and he was acquitted, though five of the men were convicted of rioting and sentenced to terms of imprisonment and fine. When this finding was reported to Lin, he refused to recognize it and reiterated that a man must be delivered up for Chinese execution. On this being refused—the reason given being that manslaughter had not been proved against anyone—Lin stopped the British trade, though in fact it had already ceased to operate as such at Canton. His object here was to be able to report a necessary stoppage to Court, for the Emperor had become uneasy on hearing a rumour that the British might not return to Canton. It had begun to strike him that perhaps Lin had gone too far and that his measures would endanger the Imperial dues remitted by the Hoppo.

Having made a paper closure of the trade for the benefit of the Court, Lin now cast about how he might force the British to surrender the culprit. To do so was not easy, as they were no longer within his grasp, but not to be thwarted, he took the unprecedented step of descending to Macao with a body of troops. As has been stated, the Chinese kept officials in Macao, having never ceded the place to the Portuguese. But though it remained Chinese property, high dignitaries and troops never entered it. When, therefore, it became known that Lin was approaching, it was believed that he would attempt to confine the British there, as he had confined them in Canton, thereby forcing them to deliver up a man, and at the same time obliging them to stop the renewed smuggling by the clippers. The Portuguese were not to be depended on; they had never been really friendly with the British; their military and naval forces were meagre to a degree and they dared not gainsay the Chinese.

Captain Elliot, whose main duty had become the safeguarding of all British subjects, held it to be unsafe for any of them to remain at Macao. The sloop, H.M.S. *Larne*, had returned to India with despatches and at the moment he had no naval support whatever. On 21 August he issued a public notice advising the British to cross the bay to Hongkong and take refuge there on the merchant fleet.

It will be recalled that the merchants kept their wives and children at Macao. They had commodious houses, set along the ridge and commanding various aspects of the lovely view, where they lived in the greatest comfort, waited on by many servants, their gardens full of flowers, ornamental trees and fishponds. Besides the merchants and their families, many Englishmen were retired there; Chinnery, the painter, was still in residence. It was a great shock for such people to be told, in the hottest month of the year, to abandon their luxurious homes at a moment's notice and live the crowded life of shipboard. But what else was to be done? They were afraid to fall into Lin's hands, knowing him to be elated by his recent success. Experience told them that Orientals were always at their worst after a victory.

Alarm, bordering on panic, was felt by some people. It had become already very unpleasant. The Chinese servants had begun to leave, the shopkeepers were getting very uncivil and even refused to deliver food, and the Portuguese, in the Latin way, made it quite clear that they regarded their guests as tiresome encumbrances. Lin and his troops were encamped north of the Barrier on the narrow peninsula leading to Macao. Since parties of his soldiers roamed the town at night it was thought unsafe to be out after dark. A letter of Chinnery's, addressed to Matheson, has been preserved, and shows the painter to have been in a pitiable state of nerves. 'I am at the top of my stairs!' he exclaims. 'Living in the greatest misery I assure you. To be away is everything to me. I should like to paint a few good pictures (at least try at it) before I'm put to the sword. Rely on it, something serious if not dreadful is coming. I feel it as certain and am in a state of anxiety beyond expression. I need not say how happy I'd be to come out if I dared. I dare not. I was out to breakfast last Sunday, and was accosted coming home; "Mr. C. you are a bold man to be walking about!" Kindly pray do look in on me . . . I passed a night of horror and presentment not to be told. I ran down to the doctor the other night in fear and trembling. I do not go out again, I think, until I cross the Beach.'

Monday 26 August was fixed for the departure to Hong-kong, a number of small vessels being procured for the purpose. The Portuguese Governor was present to see them off and with hollow gallantry saluted the ladies. *The Chinese Repository* thus sums up the scene: 'Men, women and children, all alike were hurried from their residences, to seek a secure retreat on board their ships. This was their only peaceful course. Most of them proceeded straight to Hongkong . . . The little fleet, consisting of small boats, schooners and lorchas, crowded with passengers, presented an affecting spectacle as it moved slowly away from the harbour. But we forbear to speculate on what will be the consequences of this memorable event. Would that timely and friendly interposition of western governments had prevented such an issue.'

What exactly Lin had finally decided to do at Macao is uncertain, whether to seize an English sailor or drive the British out of the place, or, on the contrary, detain them there until they abandoned further smuggling. The Portuguese Governor, who had the grand name of Adriao Accacio da Silva Pinto, informed Mr. Astell of Dent's that the Chinese intended to surround the British homes on the night of the 25th and added melodramatically 'that every European must be slain ere that should take place', though he concluded by saying he could not be responsible for British lives any longer. Matheson, writing the same day to Elliot, declared he did not believe that Lin would go to such extremes, but admitted: 'I think, however, none of our countrymen at Macao will venture to go to sleep tonight.' As, in fact, Lin did not attempt to cross the Barrier, the probability is that he wished only to frighten the British into an evacuation, believing that if they lost their homes on shore they would have to return to England, or that the wretchedness of their situation would eventually oblige them to obey him.

Certain it is that even when the embarkation was taking place he did not advance into the Portuguese settlement nor attack the boats. The schooner, *Black Joke* was, indeed, attacked on the night of the 25th, the only passenger, a Mr. Moss, having his ear cut off and being left for dead. But the seven armed rowing boats, which made the attack, were thought to have been pirates, though the coincidence was extraordinary and added to the alarm already prevailing.

Lin did not cross into Macao until September 3rd, more than a week later. His entry was termed a visit of ceremony to his Excellency, da Silva Pinto. Soon after sunrise his long procession was seen winding in, escorted by a body of Portuguese troops, which had been sent to meet it. From the Barrier it proceeded to a temple courtyard just north of the hill beyond the village of Mengha. The morning was clear and the halting place under the brow of the hill was cool. Here were waiting to receive it the Chinese magistrates of Macao. In front of the middle door of the temple were displayed presents, silver, silk, teas, pigs, and bullocks with their horns decorated with scarlet ribbons. The spectators first saw an officer on horseback. Behind him came gongmen and men holding banners, and a double straggling line of shuffling soldiers. There followed Lin in a splendid sedan, borne by eight porters and escorted by the Portuguese Guard. The rear was brought up by the Viceroy. It was remarked by those present that, though the Chinese soldiers were stout and able-bodied, they resembled European troops of the sixteenth century, and made the Portuguese Guard, a rabble of half breeds, negroes, and Goanese, by contrast appear an up-to-date force.

After Commissioner Lin had been refreshed with cups of tea and had conversed with the magistrates for half an hour, dignified and polite as he seems to have been, and so unlike what the British pictured, who judged by his actions and the incisiveness of his edicts, the procession was reformed, he re-entered his sedan, and was carried to the city gate near the Church of St. Anthony, when a salute roared from the guns of the forts. After passing the gate, the procession made a complete circuit of the town, first taking the road by the inner harbour and, after reaching the south-westerly point, turning east and parading down the whole length of the Praya Grande. By this time it had grown very hot and the soldiers, afflicted by the beating sun, straggled worse than ever, yet withal were pleased, for it was a great day, the English having fled before them. The Chinese inhabitants lined the streets, smiles too on their faces that the foreign devils were down, and had erected arches tastefully adorned with festoons of silk and laudatory scrolls, and before their doors set out tables with vases of flowers, 'in order to manifest' as a spectator was overheard to remark with stunning sycophancy 'their profound gratitude for the visit of his Excellency, the High Commissioner, who had saved them from a deadly vice and removed from them a dire calamity by the destruction of the foreign mud'.

(ii)

The Fight with the Junks

The end of August was the time when the main fleet of merchantmen always arrived. Elliot had forbidden them to go up the river to Whampoa and when the refugees reached Hongkong they found over fifty ships in the road and were accommodated in them without undue difficulty. Matheson had foreseen that his firm's establishment would have to dwell on the water for a time and wrote to his agents in Manila to send over supplies. 'Prepared breadstuffs are what appears to us will be chiefly useful, such as rusks and biscuits of various kinds, for our own use as well as for sailors—of these we should like to have a liberal supply to enable our obliging our friends when wished. Poultry with pigs and provender will be desirable, as many as are likely to come over alive . . . also some of your best beer. Send also some moderately good French claret and some seltzer water if it be had with you.' Matheson here showed his usual coolness and foresight.

The British had been at Hongkong under a week when Lin (it was three days before he entered Macao) issued a proclamation, calling on the officials and people living at Kow-loon and in the neighbourhood opposite Hongkong Island, 'faithfully to intercept and wholly to cut off from the English all supplies, that they may be made to fear and to pay tribute of fealty.' The foreigners, embarrassed by lack of food, he goes on, may attempt to land and forcibly purchase provisions. 'For this reason we make proclamation to all the gentry and elders, the shopkeepers and inhabitants of the outer villages and hamlets along the coast . . . to purchase arms and weapons . . . If any of the said foreigners be found going on shore, all and every of the people are permitted to fire upon them . . . or make prisoners of them.' Even to get water was prohibited.

Lin calculated that this order would end the matter. The ships would either have to sail up to Whampoa, be searched for opium (and their Captains be arrested if any were found), and so submit to all the old regulations of the legal trade, as when the community with its property and shipping was within the power of the Canton authorities, or they would have to go home. A third alternative existed, however; the foreigners might make a fight for it. But Lin did not believe they had the power to win a fight. How could their numbers match his? Besides, their ammunition would give out. So he argued. They must submit, abandon the drug traffic and re-enter the river to do trade in the ancient manner. Why he did not guess that they would be mightily reinforced from home, as soon as the news of the mortal affront he had inflicted on them was known in London, can only be attributed to his total ignorance of world affairs, an ignorance and a rashness far exceeding that of the Chinese Government in the past, for it had shaped its policy on the assumption that Europeans were dangerous, must be kept out or, if let in under regulations, must be soothed, handled with tact and curbed politely. There was evidently much of the fanatic about Lin. By a coincidence, on the very day that he issued this uncompromising edict, the 28 gun frigate, H.M.S. *Volage* (Captain Smith) arrived at Hongkong from India, the answer to Elliot's letter to Lord Aukland, the Governor-General, for protection.

Captain Smith reported that a smaller frigate, the 18 gun *Hyacinth*, was following. This news heartened everybody. Two frigates would suffice to protect the merchant fleet against any attack by armed junks, though there remained the danger of fireboats, a favourite Chinese weapon against ships moored in an enclosed tideway, such as was Hongkong road.

Before the *Hyacinth* came, however, an event of the gravest moment took place. Elliot was obliged to obtain provisions and water for the fleet if he proposed to stay where he was; otherwise, he would have to retire to Manila, which would much upset the arrangements with the Americans at Canton to forward teas to Hongkong. Accordingly, on 4 September he set out to see what could be done. He had with him his cutter, *Louisa*, a small armed vessel called the *Pearl*, and the pinnace of the *Volage*, in which was Captain Smith. Arriving off Kow-loon he saw three large men-of-war junks anchored in line ahead under a strong battery which seemed fully manned. Bringing up abreast of them at a pistol's shot distance, he sent the Reverend Gutzlaff, whose knowledge of Chinese made him indispensable, in a small boat to the largest junk, with instructions to present two papers to the commander. The first pleaded for water and the second for food. When the boat was alongside the junk, soldiers put out pikes to prevent the British party climbing on deck. Gutzlaff, protesting that he and his men were unarmed, was able to reassure them, and presently a man, whom he took to be a naval officer, entered into conversation with him. He could accept no papers, he said, but would be glad to know verbally what the foreigners wanted. Gutzlaff replied emphatically, food and water. The officer said he could do nothing in view of the orders from Commissioner Lin, but had no objection to reporting the matter. 'I turned then to the crew of the junk,' writes Gutzlaff in his account, 'and asked them saying: "Suppose you were without food for any length of time and debarred from buying it, would you wait until the case was referred to the higher authorities or procure for yourself the same by every means in your power?" They all exclaimed: "Certainly nobody will like to starve".' The officer, however, told them to be quiet and in an effort to get rid of his visitor, suggested he should try one of the other junks, where was a more senior officer. Gutzlaff complied and on going aboard it made his complaints and requests again, painting a desperate picture of hunger and thirst, appealing to Chinese humanity and solemnly warning them of the risk of irritating the British too far. He spoke the language very fluently and was used to haranguing the heathen for hours at a stretch. The commander of the second junk wondered also how he could get rid of him and, hitting on the same device as the first, urged him to go to the third junk, where he was certain to obtain satisfaction. Still hopeful, Gutzlaff rowed over to it after returning to the *Louisa* to consult Elliot. On the third junk he made an oration fit to move a stone, (he was an elderly and venerable old fraud of a man) and wound up with menaces, all without effect. The third commander, having no fourth to whom he could direct his visitor, sent word to the batteries on shore to clap in ball and make ready to fire. This hint was sufficient and Gutzlaff withdrew at last, the palavers having lasted for over six hours.

Elliot and Smith had been riding the swell, their impatience growing with the delay. When at last Gutzlaff rowed back to report that nothing had been effected, a boat was sent to a village further along the shore to try for provisions there. The men in charge had succeeded in making purchases and were in the act of loading the stuff into the boat, when a posse of police appeared and forced the villagers to take all back.

On the boat returning empty to the *Louisa*, Elliot, who had had a long and trying day, lost his temper. Smith was not the kind of man to act as a restraining influence, and on Elliot declaring the junks would feel his ball, the Captain seconded him with enthusiasm. The *Louisa*, the *Pearl* and the pinnace opened fire, which was briskly returned by the junks and the battery. The Chinese had five times as many cannon, but that was no advantage as their gunnery was so bad. Not a shot of theirs went home, but the junks were very severely battered. At the end of half an hour all the ammunition he had ready on deck being expended, Elliot hauled off and took his ships out of range, to get up more powder and fill his cartridges. The junks far from attempting to follow, tried to run for it into a little cove, but their sails and oars were so badly damaged that Elliot, his guns freshly supplied, was able to catch them and renew the fight. While he with the *Pearl* bore up to cut them off, Captain Smith hastened back in the pinnace to get his frigate. During this manoeuvre, the *Pearl* fell behind, and the cutter *Louisa* engaged alone the three Chinese men-of-war. But her gunnery and seamanship was so greatly superior that she drove them before her in the *Volage*'s direction. By this time it was growing late, the sun had set. Elliot was obliged to discontinue the action and with the *Pearl* went to meet the frigate. That night Smith urged that he be allowed to sink the junks in the morning and also land men to take the battery. But Elliot, who had had time to cool down and reflect, asked the Captain not to insist and declaring further action injudicious and unnecessary as the junks were already punished and the honour of the British flag upheld, he argued (and this decided the Captain to agree) that it would be unbecoming for one of Her Majesty's ships to finish what a mere cutter had carried effectively so far.

From this sea fight is generally dated the beginning of the first Anglo-Chinese War. When Elliot reported to Palmerston what he had done, he thought it necessary to excuse himself: 'The violent and vexatious measures heaped upon Her Majesty's officers and subjects will, I trust, serve to excuse those feelings of irritation which have betrayed me into a measure that I am certain, under less trying circumstances, would be difficult indeed of vindication.' What Elliot was thinking of in particular was the awkward circumstance that he had fired the first shot, and, still more awkward, that the commanders of the junks had done no more than refuse him permission to buy provisions, a permission they had no power to give. In 1637, two hundred and two years before, Captain Weddell had opened fire on the Chinese for precisely the same reason, that they refused him provisions, though he was in a truly desperate strait for food and Elliot was not. Since that date the British had never attacked the Chinese, though on a few occasions the Chinese had fired on them, as at the Bogue when frigates sought to enter against the regulations. But now on this 5th day of September 1839 an officer representing the Crown, being as vexed as was Captain Weddell on the 12th of August 1637, when he hoisted his 'bloudy Engsign' as signal to engage, followed that old sea-dog's precedent and let go all he had.

The Battle of Chuenpee

The affair of Kow-loon called forth next day a menacing
proclamation from Lin. He begins by listing Elliot's mis-
deeds: that he had failed to deliver the seaman who had
committed the murder; that he had prevented the merchant
fleet from entering the river, a complaint which indicates
how anxious was Lin to get British men and property into
his power again, in order both to exert pressure over the drug
traffic and to be able to reassure the Court that its normal
revenues were safe. The proclamation continues: Elliot's
presumption increasing he has now 'fired upon and attacked
our naval cruisers'. The navy and army will launch an
attack upon him and he will be taken to suffer just punishment at our hands. And it calls upon the Captains of the
merchantmen to desert him and come peacefully to trade or
else 'the gems and the common pebbles will be consumed
together'. The publication of this was followed by the news
that the batteries at Kow-loon had been strengthened by the
mounting of guns able to command the whole roadstead and
that a fleet of fireships was assembling. Moreover, a Spanish
brig, the *Bilbaino*, was sunk in Macao road, being mistaken
by the Chinese for a British opium clipper.

But though Lin continued his line of violent coercion, it is
interesting to observe that the local officials were so alarmed
by Elliot's attack on the junks, that they allowed the
inhabitants of Kow-loon to supply the fleet with all the
provisions and water it required. For a short time this

tendency to conciliate spread. In the course of October Elliot entered into negotiations, the object of which was to permit the merchant fleet to discharge its cargoes at Chuenpee outside the Bogue and ship the tea there, dues to be paid and business done as usual through the Hong merchants, a few of whom travelled to Chuenpee to make preparations. All went so well that some of the British thought it safe to return to their homes in Macao. The Chinese officials who were handling the negotiations even conceded that the Captains of the merchantmen need not execute a bond binding themselves to submit to the punishment of decapitation if any opium were found on their vessels. How far Lin was informed of these details is uncertain. It was Matheson's opinion afterwards that he never sanctioned the condition abrogating the opium bond, though he may not have been averse to carrying on the legal trade as a temporary measure outside the river. But in the last week of October an event occurred which was followed by his repudiation of the new arrangements and his re-issue of the proclamation he had published after the battle of the junks. A British merchantman, the *Thomas Coutts*, arrived and instead of joining the rest at Hongkong, or at Chuenpee, where some were already assembled, sailed through the Bogue and up to Whampoa. Her master, Mr. Warner, was one of those independent sort of Englishmen, of whom there are always plenty about. It seems that he had taken legal opinion on the validity of Elliot's order forbidding British ships to go up to Canton and had been advised it was unsustainable. As he was outside the opium ring and had nothing personally to fear, he signed without difficulty the penalty bond and was given a pass.

His action had the effect of undoing what Elliot had striven for since the departure of the British from Canton the previous May; it put a British ship and a British crew again in Lin's power. 'I presume to say,' wrote Elliot to Palmerston, 'that I am better versed in the particular matter

I am treat:ng, than the legal gentlemen who have arrived at the conclusion upon which Mr. Warner has acted; ... and I believe it would be difficult to point to a more reckless transaction, or to one more injurious in its results, than this of Mr. Warner.' And he explains: 'The natural consequence was a determination upon the part of the Commissioner to break off his concluded arrangement with me; and a demand for the entrance of the whole British shipping upon the same conditions as the *Thomas Coutts*, or their departure from this coast in three days, under menaces of destruction if they remained.'

It was about a month previous to this that Lin had memorialized the Emperor, giving the opinion of British naval power, which was quoted further back. The assumption, therefore, is that he repudiated the agreements partly because of the *Thomas Coutts* and partly because the force of war-junks and fire-rafts which he had been assembling was ready and, he believed, strong enough to overcome the *Volage* and burn the merchantmen assembling at Chuenpee or, in the alternative, force the merchantmen by threat of destruction to follow the *Thomas Coutts*. For the British merchant fleet of some sixty vessels, with an immense amount of property, and with almost their whole community, men, women and children, on board, to have consented to enter the river, would have been a complete victory for him and one may suppose that, to obtain what seemed so near, he was more than usually disposed to minimize the risk he was running in threatening the fleet's destruction, if he were disobeyed. It will have appeared to him that a final triumph was within his grasp; he would soon be able to report to his master that not only had he seized and destroyed the opium crop of 1838/39, but had acquired means of preventing all future smuggling, and forced the British back to the purchase of tea in exchange for legitimate commodities or silver, and under the centuries-old regulations, a state of things conceived for every reason, political and economic, to be the ideal system of trade between China and the West. That he should have been capable of so profound a mistake, not only about the power of the naval force opposed to him, but of the reinforcement from England it would certainly receive in due course, shows in what sort of a dreamland of ignorance wandered the higher Chinese mandarins. The Hong merchants would have taken a more realistic view. The very wharf coolies would have known better.

As soon as Elliot, who was at Macao, heard from Lin of the alternative to enter the river or be destroyed, he wrote to Captain Smith, acquainting him with the circumstances, and saying 'that in this grave conjuncture menacing the liberty, lives and properties of the Queen's subjects', he desired him to collect together the merchant fleet and cause it to ride at an anchorage some distance below Chuenpee called Tung-ku, and himself move to the Bogue mouth on the *Volage* with the *Hyacinth* which had just arrived, there to 'make a moderate, but firm, address in your own name to their Excellencies'.

This phrase was sufficiently explicit for an officer of the character of Captain Smith. He and his men had brooded over having been prevented from sinking all the junks at Hongkong. This time they intended to finish the job. However, the Captain managed to concoct a diplomatic letter in reply. 'I am instructed by the Admiral,' he wrote to Elliot 'to avoid by all possible means collision with the Chinese, yet taking into consideration . . . the menaces of destruction contained in the communication from the Chinese officers, it is my opinion that a firm and decided stand ought to be made.' And he enclosed copies of two addresses in his own name, one to be sent to Lin and one to the commanders of the men-of-war known to be concentrated in the Bogue mouth. The first called upon the Commissioner to cancel his proclamation threatening to destroy the merchantmen if the bond was not signed, and the second peremptorily ordered the Chinese warships to withdraw into the river. 'It will be well to do so,' this letter ended. Elliot agreed that both were well worded.

There followed 'the most serious collision which has ever taken place between Her Majesty's forces and those of this Empire,' as Elliot afterwards described the battle. On 28 October he joined Smith on the *Volage* at Macao and with the *Hyacinth* they sailed to the Bogue at Chuenpee. Though the distance is only fifty miles, it was not reached till 2 November, as the wind was strongly adverse. Both ships anchored a mile below the battery. An imposing force of war junks and fireboats was observed some eight miles away in the mouth of the river. This was the Chinese fleet, a provincial fleet, for there was no such thing as a Chinese navy, consisting of twenty-nine vessels, fifteen being men-of-war and fourteen fireboats. Such a fleet was capable of doing great damage to the merchantmen, if it attacked in darkness and with the tide in its favour. The merchantmen had guns; one of them, the *Cambridgeshire*, was heavily armed, having no less than twenty-two eighteen pounders; but a sudden night attack with fireboats would have been exceedingly difficult to repel. As Lin had plainly stated his intention to destroy the merchant fleet, if his orders were not obeyed, he would have to be deflected either by reason or force. Elliot accordingly asked Smith to begin by sending the first of the two letters already prepared.

A Lieutenant, accompanied by Mr. Morrison, son of the interpreter, rowed over to the flagship—the Admiral was called Kuan T'ien-p'ei. The two Englishmen were politely received, delivered the letter addressed to Lin, and were assured that an answer would be sent without delay.

The next day a Chinese boat containing an interpreter came alongside the *Volage*. The answer, it was stated, had come, and would the English Captain kindly send the Lieutenant to fetch it. Smith replied they should deliver it themselves. They protested, there was some delay, but eventually they went back, as if to get the letter. On their return, the interpreter handed over a package and smiled. When it was unwrapped, it was found to be Smith's letter, unopened, a cool hint of the Admiral's frame of mind.

The look-out on the *Volage* now shouted that the Chinese squadron was on the move. And there was a further complication: a British merchantman called the *Royal Saxon* chose this moment to head for the Bogue, as if with the intention of following the *Thomas Coutts'* example. This was observed and she was brought up by a shot fired across her bows. Elliot now asked Smith to send the second letter, the one addressed to the Admiral. Smith demurred. They had been treated with insolence over the first; moreover, the Chinese fleet was moving out of the Bogue mouth and standing towards them. Was it a moment to exchange letters? He knew a better way of persuading the Admiral. But Elliot, resolved not to act rashly, as he felt he had done at Hong-kong on 5 September, pressed Smith to send the second letter.

Before this could be done, however, it was necessary to take the precaution to weigh. For the frigates to ride, with the Chinese war-vessels continuing to stand towards them, was an imprudence of which Smith was the last man to be guilty; he gave orders and soon both were under commanding sail. At sight of this, the Chinese fleet, instead of continuing its course, came to anchor in a line stretching to the southward from Chuenpee point, a manoeuvre which indicated that it was neither going to attack nor expected to be attacked. During this pause Smith sent the letter to the Admiral with its peremptory order for him to go back, the two frigates being hove to, while the answer was awaited.

Admiral Kuan replied promptly: 'At this moment all that I, the Admiral, want is the murderous barbarian who killed Lin Wei-hi. As soon as a time is named when he will be given up, my ships will return into the Bogue. Otherwise, by no means whatsoever shall I accede. This is my answer.'

That the Admiral should at this stage bring up again the

subject of Lin Wei-hi, the villager who had been killed in the affray at Kow-lun nearly six months before and whose death, as Elliot had again and again assured the Commissioner, could not be fastened upon any of the sailors concerned in the riot, seemed no better than a subterfuge. What was to be done? Elliot knew well what Smith wanted to do—sink the Chinese fleet. But how could he sanction that? The Chinese, after their first threatening gesture of standing towards them, had come to anchor. On the other hand there was Lin's proclamation, with its ultimatum—submit or be annihilated. What should he do? The whole responsibility rested on him. He had had no intimation of what the Cabinet thought of any of the grave events of that year. For all he could guess, it might still be bent on peaceful negotiation. Were he now to precipitate an armed conflict between England and China, would he be upheld or would he be repudiated, cashiered, ruined? He had no means of telling. The British Empire, as he knew well, had been largely acquired by the actions of men on the spot, who did what seemed appropriate without thinking too much. His instinct, however, was to parley further; and he told Smith that an answer to the Admiral's letter would have to be devised.

But Smith had had enough; he had, over his own name, warned the Admiral to withdraw and had added the threat: 'it will be well so to do.' He was not going to be baulked by an irrelevant demand, a monstrous demand for the delivery of an innocent seaman; ample had been said already on that subject. Accordingly he resisted his chief's desire for further correspondence by the following arguments to which he was able to give a professional colour. If the Admiral were not forthwith driven back into the Bogue, he could slip past him when night fell and carry into effect Lin's threats against the merchantmen. The only alternative to driving him back would be for the frigates to return at once and keep close watch over them. But how would it look if Her Majesty's ships seemed to retire before a force moved out with the palpable intention of intimidating them? Such a retirement would not be compatible with the honour of the flag. He could not countenance it. But, as to leave the merchantmen unprotected all night with a flotilla of such dimensions at large was impossible, what alternative was there save to use force? Elliot could see no answer to this argument. Writing afterwards to Palmerston, he said: 'I could only offer Captain Smith the expression of my concurrence in his own sentiments.'

It was now about noon, with a clear sun, an easterly wind and a moderate sea. The Chinese warships were, as before, at anchor in a north-south line, and, so, at right angles to the direction of the wind. The two frigates were hove to near the south end of the line. Smith hoisted the signal to engage, and his ships, the *Volage* leading, bore away in close order, both wind and enemy on their starboard beam. In this way, and under easy sail, they ran up the Chinese line, at a distance of only fifty yards, pouring in their starboard broadsides. The first vessel to go down was a fireboat, the second a warship which blew up. The Chinese had replied with a spirited fire, but their guns, which it seemed could neither be raised nor lowered, failed to score a single hit on the hulls of the frigates, their balls flying too high as the range was so close. The frigates continued their devastating course northwards. On reaching the top of the line they turned and ran down it, this time their larboard broadsides blazing. The Chinese, whom the sudden onset had caught at anchor, had weighed or slipped or cut by now, and, when the frigates were seen returning to finish them, scattered as best they could in their damaged condition, some being deserted by their crews, who took to the boats and rowed for their lives. The conduct of the Admiral, however, was much admired. 'He bore up and engaged Her Majesty's ships in handsome style,' wrote Elliot, 'manifesting a resolution of behaviour honourably enhanced by the hopelessness of his efforts.'

Indeed, so excellent an impression did he make, that when he broke off the action and in a water-logged condition made for the shore, the *Hyacinth* which was ranging alongside was ordered not to sink him. The action was over in three quarters of an hour. By that time four of the men-of-war junks were sunk and most of the others so holed and dismasted that they could never have reached the Bogue, had not Elliot persuaded Smith to let them go, pointing out that as the object had been to cause them to retire, and that to retire was what they were striving to do, to prevent them effecting it would be supererogative. One sailor was wounded on the frigates, which had sustained only damage to their rigging. Thus ended the battle of Chuenpee, in which on 3 November 1839 two frigates of the second and third class were found incomparably stronger than a whole Chinese fleet.

Lin had a difficult letter to write to the Emperor. The complete rout of his fleet knocked the bottom out of his forward policy. But, of course, he did not tell His Majesty he had suffered defeat. He represented the collision as arising over the attempt of the *Royal Saxon* to enter the Bogue, the frigates trying to prevent her and Admiral Kuan doing his best to assist her in. In the result some cannonading took place, but the coolness of the Admiral, who was represented as 'standing erect before the mast, sword in hand and watching the action' prevented the British from having their way. And the Emperor believed this story, conceived that he had won a victory and in a Vermilion Decree commended the conduct of Admiral Kuan and bestowed upon him a high decoration.

(iv)

Jardine in London

It has been mentioned that Jardine left Canton in January 1839 just before Lin arrived. He had formed the intention, without the added incentive of what Lin was to do, of going to Lord Palmerston and pressing him to adopt a vigorous policy. As we know, his view had long been that a demonstration in force would overcome the Imperial Court's objection to a free trade.

The news of the Canton crisis did not reach London till the beginning of autumn, 1839. Jardine had not so far met Palmerston, but now feeling that his case was very much strengthened by Lin's policy of intimidation, he began to seek how a meeting could be arranged. He was well acquainted with an intimate of the Foreign Secretary's called J. A. Smith, a man who was connected with his firm. Smith solicited an interview on his behalf. Writing to Matheson on 16 September 1839 Jardine says: 'His Lordship appointed Saturday at the Foreign Office. We went there and found many people waiting, but no Lord Palmerston. Parties connected with India and China are becoming very impatient. Some talk of calling a meeting to draw up an address. We prefer doing the thing quietly if possible, though the delay is very provoking.' He was quite right in saying that the British mercantile community was becoming restive. There are various petitions from it to Lord Palmerston of about this date. For instance on 50 September 1839 thirty-nine Manchester firms connected with the cotton industry submitted a memorial pointing out that they had cotton goods to the value of half a million sterling at Canton, that those to whose care this property was entrusted had been deprived of their liberty and placed in imminent peril and that in consequence the said firms had suffered damage, and apprehended ruin. To avoid this, they asked for prompt action and reimbursement for all losses they had sustained or might sustain, and urged the making use of the present unjust attitude of the Chinese authorities to obtain a secure, sound and permanent trade in China. On 1 October ninety-six London firms petitioned in a similar sense, as did firms of Leeds and Liverpool on 4 October, and on following days of Bristol and Blackburn. Jardine could thus feel that he was not about to press Palmerston to a course of action to which the country was indifferent, but that on the contrary he had backing of the most solid kind. He was averse, however, to too public an approach, for he was very sensible to the delicacy of the matter, owing to opium being mixed up with it. The Whig administration was noted for its liberal and humane opinions. First under Lord Grey and now under Lord Melbourne, it had passed a series of enlightened enactments, such as those abolishing slavery, improving the Poor Law and providing for state education. In such a reforming atmosphere, the less said openly about the drug traffic the better, thought Jardine, or the Government would be embarrassed, and, alarmed by accusations of going to war to maintain a disreputable trade, might hesitate to take the vigorous action that was necessary. Such were the reasons that prompted him to go quietly about the business.

On 25 September he wrote to Matheson: 'You will be surprised to hear that we have heard nothing from Her Majesty's ministers respecting their intentions, nor have I seen Lord Palmerston. Mr. Smith had an interview with him three days ago, when he told him I was anxious to leave town for Scotland. His Lordship said he was desirous of seeing me, as he had many questions to ask, and added: ''I suppose he can tell us what ought to be done.'' He begged I should not leave until we had met. In his conversation with Mr. Smith he led him to believe that, as far as his own sentiments went, he was convinced serious notice ought to be taken of the gross insult and of the robbery of our drug, but would not commit himself further even to him with whom he is on intimate terms.'

Including his tenure of the post in the Grey administration, Palmerston had been Foreign Secretary since 1830, except for the short interval in 1834-5 when that office had been filled by the Duke of Wellington in Peel's Tory administration. He was the greatest figure in England, far outshining the Prime Minister, Lord Melbourne, and noted for qualities not often seen together, dash and tact, pleasantness and resolution. His policy in Europe had been highly meddlesome, and in Asia that year he had invaded Afghanistan. Jardine saw in him the very man to teach China a lesson and continued to make efforts to obtain an interview.

On 27 September he was received. The scene is given in a letter to Matheson: 'After waiting two hours J. A. Smith, Grant (our late Commodore) and your humble servant were admitted, and having taken maps, charts etc. with us, commenced by spreading them out in order that his Lordship might have a clear idea of the country with which we must cope, should Her Majesty's Ministers determine on or demand redress . . . The extent of armament, number of troops necessary, number of shipping etc., were all discussed, but no direct avowal made to coerce if necessary.' His Lordship kept the charts, saying they were holding a Cabinet meeting on the Monday following. Jardine ends the letter by declaring that he cannot believe the ministry would pocket the insult.

October and November passed without news, but on 14 December 1839 Jardine is able to report to Matheson that the Cabinet had made up its mind to act a decided part and demand reparation. That day he sent Palmerston 'a paper of hints'.

These hints he details in a further letter. A naval force consisting of two ships of the line, two frigates and two river steamers, with transports for seven thousand men, should blockade the Pei-ho River leading to Peking and demand apology for insult, payment for the twenty thousand chests of opium, and a treaty giving free trade through such ports· as Amoy, Foochow, Ningpo and Shanghai. In the event of these demands not being conceded, certain islands should be seized on the coast, the British to promise to return them when the demands were met. The operation would have two effects, the breaking down of the old closed system of commercial intercourse which Lord Macartney and Lord Amherst had striven in vain to effect by diplomacy, and the re-organization of the drug traffic on a sounder, safer basis. But the major object could be put in the front, while the second need hardly be mentioned at all.

How far Palmerston was guided by Jardine we shall see in the next section. The famous merchant prince saw the Foreign Secretary again early in February and almost immediately afterwards the Government's decision was communicated to its representatives in the East, though not to Parliament for several months. Jardine's work was done. With no idea that his health was undermined, he had, though just fifty-five, only another three years to live. He contested the Borough of Ashburton in the 1841 election, when the Whigs were defeated, and was returned to Parliament, as had been other imperial figures of a like bold character in the past. It gave him particular pleasure, he told Matheson, to feel how annoyed would be Dent, who in the old days had often laughed at the idea of his ever expecting to be elected. For two years until his death in 1843 he sat behind Palmerston in the opposition. There is extant a letter which enables us to give him his proper place in history, as not only the greatest of opium runners but as the man who exercised more influence behind the scenes during the planning of the operation to be described, than anyone else. The letter is dated 28 November 1842 and was written by Palmerston to his friend, J. A. Smith: 'To the assistance and information which you, my dear Smith, and Mr. Jardine so handsomely afforded us, it was mainly owing that we were able to give to our affairs, naval, military and diplomatic, in China, those detailed instructions which have led to these satisfactory results.' The reference here is to the Treaty of Nanking under which Britain secured the open trade in China which she had sought for centuries. The letter continues, pointing out how extraordinary it was that the information supplied by Jardine 'and which was embodied in the instructions which we gave in February 1840, was so accurate and complete that it appears that our successors have not found reason to make any alterations in them'. And the noble Lord ends, referring to the treaty: 'There is no doubt that this event, which will form an epoch in the progress of the civilization of the human races, must be attended with the most important advantages to the commercial interests of England.'

The cynic may find it amusing that civilization should owe so much to the man who had made a fortune by supplying the Chinese with opium and whose advice to the Government, while calculated to open the China market in general, was also prompted by the hope that military operations would dissolve those grievous impediments which for so long had hampered him from supplying them in the more generous measure he would have liked.

But entertaining though such a reflection may be, it obscures the broad truth of the situation, as it has here been repeatedly stated, and may be still more cogently expressed by quoting from a paper submitted to Palmerston in November 1839 by the Committee of the London East India and China Association: 'When we find the growth of opium within the territories of the East India Company is a strict monopoly, yielding a large revenue; that the drug is sold by the Government of India in public sales; and that its

destination is so well known that in 1837 the East India
Company's Government actually directed by a public notice
a large sum of money to be given as a bonus to shippers to
China of the season; when we observe that the Committees of
the House of Lords and Commons have enquired minutely
into the subject of the growth of opium; the amount it
contributed to the Indian revenue; and with a full knowledge of the place of its ultimate destination have arrived
without any hesitation at the conclusion "that it did not
appear advisable to abandon so important a source of
revenue"; when we look at the persons composing these
Committees, and those examined before them, consisting of
Ministers, Directors of the East India Company, former
Governors of India etc., etc.; men of all parties and of the
highest moral character; when we know, moreover, that the
India Board, over which a Cabinet Minister presides, has an
effective control over the East India Company and might
prevent what it did not approve—we must confess that it
does seem most unjust to throw any blame or odium attach-
ing to the opium trade upon the merchants, who engaged in
a business thus directly and indirectly sanctioned by the
highest authorities.'

(v)

The Commons Debate

We must now watch how Palmerston steered his Chinese
policy through Parliament. The despatches from the scene

of action had revealed a number of awkward points. One was Elliot's taking over of the opium for delivery to Lin in the name of the Crown. If Palmerston were to honour the implied guarantee he would have to go to the Commons with a bill for some two million pounds. But how could he hope to carry the House with him? There would be a hullabaloo. That the British taxpayer should be asked to compensate opium smugglers might result in his being laughed or hooted out of office. On the other hand, the firms concerned were pressing for payment. The obvious course was to make the Chinese find the money. That alone provided a very material reason for a military demonstration. As Palmerston thought over what to do, he began to see that he had a golden opportunity of solving all the problems which had baffled generations of statesmen. Lin had played straight into his hands. He had been naïve enough in his headlong way to proceed against the whole foreign community in Canton, innocent and guilty, interning them, starving, constraining, insulting them, driving them on to their ships, sparing neither women nor children. And all this heated zeal in a mere custom's dispute! It was a godsend. The Chinese in their long years of intercourse with the West had never had so tactless an official as Lin, who had made the British Cabinet the present of a perfect case. It would be possible for him to go to the House with that story. He would appeal to the nation's honour and get his vote. The outcry of the moralists against the opium traffic would be smothered in patriotic huzzas for the flag. Nevertheless, he had no intention of rushing into the House. The less time given the public to think the better. He would say little or nothing until all the preparations were complete. Fortunately, the expedition could start from India. Ample troops were there, ample ships. Little should leak out at that distance. Only after the expedition was launched on its voyage to China, would he inform the Commons of what he had been doing. There were risks in such a policy, but it was the only way one could get an opium war through a Whig Parliament.

A fortnight after Palmerston had had his last interview with Jardine on 6 February 1840, he wrote to the Government of India. Sixteen vessels of war mounting 540 guns, and including three of the biggest ships of the line, with four armed steamers and transports to carry 4000 troops, were to be got ready with despatch. Admiral Elliot, a cousin of Captain Elliot's, was given the naval command, and was also empowered to act as plenipotentiary along with Captain Elliot in making claims upon the Chinese Government when the expedition arrived off Canton, which it should be able to do by the end of June. Pressure was to be brought by a blockade of Canton, and of Ningpo further up, and of the mouths of the Yang-tse and Yellow Rivers, a move calculated to paralyse all China's external trade. When that was done, a force should sail north to the Pei-ho, the gate to the capital, and there demand payment for the opium seized, certain debts owed by the Hong, the expenses of the expedition, and the opening of the principal ports along the coast, Canton, Amoy, Foochow, Ningpo and Shanghai, to British trade, which should be freed of the Hong system, be controlled by Consuls ranking with Mandarins and be subject to a published and reasonable customs tariff.

These instructions only differ from what Jardine had suggested in that the force put at the plenipotentiaries' disposal was rather stronger. They were received in Calcutta in March, for by 1840 the Indian overland post had been in operation for some time. It may be assumed that preliminary preparations had already been made on the Governor-General's own authority, for he was in touch with Captain Elliot, and he will also have had some earlier hints from Palmerston.

Meanwhile in the Commons there had been a motion for papers. Members wanted to know exactly what had happened at Canton, to see the correspondence with which the reader of this book is already familiar, for all sorts of rumours were flying about. Palmerston promised papers and when on 18 February Sir James Graham, Bart., an opposition member who was to be prominent later in the China debate, enquired when they would be ready, Palmerston promised to go down to his office and hurry them up.

On 21 February Lord Ellenborough asked in the House of Lords whether the publication of the papers would be accompanied by a Government statement indicating the policy pursued and to be pursued, in the form of a message from the Crown. To which the Prime Minister, Lord Melbourne, replied shortly that 'no message would be sent down'. It was that very day that Palmerston had posted his instructions to India.

The papers relating to what had taken place in Canton in March 1839 were laid on the table at a late hour on 5 March, 1840. On the 6th Sir James Graham was on his feet demanding to know why there was no mention in them of the fight at Chuenpee in the previous November when the *Volage* and the *Hyacinth* had engaged a Chinese fleet, reports of which had privately reached him. As Lord Palmerston was not in his place, Lord John Russell, Secretary for the Colonies, replied that no official account of the naval action had yet been received, which was true, for it did not come in for another fortnight.

On 12 March, a Mr. Mackinnon, a member of the opposition, put a very bold question: 'Is there any truth in the report very generally believed that war has been declared against China?'

Evidently something had leaked out, but Lord John Russell was able to devise a prevaricating answer: 'There has been no official intelligence amounting to what the hon. Member has stated, namely a declaration of war,' he declared, though he admitted the Governor-General of India had been sent certain instructions to hold himself ready in case of eventualities. Sir Robert Peel, the leader of the opposition, then asked whether, should the rumour be true about a war, it was to be an imperial war or an armed demonstration only by the Government of India.

Lord Palmerston now intervened. Any communications, he apprehended, that might take place with the Government of China would be in the name of the Queen. Peel then asked: 'The noble Lord has stated that hostilities, if recourse to them are necessary, will be carried on in the Queen's name. Surely in so important a measure as war a formal statement will first be made to Parliament?'

VISCOUNT PALMERSTON: 'I used the word "communications", not "hostilities".'

Other questions were asked, whether instructions more precise than those mentioned had been sent out and also what course would be adopted about compensation for the opium seized. But Palmerston managed to turn off both these dangerous probes for information. Instructions had been sent, he admitted, but it would clearly not be in the public interest to disclose their exact nature. As for compensation, it would not be expedient at present to go further into that.

On 19 March, however, Palmerston could not avoid giving some information, for by then much more had got out and the press was full of criticisms. A Mr. Smith of the opposition, observing that the war-like preparations now going on in India were a matter of public notoriety, and great anxiety existed on the subject, asked whether the noble Lord had any objection to stating the object of the expedition and when it would take place. Palmerston put up Russell to reply, who reported that orders had been sent out to the Governor-General to make certain preparations. The hon. Gentleman now asked what was their object, and he would state it in these general terms—to obtain reparations for insults, an indemnification for wrongful losses of merchants' property, and security for future trade. This answer satisfied the House and the matter was pressed no further, though of course the word 'property' covered a demand for the value of the opium seized, and thereby admitted that the war in part would be an opium war, should it occur.

The situation, however, developed more rapidly than Palmerston had anticipated. While the country remained in doubt whether the Cabinet was committing it to a war in China or not, it was strongly suspected that this was the case. In reforming and humanitarian circles the idea of a war to uphold the opium trade was very repugnant, and as these were the people who ordinarily supported the Whig administration, their disapproval weakened Lord Palmerston. A section of the commercial classes was also dissatisfied. A good many firms had urged a vigorous policy, but there were others who were indignant that the administration had handled affairs so clumsily that the trade was endangered and grave losses apprehended. If the British authorities at Canton had been instructed in what terms to protest and been given sufficient support to back their demands, the present deplorable situation would not have arisen, when it had become necessary to fit out an expensive expedition and submit to all the hazards of open hostilities. Feeling ran so high that Sir Robert Peel decided that the moment was opportune to move a vote of censure, since the chances were good of defeating the Government.

The question was what line to take. For a variety of reasons Peel did not think the moral ground of the drug traffic a good one. On the occasion a few years before when the Parliamentary Committee had reported fully on the opium trade and advised against interference with it on revenue grounds, the Tory Party had raised no objection. They had, indeed, never been associated with any of the recent movements of reform. For them now to found their vote of censure on the moral ground of the traffic's iniquity would hardly be convincing; nor would it appeal particularly in those quarters to which they looked for their strongest support. Far sounder, it was argued, to censure the Government for having by carelessness and incapacity allowed a state of affairs to arise when a quantity of valuable property was endangered and when the whole future of a vast trade was clouded. A careful study of the published correspondence showed that while on his side Captain Elliot had reported at length and continually asked for guidance, Palmerston over a course of years had sent but the most perfunctory replies. Mingled with denunciations of mismanagement they might be able to embarrass the Government still further by apt references to the drug traffic, but they should put themselves forward mainly as the staunch champions of solid interests. Accordingly, a motion was drafted to the effect that the interruption of commercial intercourse with China and the hostile clashes which had occurred were due to the Cabinet's want of foresight and precaution, especially to the neglect of instructing Captain Elliot how to cope with the contraband traffic, which had got out of hand, and endangered the legitimate trade.

A debate had been inevitable in any case, for Palmerston would very shortly have had to go to the House, since the expedition would be starting from India before long. As soon, therefore, as he was apprised of the vote of censure, he fixed 7 April for the debate, confident that his majority was safe, for he held the trump card of insult to the flag and the attempts on the lives and liberties of Her Majesty's subjects.

Sir James Graham moved the vote. He began by pleading the complexity of the subject, though readers of this book, if the author has done his task efficiently, should find it far less difficult than did he or his hearers. After declaring the lively feeling he had of his own insufficiency for dealing with a matter where such mighty interests were at stake, he estimated that one sixth of the whole united revenue of Great Britain and India depended upon the China trade, for British import duties on goods from that country amounted to £4,200,000, while the income derived by India from the trade was no less than £2,000,000, though he did not emphasize that this latter figure mostly came from the opium auctions. Then, after beseeching the House to bear with him in an exhaustive statement, he went right back to the unhappy mission of Lord Napier in 1834, whose failure he ascribed to the ineptitude of the instructions drawn up by Lord Palmerston, who was Foreign Secretary up till November of that year. On the Tories' return to power that month and the assumption by the Duke of Wellington of Lord Palmerston's office, what a different order of things prevailed, even though that Government only lasted till April! He was referring to the noble and illustrious Duke's Memorandum which Members would find in the printed correspondence, a masterpiece of precision and clear thinking, indicating as it did the noble Lord's grave errors and pointing out what should be done in the future. (This was the Memorandum in which the Iron Duke, after laboriously noting his way through the mazes of the China question as it then was, had summed up by formulating the forever famous dictum: 'That which we require now is, not to lose the enjoyment of what we have got.')

On the Duke yielding place to Lord Palmerston again in April '35, the noble Lord, seemingly unable to give his mind to the problems of the trade and omitting to profit by his predecessor's notes, had done nothing whatever, leaving the gentlemen who had succeeded Lord Napier to idle at Lintin and elsewhere, ill placed to communicate with the Chinese authorities and obliged to watch the contraband trade growing so open and flagrant that it invited counter measures to the sure detriment of the tea trade. Again and again had Captain Elliot pleaded for orders whether he should attempt to regulate the opium traffic, giving warnings that it was rapidly degenerating into piracy and declaring the British name to be falling into opprobrium. But search as the speaker might in the correspondence—and he must repeat that it was a labyrinth of inextricable confusion without a clue, without an index or chronological arrangement—he had been unable to find that the noble Lord had sent out any orders beyond a few attenuated jottings which more often than not were contradicted in subsequent letters. So, unguided and unsupported from home, and with inadequate powers on the spot, Captain Elliot was left singularly ill-equipped to cope with the succession of untoward events, which resulted in England, without proper reason, being taken to the brink of war with China. Had there been proper reason, did the national honour demand it, the people would gird themselves for the conflict without anxiety, but when they saw the way things had been mismanaged, would they submit to the taxes which hostilities would involve and continue to repose confidence in an Administration, which had destroyed a great trade that had flourished for centuries, and was bringing upon them a war where success would not be attended with glory and defeat would mean ruin and unutterable shame?

The honourable Baronet's speech was of more than sixteen thousand words and will have taken over two hours to deliver. Replying on behalf of the Government there rose no less a person than Macaulay, the Secretary of State for War. He was thirty-nine years of age and besides being known as a powerful orator was already famous as a writer, his essays having by this time mostly appeared, though the *Lays* were still to come, as also *The History of England*. Young, handsome, animated but essentially simple, he was more an intellectual prodigy than a mature mind. Beginning with the debating point that the motion of censure was concerned with the past and not with the present, there being no word in the mover's speech criticizing the Government's present policy to exact reparation and obtain a settled trade, he went on to point out that in circumstances when letters took six months to arrive it was useless to send detailed instructions, because before they were to hand the situation they were devised to meet had altered. It was common knowledge that the great men who built up the empire had had the spirit to treat all orders from home as waste paper. Had they not done so, there would now be no empire. The instructions which Lord Palmerston had sent were ample, even though they were confined to a paragraph or so. Captain Elliot had not been told to bring the opium trade under control, but what would have been the use of giving him any such order, for it would clearly have been beyond his power to execute it, no matter with what authority they had invested him. To suppress a lucrative trade more was required than to issue an order. In England there was a preventive service, which cost half a million, had a staff of six thousand, and fifty cruisers, but 600,000 gallons of brandy were smuggled every year and an amount of tobacco equal to that which passed through the customs. If in England smuggling could not be stopped, what sort of an immense staff would Captain Elliot have required to put it down in China? That was surely an excellent reason why no orders had been sent him to meddle with the opium traffic.

After some more arguments of this kind, which did not close with the main reality of the case, which was that the growing of opium by the Government of India for sale in China had been allowed by successive Administrations, and that without revoking that permission it were idle to seek to regulate smuggling at Canton, Macaulay turned to the argument on which the Cabinet relied to rouse the House in its support and gave it expression in ringing phrases. This part of his speech is pure Macaulay, and at a time when his style was captivating the country it must have been an enlivening experience to hear it fortified by his eloquence. After a highly coloured description of Lin's barbarities, his demand for innocent blood, his driving from their homes of women with child, of children at the breast, he exclaimed: 'The place of this country among nations is not so mean that we should trouble ourselves to resist every petty slight, but there is a limit to that forbearance. I was much touched, and I believe others were also, by one passage contained in the despatch of Captain Elliot, in which he communicated his arrival at the factory at Canton. The moment at which he landed he was surrounded by his countrymen in an agony of despair at their situation, but the first step which he took was to order the flag of Great Britain to be taken from the boat and to be planted in the balcony. This was an act which revived the drooping hopes of those who looked to him for protection. It was natural that they should look with confidence on the victorious flag which was hoisted over them, which reminded them that they belonged to a country unaccustomed to defeat, to submission or to shame—it reminded them that they belonged to a country which had made the farthest ends of the earth ring with the fame of her exploits in redressing the wrongs of her children; that made the Dey of Algiers humble himself to her insulted consul; that revenged the horrors of the black hole on the fields of Plassey; that had not degenerated since her great Protector vowed that he would make the name of Englishman as respected as ever had been the name of Roman citizen. They felt that although far from their native country, and then in danger in a part of the world remote from that to which they must look for protection, yet that they belonged to a state which would not suffer a hair of one of its members to be harmed with impunity.' And he concluded: 'I beg to declare my earnest desire that this most rightful quarrel may be prosecuted to a triumphal close, that the brave men, to whom is entrusted the task of demanding that reparation which the circumstances of the case require, may fulfil their duties with moderation, but with success, that the name, not only of English valour, but of English mercy, may be established.'

The glow of these sentiments is not entirely dead for us, even though aware they were called forth by a picture of events, the creation largely of Macaulay's imagination. Besides animating the House, the speech told Members, for the first time officially, that there was going to be a war in

China. A Sir William Follett, who now got up to speak for the motion, admitted that the movers might not doubt the justice of a war. What they objected to was the dilatory and hesitating policy which had rendered it necessary. It was not a question of sending Captain Elliot detailed instructions. What should have been given him were adequate general powers, but he was left not only in the dark but without the legal means to do what he himself believed was proper, very different from the independent situation of such men-on-the-spot as Clive or Hastings.

Follett was answered by Sir George Staunton, the son of the Staunton who had been Lord Macartney's right hand man in the Embassy of 1795. As a page he had accompanied that Embassy and the Emperor Ch'ien Lung had complimented him on his precocity. He had also again been at Peking with Lord Amherst in 1818 and had afterwards served under the East India Company in Canton. A clever man and one who knew a great deal about the subject, he lacked weight of character and in spite of attainments, which would have sufficed to carry a stronger man to the top, remained somewhat of a nonentity. His speech for the Government was weak and inconclusive. He expressed surprise that the resolution did not call in question the rightness of the proposed expedition, a tacit admission that the Opposition considered the war, as he did, though reluctantly, to be absolutely just, an admission on their part at which he rejoiced, when he saw newspapers, supposed to reflect their views, declaring it to be atrociously unjust and dishonourable. But it would probably be no easy victory, and he urged any who might think it unjust to interpose now for it was not too late; a fast-sailing vessel might yet stop the armament. He disclaimed any knowledge of the particular policy the Government intended to pursue and he disliked he opium trade but did not see how it could be put down, though he would support a motion to that effect. The new law introduced by Lin authorizing the death penalty for

278

British smugglers might be justified, he admitted, but a little later he declared it to be monstrously unjust. With contradictions of this kind he detained the House a long while and at last sat down, having done nothing except make a confusing subject still more confusing. The sitting ended for that day with a brief speech by a Mr. Sidney Herbert which he wound up in these words: 'Unless men are blinded by faction they cannot shut their eyes to the fact that we are engaged in a war without just cause, that we are endeavouring to maintain a trade resting upon unsound principles, and to justify proceedings which are a disgrace to the British flag.'

On the debate being resumed next day, the House listened with wonderful patience to two long dull speeches by persons of little consequence, neither of whom clarified the issue by coming to essentials. In the third hour Mr. Gladstone rose to support the motion. He was then thirty years of age and had held a junior post in the Peel ministry of 1834/35. His career was before him, but he had been described by Macaulay the previous year as already 'the rising hope of the stern and unbending Tories'. What was the young Gladstone going to say? Would he keep the subject of opium in the background and speak on the motion or would his moral indignation take hold of him? It did take hold of him as he proceeded, and he inveighed against the Government with increasing violence. The latter part of the oration may be summarized in the following terms: 'Am I to be told that because the noble Lord has been a meddler in one part of the world, this is to be held an excuse for his doing nothing in another part? The noble Lord has shown that there are some things which he is ready enough to do, and those which he has done have frequently been found as mischievous as those which he did not do. I will ask the noble Lord a question. Does he know that the opium smuggled into China comes exclusively from British ports, that is from Bengal and through Bombay? If that is a fact—and I defy the right honourable Gentleman to gainsay it—then we require no preventive service to put down this illegal traffic. We have only to stop the sailings of the smuggling vessels; it is a matter of certainty that if we stopped the exportation of opium from Bengal, and broke up the depôt at Lintin, and checked the cultivation of it in Malwa, and put a moral stigma upon it, that we should greatly cripple, if not extinguish, the trade in it. I do not mean to blame the noble Lord for not having done this by means of a despatch. The interference of Parliament would have been necessary. But the noble Lord would only have had to declare us his difficulties and the Legislature would have granted him what legal power he lacked.' And looking at the Government bench he declared solemnly: 'The great principles of justice are involved in this matter. You will be called upon, even if you escape from condemnation on this motion, to show cause for your present intention of making war upon the Chinese. They gave us notice to abandon the contraband trade. When they found that we would not, they had the right to drive us from their coasts on account of our obstinacy in persisting in this infamous and atrocious traffic. I am not competent to judge how long this war may last, but this I can say, that a war more unjust in its origin, a war more calculated in its progress to cover this country with permanent disgrace, I do not know, and I have not read of. The right honourable Gentleman opposite spoke last night in eloquent terms of the British flag waving in glory at Canton. We all know the animating effects produced when that flag has been unfurled on a field of battle. And how comes it to pass that the sight of that flag always raises the spirit of Englishmen? Because it has always been associated with the cause of justice, with opposition to oppression, with respect for national rights, with honourable commercial enterprise, but now, under the auspices of the noble Lord that flag is become a pirate flag to protect an infamous traffic. No, I am sure that Her Majesty's Government will never upon this motion persuade the

House to abet this unjust and iniquitous war. Yet without pronouncing upon the abomination of the traffic and the war, the charge against the noble Lord is equally complete. In whatever sense he ought to have interfered, he ought to have interfered with spirit and effect, nor allowed the drug traffic to have gone to the extent which it has reached. If the noble Lord had ever read those papers—yes, I repeat, if the noble Lord had ever read those despatches—for it is to me a matter of doubt whether he has read them . . . Gentlemen may cheer, but I will never believe that he has read them, till I hear him make with his own lips a declaration to that effect. Yes, I want to hear that declaration from himself. The noble Lord has certainly done all in his power to keep us in the dark with respect to them and now, when at last he condescends to give them to us, he gives us them in one vast rude and undigested chaos which the wit of man is incapable of comprehending. I therefore think it more charitable to believe that the noble Lord has never read these despatches than to suppose that, having read them, he was so ignorant of his duty as to make no application to Parliament. The noble Lord is chargeable; on his head and on those of his colleagues responsibility rests for the indolence and apathy which have brought about this pass, unless the House should deem fit to negative the motion of my right honourable Friend and, if it does, it will become a voluntary participator in that great and awful responsibility.'

The independence of Gladstone is well shown in this indictment. He was not speaking as a party man to a party motion with the primary object of displacing the existing Government, but as a statesman voicing the conscience of his country. The Opposition had, of course, no objection to the speech in so far as it discredited Palmerston and the Whigs and so contributed to carrying the motion, but the prospect of having itself to suppress the opium trade at source and of being faced with the problem of Indian revenue and the financing of the tea trade, should the Government have to resign as the result of the motion, was hardly one it could anticipate with confidence. The House adjourned shortly afterwards without anything further of importance being said.

On the third and final night of the debate, Peel, as leader of the Opposition, rose to sum up at a late hour. His speech, which was a long one, was made to a House grown impatient for a decision after three nights spent in listening to a confusing and inconclusive wrangle, which often wandered far from the point, the limits of the subject being difficult to determine. Peel decided to take it back to the point—the omission by Lord Palmerston to give the British representative in Canton sufficient instructions and powers in a difficult pass, thereby bringing on a situation which could only be resolved by war. The tenor of his speech will be gathered from the points which follow. The most effective way of carrying a vote of censure, he declared, would have been a motion denouncing the opium trade and deprecating the war. But he did not deny the necessity of hostile intervention, for violent outrages had been committed by the Chinese. A war was necessary owing to these outrages, but they would not have taken place had the Government shown a reasonable foresight. The country could not now avoid war, for its honour was engaged, but should withdraw its confidence from a ministry which had unnecessarily got it into an embroglio from which only the arbitrament of war could extricate it. His references to the drug traffic were from the same angle—when report was made to Palmerston that it was becoming a matter of acute difference between China and England, he should have applied himself diligently to the problem, but in fact did nothing. Thus Peel declined to follow Gladstone along the path of moral indignation. We may suppose that he would have done so, had he really thought he could carry the House. But evidently he feared that Macaulay's speech about the flag and the sacred duty of protecting British subjects overseas from the presumption of foreign tyrants had expressed the deepest convictions of many members and that a majority would insist on an armed demand for redress, no matter how iniquitous the drug traffic might be. But his case against Palmerston of having let things drift into a state of war was not as damning as he could have hoped, because a solid body of commercial opinion, well represented in the House, had been wanting a naval demonstration for a number of years, believing that to be the only way the Chinese could be forced to make a modern commercial treaty. Those of that opinion, therefore, would never blame Palmerston for bringing on, whether by right or otherwise, the very armed intervention for which they had long been asking. Moreover, when all was said, it remained a paradox to call a war just but the Ministers who had undertaken it misguided.

Feeling that he had little to fear, Palmerston rose to answer for the Government. He was fifty-six, his age being greater and his Parliamentary experience longer than Peel's, while over Gladstone he towered in years and worldly wisdom. Throughout he freely mingled banter with severity, seeking as much to laugh, as to beat, down the vote. We may listen to him here and there. 'If the resolution of the right honourable Baronet who opened the debate were not so pointedly directed at the department, which I have the honour to fulfil, I should not—and I wish to say it without meaning the slightest offence—think it necessary to address myself to a motion so feebly conceived and so feebly enforced.' Was it necessary to keep the House talking for three nights on the question whether certain answers to certain letters should have been more or less precise? The Duke of Wellington had been warmly felicitated for answering one letter the day after it was received. He could show—and he demanded the credit for it—that he had answered two letters the day after they were received. 'I gave the Superintendent instructions, and have been blamed because they were not long enough. Gentlemen who make long speeches think, I suppose, that I should write long letters. They imagine that precise instructions contained in a few but significant words are not proportioned to the length that they had to travel; they imagine that when you write to China your letter should be as long as the voyage.' And what were the added instructions they expected him to have given? They had not dared say out what they were, but had implied that he should have told Captain Elliot to expel every smuggler and drive away every clipper. But such a monstrous and arbitrary power and open to grave abuse no Government had ever entrusted to its representatives, for it was totally at variance with English law. And supposing such instructions to have been sent, they would have been no better than waste paper without the force to give effect to them. 'I wonder what the House would have said to me, if I had come down to it with a large naval estimate for a number of revenue cruisers to be employed in the preventive service from the river at Canton to the Yellow Sea for the purpose of preserving the morals of the Chinese people, who were disposed to buy what other people were disposed to sell them. Why, the House would have granted me not a single farthing. Nay, I verily believe that if I had set out to execute the laws of China on behalf of the Chinese Government, and had attempted to establish a vigilant police to do in China what our police cannot accomplish here—namely, put down smuggling—the House would not have treated my proposals with serious levity, but would absolutely have laughed them out of court.' That there was no need for any such suppression in China when all the Government had to do was to stop the growth of the poppy in India, he answered by pointing out that the motion did not state that any measure should be taken to diminish that growth, and, in parenthesis, declared his doubt whether the usual effect of destroying a monopoly would not ensue with a vast increase of the product, in this case probably an uncontrolled cultivation in Turkey, Persia or those Indian states in whose

internal administration Britain had no say. And he turned
on the mover a flood of persiflage. 'The motion of the right
honourable Baronet, steering clear of all the difficulties of
the case, evading all the real circumstances, attempted by a
side wind bearing upon an incidental part of these transactions either to cripple the measures which Her Majesty's
Government had adopted for the accomplishment of the
objects which they had in view, or else to take the matter
out of their hands in order that the right honourable
Baronet and his colleagues might themselves reap the har-
vest of which Her Majesty's Government had sown the
seed.' At this sally there were Whig cries of 'Hear!'. But
perchance, went on the noble Lord in a roguish tone, 'it was
only out of kindness and compassion that the right honourable Baronet has come forward nobly, volunteering in his
own person to bear the consequences of impending and
inevitable defeat.' Nevertheless, he dared hope that his
honourable friend might be spared the exhibition of his
generosity, since the objects of the expedition would probably be accomplished without resorting to hostilities, for
the Emperor, a very different person from Mr. Commissioner
Lin, would be brought to that sense of justice which was
generally said to inspire him and would be eager to end the
dispute with an amicable settlement. And changing his tone
again, he declared solemnly that until redress had been
obtained for the many humiliations heaped upon British
subjects from the time of Lord Napier or before, there could
be no self-respecting trade. At this point he read out a
petition which, he said, he had recently received from the
China firms 'that unless measures of the Government are
followed up with firmness and energy, the trade with China
can no longer be conducted with security to life and property
or with credit or advantage to the British nation,' its signa-
tories headed by his secret counsellor, Jardine. His final
point was strong and unexpected, and calculated to reassure
the House that the war would lead to no international com-

plications. Here was a memorial, he said, holding it up, which the American merchants of Canton had presented to Congress in January 1840, in which they denounced Lin as a robber and gave it as their belief that if a naval force from England, France and America appeared on the coast a treaty could be obtained placing foreign trade on a safe footing, and that without bloodshed.

Sir James Graham rose to reply, as mover of the motion, and began by saying that if the House would permit him, he would like to follow the noble Marquis through the various parts of his speech. But it was very late and members were heartily tired of the subject. There were cries of 'Divide, divide!' and when the honourable Baronet attempted to continue, he was howled down by reiterated shouts of 'Divide!'. After further efforts to be heard, he gave way at length and resumed his seat. Nevertheless, it was a close thing: the motion of censure was defeated by only nine votes.

Chapter VI

WAR

(i)

A Smuggler's Sea-fight

We left Captain Elliot on 3 November 1839 victorious over the best fleet that Lin could send against him and we saw how the latter represented the collision to Court as one more example of the disgraceful behaviour of the Outer Barbarians. In Europe a naval action of the sort would have created a state of war between two countries, but in Chinese political thought there was no such thing as war. Since the Son of Heaven swayed the whole world, the fight at Chuen-pee Point could be no more than a civil breach of the peace, when the Celestial authorities, having failed to soothe the rebellious Foreign Devils, were obliged to punish them for their boisterous conduct. To soothe and admonish in the right sequence and proportion, that was the secret of sound diplomacy. But this policy, which had been remarkably successful for centuries, was not working so well now, for Lin had been obliged to admonish more often than he soothed. His triumph in getting the opium had encouraged him to believe that he could continue to admonish with safety. Now, however, some of the Emperor's advisers were beginning to whisper that his actions might lead to the very situation which it had always been the main object to avoid, a greater rather than a lesser intrusion of the Barbarians. But these voices of warning had not yet the Emperor's ear. He continued to support Lin. He did not know that an

288

VIEW FROM KOWLOON ACROSS TO HONG-KONG

from an aquatint by J. Prendergast

THE FALCON, FLAGSHIP OF JARDINE AND MATHESON'S OPIUM
CLIPPER FLEET
from a contemporary print

expedition of formidable proportions was preparing; and between November 1839 and June 1840, when the expedition arrived, he gave no instructions to return to soothing. But though he made no concessions nor sought to restore old trading relations, in fact there was a lull, due more to deadlock than to any decrease of crisis, for the Chinese were unable to get at the British, and the British could do nothing until they were reinforced.

In December 1839 there were thirty-two merchantmen at anchor in Hongkong and the road north of it, Tong-ku. They were managing to tranship their cargoes by arrangement with the neutral Americans and were receiving tea so steadily that Elliot was able to report to Palmerston: 'It is a striking and gratifying fact that up to this time the lawful import trade of the current year has been done more advantageously than any of a like period since the close of the Company's Charter in 1834.' During these months the merchants and their families moved, sometimes to Macao and sometimes back to shipboard, according as tension declined or increased.

The drug traffic, too, was doing exceedingly well. This may be illustrated again from the records of Jardine and Matheson. After the firm had delivered the odd six thousand chests, which was its share of the 20,000, it had five hundred left in stock. At Singapore waited its schooner, *Hellas*, with a thousand more on board, the first of the new crop. She was ordered to Manila, where the young Jardine, a nephew, was waiting to start operations, the Spanish Government of the Philippines having given him every facility. On the arrival there of the *Hellas*, he had six schooners at his disposal and with these offered the drug along the China coast. The firm's receiving ship, *Hercules*, was anchored at Hongkong and was used as a post office and treasury. The demand was small and about £140 a chest, but at Singapore, where the new crop was accumulating, the price was only £50. Matheson, being convinced the demand and the price would rise when the coast Mandarins recovered from their fright at Lin's measures of repression, decided to buy at Singapore, a departure from the firm's usual practice of confining itself to carrying and sale on commission. In June 1839 he purchased nearly £30,000 worth there and ordered another £8,000 worth from Calcutta. These purchases put him ahead of Dent and the other opium runners, and for nine months he had a virtual monopoly of the drug. His profits over the season averaged 200%. By April 1840 competition had become severe and profits less certain, and the firm returned again to its previous commission policy. In this way it far more than made up the value of the surrendered 6,000 chests, and still held the Crown's guarantee, given by Elliot, that it would be compensated for that loss, as, indeed, it eventually was. Thus the opium seizure, though represented as a high-handed action and insult that required to be avenged, was in point of fact enormously profitable to this firm. Their fleet of a dozen or more vessels was splendidly equipped, heavily armed and manned by crews as bold as could be desired. The flagship was the *Falcon*, a brig formerly the property of Lord Yarborough. She was a full-rigged ship, massively but beautifully masted in rake and proportions. Her yards and spars were equal to those on a ship of twice her capacity. It was her breadth of beam that enabled her to carry such a spread. Her fittings were unusually elegant, substantial and costly. Where metal was employed it was mostly brass and copper, and this included even the belaying pins. The stanchions, skylights and coamings were of mahogany. The officers' cabins were extravagantly luxurious. Of her, one of her mates wrote in the *Yachtsman*: 'She was easy, handy and smart in every evolution. She swam like a duck and steered like a fish. She was fast, yet dry, lively yet stiff. No academician draped a classical figure with more consummate taste than that with which our sailmaker draped the *Falcon*. Nothing in still life could be more picturesque than her sails which, unfurled at anchor or in a calm, fell in full heavy graceful folds from her yards and booms. Nothing could confer so strikingly the same triumph of art, when the same sails were filled and trimmed, in the first case presenting a cloud of swelling segments, pressing forward in living rivalry, in the second place held like boards by sheet, tack and bowline, the rounded luff and foot leaving no rift twixt spar and canvas; in both cases gladdening and satisfying a seaman's heart. We trusted more to spread than to hoist; and in going free the show of canvas upon our square yards, further extended by lengthy stern-sail booms, would leave the observer in no doubt of the pressure under which the beautiful fabric trembled and vibrated in its headlong career. It was in the *Falcon* I began to comprehend a singular belief that prevails among seamen. She appeared to resent every neglect of her handling and rebel at once against any over pressure or any tampering with her trim, so that our common expressions, that she was complaining or sulking or huffed or offended, seemed to us rightly applied. "She can do everything but speak" was a common remark among the crew.'

That heartfelt testimony, that reads almost like a bit of Conrad, though written by a smuggler of his opium clipper, is the authentic voice of seafaring England.

The Chinese authorities sought, when they could, to sink or capture these vessels. In May 1840, just before the expedition's arrival, the *Hellas* (Captain Jauncey) was lying becalmed off the *Brothers*, islets on the coast at Namoa near Swatow. Close by were eight junks and three large rowing boats, which Jauncey mistook for traders, until they got out their sweeps and closed in on his schooner. He cleared for action, but the junks came up astern so that his broadside could not bear. When close enough their crews flung oil pots on to his decks, and set him afire, and in the confusion thought to board and overwhelm him. But while some of the *Hellas* crew dealt with the flames, others leaped on to the junks and fought with sword and pistol. For four hours a hand to hand struggle raged, it being never possible to use the schooner's cannon. A Malay tindal cleft the captain of one junk to the chin, and the mate, McMinnies, boarding another with two native mates did such mischief that the Chinese jumped overboard and swam for their lives. In the fight Captain Jauncey lost an eye. At last a breeze filled his sails and he was glad to escape. Twenty-five of his crew had nasty wounds. The *Chinese Repository* mentions Jauncey's arrival at the Macao hospital, and, though a journal that never showed approval of the drug trade, deeply condoled with him.

But the firm's Captains were very serious men, more serious than the partners always found convenient. We find in one of Matheson's letters: 'The *Gazelle* was unnecessarily detained at Hongkong in consequence of Captain Crocker's repugnance to receiving opium on the Sabbath. We have every respect for persons entertaining strict religious principles, but we fear that very godly people are not suited for the drug trade. Perhaps it would be better that the Captain should resign.'

Thus, while Parliament debated and the expedition was got ready, both the legal and illegal trade flourished in a manner and to a degree that differed considerably from the gloomy picture of danger and privation painted by the Government and which had enabled it to justify itself.

Lin is dismissed and succeeded by Kishen

In its issue of June 1840 the *Chinese Repository* noted: 'The British expedition to the East yet excites but little interest among the Chinese. Some even seem to doubt its coming, though preparations are making to resist they know not what. The state of public affairs here (i.e. Macao) and the vicinity remains quiet. With deep anxiety we await the arrival of the expedition and its consequent events.' Before June was out sixteen men-of-war, four armed steamers of the East India Company, and twenty-seven transports, carrying 4000 Irish, Scotch and Indian troops, had arrived. The fleet consisted of three seventy-fours, the *Melville* flying the flag of Rear Admiral the Honourable George Elliot, Commander-in-Chief and Plenipotentiary; two first class frigates, forty-fours; three second class, twenty-eights; with eight sloops carrying from eighteen to ten guns. This fleet, which assembled gradually in the vicinity of Hong-kong, was far larger than any the Chinese had ever seen. But Lin was not intimidated. He issued a public edict, which if it represents his real belief shows that he mistook the object of the expedition. 'English warships are now successively arriving at Canton, and though it is certain that they will not venture to create disturbances, nevertheless, like rats they will enter all the ways in order to protect those base followers who sell opium.' And he ordered the fortifi-

cations to be improved and the formation of a sort of Home
Guard of fishermen, boatmen and villagers, their duty being
to attack any soldiers who landed and burn the ships, if
possible, with fireboats. He apostrophizes these unarmed
ragamuffins thus: 'Valiant heroes, let not the heads of the
base foreign devils long be wanting! Establish your character! Act like men! So will you be possessed of an excellent
name and rich rewards.' And he described himself as sitting
in his office with a scale of rewards hanging on the wall:
twenty-thousand dollars to be paid for a seventy-four (with
discount of a hundred dollars for each gun less); five
thousand for a naval commander alive, or one third of that
sum dead; white rank and file a hundred, coloured twenty.
And he assured his heroes that the usual 10% commission
would not be deducted by the issuing officials. So, as best he
might, did Lin prepare to sink the British fleet and take
captive its men, the meticulousness of his absurd arrangements making them the more preposterous.

We already know in general of what the British plan consisted, that it was to seize a port or two up the coast, appear
in force at the mouth of the Pei-ho, make demands direct to
the Emperor through his appointed plenipotentiary, and by
this demonstration of power, coupled with a promise of
withdrawal, obtain open trade, compensation and a fixed
emporium. Accordingly, at the end of June the expedition
sailed north to put this plan into action. Elliot's inclination
was to avoid serious fighting and to obtain satisfaction by
threat and negotiations. He was naturally of a humane
temper, but his attitude had also a practical side: general
hostilities would interfere with the trade and might be
protracted, while armed diplomacy should yield very rapid
results. Matheson, however, was not so sanguine and wrote
that the more tender Elliot showed himself about the trade,
the stiffer the Chinese would become, for it had always been
a cardinal belief of theirs that the British could not exist
without tea and, incidentally, rhubarb, which at that time

we got from China, and so could not hold out long if the trade were stopped.

Elliot had been sent a letter from Palmerston for delivery to the Chinese Government. In it the 20,000 chests of opium are described for the first time as having been surrendered only as a ransom for the lives of the British at Canton. It contained a demand that the opium be restored or its equivalent in cash paid, and enumerated the other demands we are already familiar with. This letter had to be delivered and, as the warships sailed north along the coast, some of them stopped near Amoy, three hundred miles up, and tried to send it ashore to the authorities there under a flag of truce. But the Chinese had never heard of such a flag and, when informed of its significance, still refused to allow any British sailors to land. The attempt was abandoned and the fleet proceeded on another four hundred miles to Chusan Island, south of the estuary of the Yang-tse River. The chief city of the island, Ting-hai, was summoned to surrender on 4 July and, when the Governor refused, the place was occupied by landing parties next day without opposition, for the Chinese were totally unprepared to resist. It was placed under a British administration, old Gutzlaff being made one of the magistrates. As his Honour, the City Magistrate, this is the last we hear of the Prussian missionary.

Leaving some ships to blockade the Yang-tse mouth, the fleet sailed on to the mouth of the Pei-ho, another eight hundred miles. This put the British within a hundred miles of Peking. Here at last the letter was delivered to a Manchu dignitary, Kishen, who was Grand Secretary, and Viceroy of the Metropolitan Province.

When the Emperor received it and realized that Lin's policy had led to the Barbarians arriving in force almost at the gates of the capital, he had a revulsion of feeling against his trusted representative and sent him a violent letter of dismissal: 'You have dissembled to Us,' he pronounced, 'disguising in your despatches the true colour of affairs. So far from having been of any help, you have caused the waves of confusion to arise. A thousand interminable disorders are sprouting. You have behaved as if your arms were tied. You are no better than a wooden image. And as We contemplate your grievous failings, We fall a prey to anger and melancholy. Your official seals shall be immediately taken from you and with the speed of flames you shall hasten to Peking, where We will see how you may answer Our questions. Respect this! The words of the Emperor.' Lin was tried and exiled to Ili, a cold frontier town with no amenities.

Meanwhile the Grand Secretary Kishen, one of the richest Manchu officials in the empire, was appointed Plenipotentiary to negotiate with the two Elliots, which he began to do on 30 August. His instructions were to soothe and employ every finesse to induce the Barbarians to leave the capital and go back to Canton. By a lavish use of flattery and promises he effected this in a fortnight. 'Let us all adjourn to Canton where it is so much easier to ascertain the facts in dispute. I can assure you His Majesty is most graciously inclined. He understands how provoking Lin must have been, and loving, as he does, strangers from afar, you may rest assured of his vast condescension. Let us adjourn, therefore, to the provincial city, and I can promise that you will be wholly satisfied.' Such was the gist of his protestations, which sapped the warlike resolution of the two Elliots. In his letter to the Emperor written on 17 September, two days after they had departed with the fleet, he explains how he succeeded, using a phraseology suitable for the Imperial ear: 'Although the Barbarians are bold and defiant, and scarcely amenable to reason, nevertheless they soon became well disposed on receiving words of praise. Indeed, I found that even if in a boastful mood they could be moderated by pleasant phrases. But Your Majesty is daily confronted with innumerable problems. These trifles do not warrant a turn of the Holy Glance.'

The Plenipotentiaries sailed south in good spirits. Writing to Matheson, Captain Elliot confidently declared: 'We have not brought you back a great waving olive branch, but I think we have a twig of the blessed plant in our portfolio. So far as I can judge, the Court has deliberated upon peace or war and decided that peace is the wisest course.' He and the Admiral put in at Ting-hai to inspect, where an armistice was arranged, if one may speak of an armistice after such token hostilities. By 20 November they were back at Macao.

This withdrawal by the British, when, as it were, they held the Court by the throat, the Chinese misinterpreted as weakness. The Barbarians must be less formidable than was thought. Before his dismissal Lin had written to the Emperor: 'People may say that our junks and guns are no match for the British, and that ingenious diplomacy is preferable to a protracted war. But O they do not know!' This view now began to receive support again. As things stood China had lost Ting-hai, but that was all. Only about a thousand British troops had been landed and half of them were suffering from fevers and dysentery. When the Imperial forces were assembled, they could retake the town. Meanwhile Kishen should be sent to Canton with orders to draw out the negotiations and give time for the army to concentrate and strike. The Emperor, who, when the British were at the Pei-ho mouth, had expressed some moderate sentiments, under the influence of these views now noted in vermilion: 'After prolonged negotiation has made the Barbarians weary and exhausted, we can suddenly attack them and thereby subdue them.'

Quite ignorant that the discussions were to be fictitious, Elliot (his cousin, the Admiral, had fallen ill and gone home) began putting the British case to Kishen, who had taken Lin's place as special Commissioner at Canton. But by the beginning of January 1841 he realized that he was being played with and that he must use the force at his disposal to bring the Chinese to their senses. The blow he believed

297

would have this effect was to seize the two forts at the mouth of the Bogue, Chuenpee on the east and Tycocktow on the west, for the Chinese were very sensitive about the gate to Canton. Accordingly, early on 7 January 1841, line-of-battleships with frigates, steamers and transports moved in to the attack. The engagement lasted from 9.30 to 10.30 a.m. Both forts were taken, 500 Chinese being killed and 300 wounded. There were no fatal casualties on the British side. Nothing now prevented the fleet from entering the Bogue and capturing the two inner forts and that on Tiger Island, thereby laying open the way to Canton. But Elliot called off the action, being of opinion that enough had been done to force Kishen to agree to the demands which had been discussed for so long. 'I hope we shall settle without further bloodshed,' he wrote to Matheson. 'The Commissioner knows that we can take much more than he would like to lose whenever we please.'

Kishen, in fact, immediately became amenable. By 20 January an agreement, known as the Convention of Chuenpee, had been drawn up and signed by him and Elliot, acting as plenipotentiaries for their two countries. Its terms were shortly these: cession of Hongkong to the British Crown; an indemnity of six million dollars by annual instalments of a million; official intercourse to be on an equal footing; trade to be re-opened at Canton and carried on there until Hongkong was ready.

Elliot and Kishen are dismissed

Elliot thought he had secured everything that was necessary. The island of Hongkong was a strong place with a grand harbour. The firms could build their warehouses on the north shore and as it was ceded territory organize the trade as they liked without interference, without regulations and without the Hong merchants. That would be the real free trade they had wanted for so long. The indemnity was not very high; it only just covered the bare market price of the opium at the time of seizure, and so left out of the reckoning the Hong debts and the cost of the expedition; but he knew that the firms had, in fact, benefited by the seizure and the compensation would be clear profit. Moreover, the general trade would rapidly expand under the favourable circumstances of the new port, so that a stiff indemnity was not an urgent requirement. The expedition, too, had not been expensive, having accomplished its task in under six months. And it was a great satisfaction that there had been so little bloodshed.

Matheson, who was generally inclined in his letters to call Elliot too mild and hesitating, had no criticisms on this occasion. Writing to Jardine he expatiates on the advantages of Hongkong and expresses himself as pleased and confident of the future. That there was not a word about the drug traffic in the Convention was a matter of satisfaction. Opium could be stored at the new port without contravening the treaty, and distributed thence with far greater propriety.

Kishen was also pleased. His face had been saved, he thought. With the cession of Hongkong, Ting-hai was returned and he felt the Emperor would be much pleased at the exchange, for Ting-hai was a large town half way to the capital, from which Nanking, the second city of China, could be threatened and the vast trade of the Yang-tse blocked with ease, while Hongkong was a barren rock far in the south. He had cheated the Barbarians and extricated the Empire from a threatening pass. As for the six million indemnity, the Hong merchants would be squeezed to get that.

But the glow of satisfaction felt by both the British and Chinese plenipotentiaries was to be rudely extinguished by their respective masters. As soon as the news reached Palmerston he wrote a crushing letter to Elliot. It is dated 21 April 1841. Since his dressing down in the Commons for not sending out East precise and ample instructions, and in spite of his sarcastic disclaimers that it was practicable so to instruct a man on the spot, he had addressed lengthy epistles to his representative. Elliot had received the most exact orders how to use the force under his command and what he was to get from the Chinese Government. But accustomed as he had been to meagre directions, to depending upon his own judgment in emergencies, and to the subsequent approval which Palmerston invariably had accorded his actions, he had only carried out as much of what he was told to do as he deemed expedient in the circumstances as they were unfolded. As plenipotentiary he imagined that he had that discretion, but Palmerston now showed him that he had not. Here are some extracts from his letter: 'You have disobeyed and neglected your Instructions; you have deliberately abstained from employing the Force placed at your disposal; and you have without sufficient necessity accepted Terms which fall far short of those you were instructed to obtain. You were instructed to demand full compensation for the opium which you took upon you two Years ago to deliver up.

To ask Parliament to pay the money was out of the question. You have accepted a sum much smaller than the amount due to the opium holders. You were told to demand payment of the expenses of the expedition, and payment of Hong debts. You do not appear to have done one or the other. You were told to retain Chusan (Ting-hai) until the whole of the pecuniary Compensation should be paid, but you have agreed to evacuate the island immediately. You have obtained the cession of Hong-Kong, a barren Island with hardly a House upon it. Now it seems obvious that Hong-Kong will not be a Mart of Trade, any more than Macao is so However, it is possible I may be mistaken in this matter. But you still will have failed in obtaining that which was a Capital point in our view: an additional opening for our Trade to the Northward. You will no doubt, by the time you have read thus far, have anticipated that I could not conclude this letter without saying that under these circumstances it is impossible that you should continue to hold your appointment in China.'

This despatch no doubt reflected the feeling in Parliament and in the country. Having started, though slowly and with some misgivings, on a war mixed up with the opium traffic, the public had become excited by the exploits of their army and navy and wanted as glorious a victory as possible. The young Queen Victoria is seen expressing this national indignation. On 10 April she wrote to the King of the Belgians: 'The Chinese business vexes us much, and Palmerston is deeply mortified at it. *All* we wanted might have been got, if it had not been for the unaccountably strange conduct of Charles Elliot . . . who completely disobeyed his instructions and *tried* to get the *lowest* terms he could.' The Cabinet repudiated the Convention of Chuenpee and sent out Sir Henry Pottinger to relieve Elliot, get a larger indemnity, re-occupy Ting-hai and demand trading ports.

Distances being as they were, Elliot remained in ignorance of all this till the despatches arrived in August. That the

Convention of Chuenpee was null and void, however, he learned quite soon from the opposite quarter. Shortly after it was signed, Kishen received a letter from the Emperor, but before His Majesty knew of it, which contained sentiments wholly irreconcilable with its terms. In it, among other things, the Dragon said: 'The Celestial Empire treats the Outer Barbarians with favour and compassion. When they are obedient, We never omit to show them friendliness and good will, for We strive for universal peace. The English Barbarians, however, knew not to repent, but daily increased their insolent violence. It would not have been difficult for Us to call forth our troops and annihilate them utterly. But We gave consideration to the fact that the said Barbarians presented addresses in which they asked for redress of certain grievances.'

This way of describing the war to date should not cause surprise; it was a rendering of events drawn strictly upon precedent.

The Dragon continues: 'To insure fairness for all, We Delegated our Grand Secretary, Kishen, to proceed to Canton and there examine the matter. On arrival he explained everything to the Barbarians, but they still dared to make excessive demands. We had declared them long ago to be fickle of temperament. Wherefore We have instructed the best provincial troops to hasten to Canton and there to extirpate them.' Kishen is enjoined to encourage his troops to fight with bravery. The rebel leader (Elliot) should be subdued and brought to Peking for punishment.

This Edict was not pleasant reading for Kishen who had just signed away Imperial territory, and his reply to the Emperor shows him in a panic. He begins: 'After I, your slave, have perused the Sainted Words commanding me to wage war rather than follow diplomacy, I have this to submit: whatsoever concessions I promised the Barbarians were made with the understanding that I should on their behalf petition for their grant. But O! I am ignorant and what I have done will not meet with the approval of Your Majesty. I tremble more than words can describe. As I, your slave, thought over the situation, I concluded that what happens to me can only be insignificant, but what affects the whole nation is of tremendous importance.' And he hints that what he has done, though it may mean his disgrace, has saved the people from great tribulation, for after consulting with the Tartar General, he learnt that defeat would be inevitable. 'I, your slave, have actually abandoned all food and sleep, so terribly worried am I by the situation. But the Barbarians have pledged themselves to return all they have captured. I beseech the Heavenly Face to take the lives of the masses into consideration, and grant to us poor mortals extraordinary favour. The work of extirpation can be carried out later. I, your slave, have throughout acted for the general welfare. There is not a shred or sign of timidity in me.'

But the Dragon was not moved by such a plea, and when he had perused a copy of the Convention, which Kishen appended to his letter, he replied: 'After Kishen arrived in Canton, he willingly succumbed to the wiles of the rebel Barbarians. Repeated warnings failed to awaken him. Hongkong is an important place. How could the said Kishen allow the rebel Barbarians to occupy it officially? A misdemeanour so high shows indeed that he has no conscience. Let him be deprived of his post and imprisoned. All his properties are to be confiscated to the Government.'

On 12 March the luckless Grand Secretary was seen leaving Canton in chains. On arrival at Peking he was tried on thirteen counts before the Council of State and condemned to death. His property was a windfall for the Imperial treasury. He was found to own 425,000 acres of land, 13,500 ounces of gold, six million pounds sterling worth of silver, eleven boxes of jewels, besides houses and shares in ninety banks and pawnbrokers' shops, the total being estimated at £10,000,000. Yet this fortune of a Chinese Civil Servant was far from unprecedented, and may be declared modest when we recall that Ho Shen, Grand Secretary under Ch'ien Lung some fifty years earlier, was found on impeachment to have savings that amounted to three hundred million pounds. Yet it was very welcome at this time, providing the Court with ample compensation for all losses incurred in the war. Kishen was not executed, however, but exiled to the Amur River, in which frozen region he passes out of history. Elliot, dismissed his appointment for getting what Kishen was impeached for giving him, did much better. He too passed out of history, but continued to be employed by the Crown. His subsequent places of residence, though like Kishen's they amounted to exile, were a gilded exile. He became in turn Consul-General in Texas, Governor of Bermuda, Governor of Trinidad and Governor of St. Helena. And they made him a Knight and an Admiral on the retired list. Thirty-nine years of age at the time when he conducted the war against China, he was seventy-four when he died. It does not seem that he ever wrote his memoirs, though at St. Helena in his sixties he must have had, one supposes, ample leisure. But he will certainly have mused on how as a young man, from December 1836 to August 1841, almost five years, he directed, as the Crown's chief administrator in China, affairs of the first magnitude, amounting as they did in sum to the entry into China's forbidden close, into the Far East's very heart, of the energies and ideas of the Western world, an irruption fatal in the end to the Great Pure Dynasty, and which enthroned the dominant white races as masters of the whole globe, a mastery against which the Japanese counter-attacked exactly a hundred years later and which they had not the strength to shift.

ATTACK AND CAPTURE OF CHUENPEE
from a painting by Thomas Allom

PORTRAIT OF HOWQUA
from an unfinished painting by George Chinnery

The Sequel

The rest of the story can only be related as epilogue. To recount it at large would entail bringing in a set of fresh characters. A rule of dramatic composition insists that fresh characters cannot be brought in at the last scene without weakening the effect of the whole theme. This rule is not inapplicable to historical composition. What reader of this book would find it endurable at this stage to be introduced to Sir Henry Pottinger, Elliot's successor, and to Kiying, who took Kishen's place? Nevertheless, the sequel must shortly be indicated, for the story now rests in the air, and the question—what happened in the end?—demands an answer.

The Convention of Chuenpee of 20 January 1841 being repudiated by the Emperor in February, preparations to renew hostilities were observed by Elliot and to anticipate them he broke through the Bogue and on 2 March brought his warships up to Whampoa. There was another truce, trade even being re-opened, and the season's tea rapidly shipped. But during April the Chinese continued their preparations to attack and at 11 p.m. on 10 May loosed fire rafts against the British ships and plundered the Factories, which had been evacuated just in time. On 27 May when Elliot was about to counter by an assault on Canton itself with 2,395 men and artillery, the Chinese faltered and ransomed the city by paying six million dollars. The British forces then withdrew outside the Bogue. Elliot's reason for not occupying Canton was his fear that his small force would be swallowed in the warren-like streets and become unruly with drink and loot.

In June, though of course the ceding of Hongkong had been cancelled, the British settled there and laid out the new city. Elliot seems to have been at a loss what to do next, and had taken no further action when Sir Henry Pottinger, his successor, arrived on 10 August. On Elliot leaving for home, Pottinger set out to do again what Elliot had done once and which had been undone by the Convention of Chuenpee, namely, to recapture Ting-hai and to make the original demands for a final settlement of all outstanding questions. He started north on 21 August 1841, took Amoy en route on the 26th and Ting-hai on 1 October, and after seizing certain other cities in the vicinity to secure his position, he returned south in January 1842 and continued the organization of the tea trade at Hongkong so that the seasonal shipments could be made. To enable him to finish the war before the next season began, his troops were doubled by a reinforcement which brought his numbers to 10,000 and as it was thought in London that to take Nanking, on the Yang-tse just north of Ting-hai, would be more effective than to go again to the Pei-ho mouth, he was now instructed to move against that city, the second capital. He was not ready, however, to do this until May 1842, by which time the tea had been shipped home. When he did start his course was rapid and irresistible and his victory complete, though he had to meet some picked Manchu troops, who in the decadence of the Empire had preserved the traditional valour of their ancestors, the northern tribesmen that had overrun China two centuries before. They fought to the last man at Chapu and Chin-Kiang, a town on the Yang-tse, the fall of which uncovered Nanking and convinced the Chinese that resistance was hopeless. Not, however, until the British were moving to its assault on 14 August, did the Chinese signify that they would meet their demands, the Grand Secretary, Kiying, having memorialized the Court that 'should We fail to take advantage of the present occasion and ease the situation by soothing the Barbarians, they will run over the country like beasts, doing anything they like.'

There followed at once the Treaty of Nanking. This treaty was a dictated peace and forced the Chinese to grant everything the British had been asking for from the time of Lord Macartney in the eighteenth century, as well as give satisfaction for Lin's seizure of the opium two years and six months before the event, which had been the immediate cause of the war, or rather had afforded Palmerston an argument sufficiently potent to move the Commons to indignation and, so, get them to sanction the armed demonstration, which a long line of experts had declared was the only way to persuade China to abandon her policy of seclusion and emerge into the modern world of trading states. As the reader is by now thoroughly conversant with what the British mercantile community wanted, it will suffice to state in the briefest fashion the contents of the treaty. Hongkong was ceded to the British Crown absolutely. In addition five ports in a line up the coast afterwards called Treaty Ports, were opened—Canton, Amoy, Foochow, Ningpo and Shanghai—where British merchants could reside with their wives permanently, having their Consuls and courts, with the right to import under a fixed Customs tariff and without being obliged to buy and sell through Hong merchants. These were the clauses which redressed all the old grievances and opened China to the West. In the matter of the opium seizure, the Chinese were to pay six million dollars, the estimated value of the 20,000 chests at the time of seizure, though not their cost price as the market had fallen. This payment was not to be regarded as money compensating smugglers for the loss of contraband, but as indemnity for property which had had to be surrendered as ransom for the lives of British subjects, who otherwise might have been put to death; and as such the payment was described in th treaty. So was put in practice Macaulay's declaration in the Commons that the British Government would ever seek to defend its subjects against spoliation and violence, whether they were in the right or whether they were in the wrong, a view of its duty which has always been cordially encouraged by the commercial community. Needless to say, the Chinese did not agree that ransom came into the transaction; the opium was surrendered on demand under the customs' law after a warning that neglect to surrender it would be visited by the penalty of the law, precautions being taken that the transgressors in question should not be able to escape beyond the jurisdiction of the courts. But as it was a dictated peace, they had to sign the clause that the surrender was ransom. They also had to pay another fifteen million dollars to cover the cost of the expedition and outstanding debts.

In spite of getting all that was wanted to establish an up-to-date legal commerce with China, the British did not undertake on their side to stop illegal commerce, which, as was pointed out in the House of Commons, could have been done by getting the Indian Government to reduce poppy cultivation and prohibit the export of the prepared drug. But though by September 1842 Palmerston had gone out with the Whigs, and the Tories had come in under Peel, the new Cabinet was afraid, in spite of the anti-opium speeches of some of its supporters on the 1840 vote of censure, to endanger the stability of the Indian revenues by calling on the Governor-General to take so drastic a course. Accordingly, nothing was said in the treaty about the very subject which had caused the first Anglo-Chinese war to be fought when it was, except that 'it was hoped smuggling would cease'. With the added facilities of five Treaty Ports and an emporium at Hongkong, its volume in fact, increased rapidly and enormously. At first it was feared that a proclamation should be taken seriously which Sir Henry Pottinger thought it prudent to issue and which declared that opium ships sailing under the British flag would, if found in the

Treaty Ports, have their cargoes confiscated. Matheson even, for a time used the Danish flag on his runners. But this subterfuge was not necessary for long. The infant port of Hongkong was unable to do without the silver which the opium firms could supply nor could the Government of India contemplate a slump at its auctions. We find Matheson writing on 21/4/'43: 'The Plenipotentiary has published a most fiery proclamation against smuggling, but I believe it is like the Chinese edicts, meaning nothing, and only intended for the Saints in England. Sir Henry never means to act upon it and no doubt privately considers it a good joke. At any rate he allows the drug to be landed and stored at Hongkong.' This firm later anchored in Hongkong harbour a very large receiving ship, the *Bomanjee Hormusjee* of 866 tons burden, and also built a granite storehouse on shore. In all it maintained eleven receiving ships and six runners along the coast, keeping them supplied from India by a fleet of five crack clippers, at an annual cost of a quarter of a million dollars. The import figures show vividly the effect of the war on the drug trade. The number of chests rose from the 20,000 at the time of the seizure in 1839 to 39,000 in 1845, and 52,000 in 1850. In 1850 the Government of India was deriving five and a half millions of revenue from opium out of a total revenue of twenty-seven and a half millions. Without these five and a half millions, it was innocently asked, how could the Government continue its beneficent plans for education and hospitals and put the Indians on the road to civilization?[1]

The reader, before I close, will want to know what happened to Matheson. He too became an M.P., being elected on his return to England to the seat which Jardine left vacant by his death in 1843. The sum of £574,000, only a small part of his great fortune, we may suppose, he spent on purchasing and improving a house and estate at Lewes, where he lived till his death at eighty-two.

[1] The opium traffic continued until 1908.

Howqua also retired. With the abolition of the Co-Hong his principal occupation was gone. But in spite of a last squeeze, when the Chinese Government forced him and his confrères to find a third of the indemnity[1] for the opium, he still had a very ample fortune and we may picture him in his palatial courtyards and pavilions surrounded by a more real luxury than Matheson can have achieved at Lewes. And he has received a posthumous translation his *vis-à-vis* has not. The other day I was looking at recent acquisitions by the Tate Gallery. There he was, painted by Chinnery. Howqua in the Tate! What could express more blandly the perpetual smile that History wears?

[1] The remainder the Chinese Government got from the Consoo Fund, which was contributed British Money, see pp. 67-8. This Fund paid also the general indemnity. Thus the British were only getting some of their own money back.

Authorities

The authorities on which this book is founded are generally cited at their place in the text. The following note amplifies that information.

The principal source is the *Correspondence Relating to China*, 1834-39, which gives all the British Government's instructions to its representatives at Canton, all the despatches which passed between the two, and the Parliamentary Report on the enquiry into the seizure of the opium by Lin in 1839. This volume, which contains nearly nine hundred pages, is the bones of the matter. H. B. Morse in his *International Relations of the Chinese Empire*, published 1910, works over the *Correspondence* in a methodical way and gives a dry, abbreviated, but wholly reliable, summary of the story told at large by me. The next most important source is the first twelve volumes of the *Chinese Repository*, a quarterly paper published in Canton and Macao during the currency of the events recorded. It editors are unknown to me by name; they were not members of the mercantile community but Protestant missionaries. It is a voluminous work, each volume containing some 650 pages, and as the print for the most part is so small that there may be as many as 1800 words on a page, the words in the twelve volumes amount to the content of a hundred ordinary books. The greater part is given up to essays upon Chinese history, literature and travel, but a quantity remains of record of current events, comment thereon, and transcriptions of documents both English and Chinese. The tone throughout is impartial and, where it does not touch religion, quite liberal.

The third of my principal sources is the archives of the firm of Jardine and Matheson. The archives, which have been presented to the Cambridge University Library, consist of 77 volumes of letters, 66 volumes of account books and journals and 68 boxes of letters. I did not consult these papers myself, but a gentleman who had previously been given permission to examine them and had compiled a typescript volume of extracts and comments, containing 490 pages, kindly placed this valuable source at my disposal. No previous historian has had access to these private papers and by using them in the present book I have been able to give a much more detailed and picturesque account of the drug traffic than has before been possible.

Hansard, of course, is the authority for the great opium debate in the Commons (Vols. 52, 53, 54).

For local contemporary colour the two books *The 'Fan-Kwae' in Canton before Treaty Days 1825-1844* by the American merchant W. C. Hunter, and *The Fan-Qui in China in 1836-1837* by C. T. Downing, the British doctor, are vivid and entertaining.

Besides Morse as above cited the only other modern book treating the subject in a general way is *A Critical Study of the First Anglo-Chinese War* by P. C. Kuo, published Shanghai 1935. The author has read all the British sources, except the afore-mentioned archives, and also what original authorities exist on the Chinese side. The book, however, is dry, and too abbreviated to be entirely clear, and has some bias for the Chinese side, though it attempts to hold a balance. Its chief value is the information it provides drawn from Chinese histories and the translation it gives of some fifty Chinese memorials and edicts, some of which are not in the *Correspondence* or the *Chinese Repository*.

Index

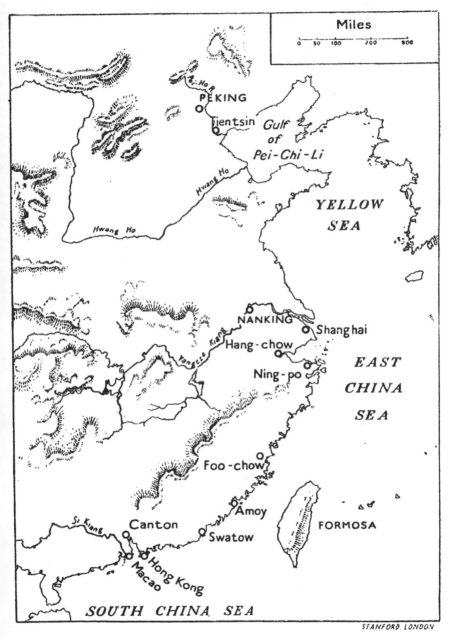

Miles

0   50   100   200   300

Ho R.

PEKING

Tientsin   *Gulf of Pei-Chi-Li*

Hwang Ho

Hwang Ho

Hwang Ho

YELLOW SEA

NANKING

Yangtze Kiang

Hang-chow   Shanghai

Ning-po   *EAST CHINA SEA*

Foo-chow

Amoy

Si Kiang   Canton   FORMOSA

Swatow

Hong Kong

Macao

SOUTH CHINA SEA

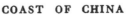

COAST OF CHINA